African Linguistics and the Development of African Communities

La linguistique africaine et le développement des communautés africaines

Edited by / Sous la direction de
Emmanuel N. Chia

COUNCIL FOR THE DEVELOPMENT OF
SOCIAL SCIENCE RESEARCH IN AFRICA

© Council for the Development of Social Science Research in Africa, 2006
Avenue Cheikh Anta Diop Angle Canal IV, BP 3304 Dakar, 18524, Senegal
Web site: www.codesria.org

All rights reserved

ISBN: 2-86978-160-1   ISBN-13: 978-2-86978-160-3

Typeset by Hadijatou Sy

Cover designed by Ibrahima Fofana

Printed by Lightning Source

Distributed in Africa by CODESRIA

Distributed elsewhere by
African Books Collective, Oxford, UK
Web site: www.africanbookscollective.com

The Council for the Development of Social Science Research in Africa (CODESRIA) is an independent organisation whose principal objectives are facilitating research, promoting research-based publishing and creating multiple forums geared towards the exchange of views and information among African researchers. It challenges the fragmentation of research through the creation of thematic research networks that cut across linguistic and regional boundaries.

CODESRIA would like to express its gratitude to African Governments, the Swedish Development Co-operation Agency (SIDA/SAREC), the International Development Research Centre (IDRC), OXFAM GB/I, the MacArthur Foundation, the Carnegie Corporation, the Norwegian Ministry of Foreign Affairs, the Danish Agency for International Development (DANIDA), the French Ministry of Cooperation, the Ford Foundation, the United Nations Development Programme (UNDP), the Rockefeller Foundation, the Prince Claus Fund and the Government of Senegal for support of its research, publication and training activities.

Contents

Acknowledgments vii

Contributors viii

Introduction and Overview
Emmanuel N. Chia x

Section I
African Linguistics: A Tool for Development

Chapter 1
Langues africaines, garant du succès du NEPAD 1
Maurice Tadadjeu

Chapter 2
African Development: Focus on the Nigerian Milieu
Adeyemi Adegoju 13

Chapter 3
Langues et intégration sociale
Engelbert Teko Domche & Lem Lilian Atanga 24

Chapter 4
What Can Linguists Do to Counteract the Spread of AIDS?
Nguessimo Mutaka & Swiri Roseta Ade 33

Chapter 5
Les enjeux de la traduction en langues africaines: le cas du Cameroun
Moïse Ateba Ngoa 46

Chapter 6
Développement des langues gabonaises : État des lieux et perspectives
Daniel Franck Idiata 54

Chapter 7
L'identification d'une unité-langue par l'auto-évaluation: cas du giziga, langue tchadique, dans l'Extrême-Nord Cameroun
Etienne Sadembouo 67

Chapter 8
Critères de généralisation de l'enseignement des langues maternelles dans le système éducatif
Gabriel Mba 78

Chapter 9
Efforts and Challenges Involved in Establishing an Adult Literacy Model for Cameroon
Emmanuel Nforbi 88

Chapter 10
The Rivers Readers Project as an Attempt to Develop Communities
Kay Williamson 98

Chapter 11
Barriers to Effective Implementation of Multilingual Education in Cameroon
Blasius Agha-ah Chiatoh 103

Chapter 12
Rescuing Endangered Languages for National Development
Emmanuel N. Chia 115

Chapter 13
Of the Tongue-Tied and Vanishing Voices: Implications for African Development
Okwudishu Appolonia Uzoaku 129

Section II
Applied Linguistics

Chapter 14
Initial Assessment of the Performance of Lamnso PROPELCA Children at the First School Leaving Certificate Examination
Emmanuel N. Chia and Laura Berinyuy Jumbam 141

Chapter 15
A Linguistic-Based Language Teaching Model for Deaf Communities
John Ogwana and Puis Tamanji 154

Chapter 16
The 'S' in 'Esp: Will Teachers' Knowledge of the Learners' Speciality Make a Difference?
Ludwig N. Metuge 171

Section III
Sociolinguistics

Chapter 17
The Pidgin Factor in the Development of the Niger Delta Region of Nigeria
Rose O. Aziza 184

Chapter 18
Kamtok (Pidgin) Gaining Ground in Cameroon
Miriam Ayafor 191

Chapter 19
Towards the Universals of Loan Adaptation: The Case of Cameroonian Languages
Ayu'nwi N. Neba, Beban S. Chumbow and Puis N. Tamanji 200

Section IV
Syntax

Chapter 20
Feature Checking in Optional Wh-Phrasal Movement in Denya
Samson Negbo Abangma 221

Chapter 21

Constituent Structure of the Associative Construction in Grassfields Bantu

Puis N. Tamanji & Gratiana L. Ndamsah.. 229

Acknowledgments

Emmanuel N. Chia

The task of editing these proceedings fell on me in my capacity as the Chairman of the Local Organising Committee of the 23rd Congress of WALS. Obviously, editing a vast range of papers on different areas of the language sciences could not be done easily and efficiently by any single person. I would therefore like to acknowledge a debt of gratitude for the editorial assistance given to me by the following eminent scholars:

Professor Beban Sammy Chumbow,
Dr Philip Ngessimo Mutaka,
Chief Dr Samson N. Abangma,
Dr Charles Atangana Nama,
Dr Robert Hedinger,
Dr Stephen Anderson,
Dr Pius N. Tamanji.

I am particularly indebted to Mr. Ayu'nwi N. Neba who diligently worked in the secretariat, tracking down all correspondences, keeping tacks on all the abstracts, conference documents and often making very useful suggestions and Mr Moïse Ateba Ngoa who took care of the nitty gritty of the French spelling and syntax.

Since nothing would have been done without material and financial assistance, I would like to place on record the following sponsors for their invaluable contribution:

The Ministry of Higher Education
The University of Buea
The University of Ngaoundere
The UB Staff Development Grant
The Summer Institute of Linguistics (SIL)
The Advanced School of Translators and Interpreters
The Faculty of Arts (UB)
NACALCO

I must also register my immense appreciation to the postgraduate students who provided invaluable assistance in the material organisation of the day-to-day business of the congress.

Finally, I would like to express my deep appreciation to Ms. Rita Ekukole and Johanna Njumbe who served sacrificially as secretaries of the congress, typing sometimes from very difficult handwriting.

Contributors

Adeyemi Adegoju is a Ph.D. candidate in the Department of English at the University of Ibadan, teaches Discourse Analysis and Stylistics in the Department of English Studies and Mass Communication at Adekunle Ajasin University, Akungba-Akoko, Nigeria.

Ayu'nwi N. Neba teaches Linguistics at the University of Buea, Cameroon. He is currently working towards a terminal degree and doing research on tone in African Languages. His research interest is in the area of Language Education and Language Use, and Phonology.

Beban Sammy Chumbow is a Professor of Linguistics. He has published extensively both on African languages and on exoglossic languages. He is presently rector of the University of Yaounde 1 in Cameroon.

Blasius Gha-h Chiatoh is a field researcher at the Centre for Applied Linguistics in Yaounde, Cameroon. He has published widely in various scientific journals both national and international.

Daniel Frank Idiata est linguiste, spécialiste d'acquisition du langage chez les enfants. Inscrit au Cames au grade de Maître-Assistant en 2003, il est responsable du cours de psycholinguistique au département des sciences du langage de l'Université Omar Bongo de Libreville. Il mène des recherches sur l'acquisition des langues bantu et sur le développement des langues et les politiques linguistiques en Afrique.

Engelbert Domche is a lecturer of Linguistics and African languages and currently the Head of Department of the Department of African Studies of the University of Dschang, Cameroon.

Emmanuel N. Chia is Professor of Linguistics and currently Deputy Vice Chancellor in charge of Research and Cooperation at the University of Buea, Cameroon.

Emmanuel Nforbi, Lecturer of Applied Linguistics at the University of Dschang Cameroon. He is also a field researcher on the development and use of African languages in Education. He is affiliated to NACALCO.

Gabriel Mbah: Researcher and lecturer of Applied Linguistics at the University of Yaounde 1, Cameroon.

Gratiana L. Ndamsah: Lecturer of Linguistics at the University of Yaounde 1, Cameroon.

John Ogwana: Lecturer of Applied Linguistics in the Department of Linguistics and African languages, University of Yaounde 1, Cameroon.

Contributors

Kay Williamson: Professor of Linguistics at the University of Port Harcourt, Nigeria

Laura Berinyuy Jumbam: Postgraduate student of Linguistics at the University of Buea, Cameroon.

Lem L. Atanga is a lecturer of the University of Dschang, Cameroon but is currently doing a PhD in the University of Lancaster, UK in the area of Language and Gender. Her research is based on a Critical Discourse Analysis of Gendered Discourses in Cameroonian Political Systems.

Ludwig N. Metuge: Lecturer of English and Second Language acquisition. Currently Director of students' affairs, University of Buea, Cameroon.

Maurice Tadadjeu: Professor of Linguistics at the University of Yaounde 1. Director of the Centre for Applied Linguistics and of NACALCO, Yaounde, Cameroon.

Miriam Ayafor : Lecturer of English Language at the University of Yaounde 1, Cameroon. Her interest is in the area of sociolinguistics and Pidgin English use in particular.

Moise Ngoa Ateba is a lecturer in translation at the Advanced School of Interpreters (ASTI), University of Buea Cameroon.

Ngessimo Mutaka: Professor of Linguistics at the University of Yaounde 1, Cameroon. Author of *Introduction to African Linguistics, A Research Mate in African Linguistics* and *Wish I had Known*.

Okwudishu Appolonia Uzoaku: Lecturer of Linguistics at the university of Abuja Nigeria.

Pius Tamanji: Associate professor of Linguistics at the University of Yaounde 1, Cameroon.

Rose O. Aziza: Lecturer in Linguistics in the Department of Languages and Linguistics Delta State University Abraka, Nigeria.

Sadembouo Etienne: Researcher at the Centre for Applied Linguistics and Lecturer at the University of Yaounde 1, Cameroon.

Samson N. Abangma: Associate Professor of Linguistics, now at the University of Dschang, Cameroon.

Swiri Roseta Ade: Postgraduate student in Linguistics at the University of Yaounde 1, Cameroon.

Introduction and Overview

Emmanuel N. Chia

The chapters in this volume cover some of the presentations made during the 23rd Congress of the West African Linguistics Society (WALS) that was held at the University of Buea, Cameroon, 7–9 August 2002 on the theme of 'African Linguistics as a Tool for the Development of African Communities'. An attempt has been made to select more of the papers that highlight this theme. This bias is reflected in the keynote and theme papers as well as the panel discussion held with the Cameroon Radio and Television in Buea during the congress. Since the congress is an important biannual event of WALS, a wide range of issues of interest to the participants were also discussed.

The chapters are organized into four sections. Section I brings together the keynote and theme papers, the rest of the papers fall under sections II–IV: Applied Linguistics, Sociolinguistics and Syntax. The participants had the liberty to submit their papers for publication either in the Congress Proceedings, the *African Journal of Applied Linguistics* (AJAL), or in the *Journal of West African Languages* (JWAL). These papers were selected, first of all, on the basis of their relevance to the congress theme before other areas of language study were considered. They were sorted and referred to specialists in relevant fields for assessment. It must be indicated also that some of the authors who initially opted to have their papers published in the proceedings did not return their papers at all, nor return them formatted as requested and others did not go through the review process in time or at all. The nonavailability of some of the peer reviewers resulted in the delay of the publication of this volume. In other words, not all papers submitted in preparation for the congress and presented subsequently are published in this volume.

Section I: African Linguistics as a Tool for Development

This section of the introduction gives a summary overview of the theme papers presented at the 23rd Congress of WALS, further distributed into sub-areas of focus, such as, the role African languages play in the development of these languages, the problems of African MT education and the threat to minority languages of Africa. There is however considerable overlap in the treatment of these subthemes.

The Role of African Languages in the Development of African Communities

In his paper, Tadadjeu demonstrates the historic role African languages must play in the realization of the plan of action of the New Partnerships for African Development (NEPAD), tabled in July 2001 by the African Union in order to jump-start the economic and social development of the continent. African languages, Tadadjeu strongly argues, will be able to discharge this duty honourably thanks to the generalisability of three research projects, namely, the Operational Research Programme for Language Education in Cameroon (PROPELCA), Basic Standardisation of African Languages (BASAL) and the Satellite Communication Network in African Languages (CONAL) initiated in Cameroon. Using a historico-comparative approach, Adegoju's contribution underscores the instrumentality of African languages to usher in development to their communities. With particular focus on Nigeria, he identifies three areas: agriculture, food technology, and trado-medicare which only require the touch of local languages for a turn-around. Since no country ever developed using a foreign language, Adegoju argues, African linguistics must look inwards to explore the enormous potential of African indigenous languages as a veritable tool for the sustainable development of Africa. Another role that African languages can play is in national integration. This role is articulated by Domche and Atanga who, from the premise that whoever masters his language masters his social, economic and political environment, argue that language is a determining factor in social and national integration. Focusing on the Cameroonian multilingual context they stress the need for a language policy that takes into consideration all the languages of the nation if national integration is to be attained.

On the spectre of the AIDS pandemic decimating large populations of Africa and compromising the development of its communities, several participants at the conference questioned what linguists could do to counteract the spread of the disease. In a contribution presented in the format of a case study following Dell Hymes' (1962) seminal paper on the ethnography of speaking, Mutaka and Ade's study on the Mankon community makes a strong case for a better way to learn about the sexual behaviours of African language speakers in their cultural contexts. Knowledge of these patterns of behaviour should lead ultimately to new strategies of fighting the AIDS pandemic in Africa. In another contribution Ateba, through the eyes of a professional translator, states emphatically, that despite the marginalisation of African languages during the colonial and neo-colonial periods on the wrong pretext of their backwardness, these languages have no rivals in their capacity to convey and disseminate information.

The Development of African Languages

Most of the foregoing contributions point to the absolute necessity to develop African languages as a condition for them to accomplish the roles assigned to them, while the contributions in this subsection explore the issue further. Idiata examines the linguistic situation of Gabon, tracing the chequered history of the development of Gabonese languages through the colonial period to the present. He concludes that until all sectors of society are actively involved in language development efforts, and speakers of these languages accept that their languages are not inferior tools in national development, success will not be achieved.

The process of language development begins with its identification. Aware of the difficulties involved in identifying a language in complex multilingual settings characteristic of Africa in general, Sadembouo proposes another approach, that of auto-evaluation using Giziga, a Chadic language, as a case study. He reiterates that language identification along with the demarcation of its dialects is a preliminary step in language development. Assuming that language identification has been followed by basic linguistic study, appropriate development of orthography and materials production leading to the introduction of the language into the formal school system, Mba outlines four types of generalisation of mother tongue education: oral, informal, zonal and national and then presents some criteria – scientific, technical economic, socio-psychological, and political (arranged in order of hierarchy) which must be considered if MT education generalization is to be successful. The same criteria would be used to assess progress in MT education. Nforbi's contribution seeks for an adult literacy model in a multilingual country like Cameroon. He examines the challenges involved in combining both national and official languages in the educational enterprise, identifies the components of such a system and discusses them with lively examples drawn from several language communities.

Problems of Mother Tongue (or Bilingual) Education Implementation

Developing indigenous languages and introducing them into the school system is riddled with intractable problems. Williamson discusses practical problems borne of an attempt to develop the communities of the Rivers State in Nigeria through the introduction of reading material in the local languages. The enormity of the problems encountered, for example, the lack of commitment at both the state and local government levels, calls for serious debate and reflection on the fate of African languages, particularly the minority languages, placed alongside predator languages such as English and French. Chiatoh, following in the same vein, identifies what he considers 'barriers to effective implementation of multilingual education in Cameroon'. According to him, the factors include: the lack of political will, the unwritten nature of these languages, the dearth of teaching materials and of human and financial resources, and community resistance among others. He then concludes by suggesting ways such as local ownership, private and institutional partnership etc., to overcome the barriers.

Rescue of Endangered Languages for Development

The last sub-section deals with African minority languages that are threatened with extinction. Chia defines and attempts to identify those Cameroonian languages that face this threat, and sketched indices and processes of language endangerment and suggested measures to rescue them for use in national development.

Okwudishu's paper, 'Tongue-tied and Vanishing Voices: Implications for African Development' tackles the Nigeria version of Chia's treatment of Cameroon. She highlights the threat to the world's linguistic heritage, then beams her searchlight on Nigerian communities whose languages have fallen victim to extinction. As glaring examples of languages under threat of extinction, she focuses more specifically on the displaced indigenous populations of the Federal Capital Territory—Abuja. In conclusion, and in line with the Asmara declaration, she makes pertinent suggestions and recommendations for rescuing those indigenous languages of Africa teetering on the brink of extinction.

Section II: Applied Linguistics

In the first of these contributions Jumbam and Chia reports on a comparative study of the First School Leaving Certificate (FSLC) results of English monolingual Lamnso children and Lamnso–English bilingual children of the Language Education Research Programme (PROPELCA) in Cameroon. The tentative results show that the bilingual children have an edge over the English monolingual children. The necessity of early childhood education in the child's mother tongue is highlighted and a number of recommendations are made. Ogwana and Tamanji propose a language teaching model for the deaf, a model principally based on linguistic considerations and which combines two methods (sign language and lip-reading) in practice in Cameroon. This model, according to the authors, has the potential of bringing all categories of deaf children to communicate simultaneously through both lip-reading and sign language, thus affording learners the opportunity to live normal lives insteadof being secluded from society. Metuge's paper is based on the hypothesis that a mastery of the second language (L2) learner's area of interest by the L2 teacher would lead to significant progress in the learning task. In this study, the performance of a control class is compared to that of an experimental class in which the teacher adequately mastered the specialty of the language learner. The results show that the performance of the experimental class is better and the author makes some interesting proposals.

Section III: Sociolinguistics

This section has three contributions. The first two focus on Pidgin English. Azizia studies the Pidgin factor in the development of the oil-rich Niger Delta region of Nigeria, an area of complex linguistic heterogeneity. Precisely because of this heterogeneity, Nigerian Pidgin (NP) English is the most commonly used language. Because of its intensive usage it has interfered and considerably modified and impoverished the phonology of the local languages. Interestingly, instead of the vehicular Pidgin, the author argues very strongly for the development of the indigenous languages in any meaningful development of the region. On the other hand Ayafor who studies the Pidgin English in Cameroon which is fast developing into an African language argues for its official recognition, the negative attitude towards it notwithstanding. In situations of language contact such as described in the Niger Delta, Nigeria and Cameroon above, languages borrow from each other and coin new terms to expand their lexicon. Neba, Chumbow and Tamanji examine the processes involved in loan adaptation across a wide spectrum of African languages and identify very interesting universal tendencies.

Section IV: Syntax

Following earlier publications (Abangma 1987, 1992) in which the author claimed that a wh-phrase in Denya may either stay *in-situ* or appear at the beginning of the clause, but without explaining why, Abangma now uses the Minimalist Programme (Chomsky 1993, 1995) to suggest that the optionality of wh-movement in this language should be traced to the point in the lexicon where selection of lexical items is performed. The assumption is that in Denya like in some other languages that permit optional wh-movement, two derivations containing wh-movement may converge because the items selected for the numeration may or may not contain C. The one with C will cause the wh-phrase to move to spec-CP. The one that does not contain C will allow the wh-phrase *in-situ*.

Tamanji and Ndamsah on their part examine the internal constituent structure of the associative construction in the Grassfields Bantu languages to account for the different patterns of agreement in the construction. The article goes beyond the possessive relation to the inventory and description of a variety of semantic relations that hold between the genitive noun and the head noun in the associative construction using illustrations from Bafut and Limbum. The study shows that while some genitive phrases are frozen with the head noun into some sort of compound, some are modifying adjuncts and others arguments of the head noun. Following this analysis, they propose that different genitive phrases should occupy distinct positions in the phrase structure representation. The agreement relation between the head noun and the associative morpheme is accounted for in terms of Chomsky's Specifier-Head agreement while the absence of agreement between the two is accounted for by a Feature Uniqueness Condition (Tamanji 2001).

References

Abangma, S.N., 1987, *Modes in Denya Discourse*, Dallas SIL & University of Texas at Arlington.

Abangma, S.N., 1992, 'Empty Categories in Denya', Ph.D Thesis, University of London.

Asmara Declaration, 2000, 'Declaration Made during the Conference of African Scholars on the Theme: "Against All Odds: African Languages and Literatures into the 21st Century"', Asmara, Eritrea, Jan 11-17.

Chomsky, N., 1993, 'A Minimalist Program for Linguistic Theory' in I. C. Hale and S. J. Keysa (eds) *The View from Building 20*, Cambridge Mass: MIT Press, pp. 41-58.

Chomsky, N., 1995, *The Minimalist Program*, Cambridge Mass.: MIT Press.

Hymes, Dell H., 1992, 'The Ethnography of Speaking' in Thomas Gladwin and William C. Sturtevant (eds.), *Anthropology and Human Behavior*, Washington D.C.: Anthropological Society of Washington.

Tamanji, P., 2001, 'Concord and DP Structure in Bafut', Ms University of Yaounde I.

Section I

African Linguistics: A Tool for Development

1

Langues africaines, garant du succès du NEPAD

Maurice Tadadjeu

Introduction

L'objet de cet article est de montrer comment les langues africaines peuvent garantir le succès du Nouveau partenariat pour le développement de l'Afrique (NEPAD). Pour ce faire, le NEPAD sera succinctement présenté à travers, d'une part, l'énumération des dix super-priorités qu'il vise et, d'autre part, les principes de participation de la société civile à sa mise en œuvre.

Le rôle historique que les langues africaines sont appelées à jouer sera illustré par trois programmes initiés au Cameroun, à savoir le Programme opérationnel pour l'enseignement des langues au Cameroun (PROPELCA), le Programme de standardisation de base de toutes les langues africaines non écrites (BASAL), et le Programme du réseau de communication par satellite en langues africaines (CONAL). Le dénominateur commun de ces programmes est leur généralisabilité sur l'ensemble du continent africain, ce qui remplit déjà l'un des critères fondamentaux du NEPAD.

Mais ce qui est capital ici, c'est de montrer qu'en 2002, l'Afrique dispose suffisamment de ressources humaines (savoir et savoir-faire), technologiques et même financières pour utiliser toutes ses langues dans la mise en œuvre du NEPAD. Plus particulièrement, les professionnels des langues africaines ont la possibilité, et donc le devoir historique, d'impliquer toutes les populations du continent, à travers leurs langues, dans la réalisation de ce « Plan Marshall » appelé NEPAD, qui a toutes les chances de commencer à sortir l'Afrique de la misère.

Ces professionnels travaillent dans des cadres institutionnels solides, tels que les Départements des langues africaines et/ou de linguistique de nos universités, des sociétés savantes comme la Société linguistique de l'Afrique de l'Ouest (SLAO), des associations continentales comme la Fédération des académies des langues africaines et associés (FALAA) et même la nouvelle Académie africaine des langues (ACALAN) créée en juillet 2001 en tant qu'organe technique de l'Union africaine (UA) dans le domaine des langues. La tâche qui interpelle les linguistes africains est donc parfaitement à leur portée.

Le NEPAD

Le Nouveau partenariat pour le développement de l'Afrique est le plan d'action de l'Union africaine, initié par des chefs d'état africains et adopté au Sommet de l'OUA/UA à Lusaka, en Zambie, en juillet 2001. Ce plan vise à faire décoller le développement économique et social de l'Afrique au cours des 10 à 15 prochaines années, à travers la réalisation des super-priorités sectorielles.

Les super-priorités du NEPAD

Dans un document intitulé « Le NEPAD expliqué », la vice-présidence du Comité de mise en œuvre du NEPAD (République du Sénégal) écrit en avril 2002 :

> Le NEPAD estime que, s'il est vrai que tout est prioritaire en Afrique, il y a quand même des super-priorités, sortes de fondements sans lesquels il n'y a aucune possibilité de développement. C'est pourquoi, le NEPAD propose un partenariat avec les pays riches en vue de la conception en commun et de l'exécution d'un plan d'urgence de super-priorités.

Le document sus-cité énumère donc les dix super-priorités du NEPAD qui sont les suivantes:

1. **La bonne gouvernance politique** : elle se concrétise par une démocratie se traduisant par des élections libres et honnêtes ainsi que des institutions démocratiques, le respect des droits de l'homme, de la femme et de l'enfant, la transparence dans la gestion du patrimoine public, l'éradication de la corruption.

2. **La bonne gouvernance économique** : celle-ci se concrétise par les flux de capitaux privés, par une justice indépendante et honnête dans les litiges impliquant des investisseurs étrangers, par la gestion honnête et transparente des sociétés privées, etc.

3. **Les infrastructures** : il s'agit des routes transafricaines, des chemins de fer, des ports et aéroports, et des transports qui sont des éléments de coûts qui pèsent sur la compétitivité des produits africains appelés à être vendus à l'étranger. Au surplus, les infrastructures sont amplificatrices et créatrices d'activités économiques.

4. **L'éducation** : le document reconnaît que, aujourd'hui, les ressources humaines sont le facteur le plus important de la croissance économique parce que facteur entrant directement dans la production : créativité, inventivité, productivité. L'Afrique ne pourra se développer qu'en investissant massivement

dans l'éducation et la formation de ses enfants. L'éducation primaire pour tous les enfants en âge scolaire est l'objectif super-prioritaire recherché dans ce secteur.

5. **La santé** : C'est un pari important pour l'Afrique à cause de son taux très important de mortalité dû à des maladies endémiques : malaria, tuberculose et sida. C'est pourquoi la bataille de la santé est une super-priorité indiscutable pour l'Afrique.

6. **Les TIC** : les technologies de l'information et de la communication ont l'avantage d'être accessibles à tous les peuples en ce sens qu'elles ne demandent que de l'intelligence. Cette dernière est heureusement répartie de façon équitable entre les communautés humaines. Les TIC constituent un facteur de contact permanent, d'échanges de biens et services à la même vitesse pour tous, c'est-à-dire à la vitesse de la lumière.

   Au plan économique, les NTIC produisent des services générateurs de revenus élevés. L'accès à ces nouvelles technologies doit être assuré aux populations africaines dès la petite enfance et il doit être étendu à toutes les activités, de l'agriculture à l'industrie, aux transports, aux services et aux échanges.

7. **L'agriculture** : l'Afrique a un retard énorme en agriculture qui se traduit par sa dépendance alimentaire ; ce qui est difficilement concevable pour un continent immense qui dispose de tant de terres fertiles et d'eau. Au moment où les consommateurs occidentaux se détournent des produits agricoles de leurs pays affectés par les pesticides, l'agriculture biologique offre à l'Afrique une opportunité sans précédent de produits d'exportation pour gagner les devises nécessaires au financement de son développement.

8. **L'énergie** : l'énergie est une dimension du développement bien connue. Or, la plupart des pays africains ne sont pas producteurs de pétrole et ne disposent que d'énergie hydraulique très mal répartie sur le territoire. De sorte que la plupart des pays sont dépendants des fluctuations des cours du pétrole. Leurs gouvernements sont donc obligés d'augmenter les prix du pétrole lorsque le prix du brut augmente. Ceci se traduit par un effet immédiat sur les conditions de vie des travailleurs et plus généralement des populations. Certains pays africains qui disposent de gaz ont déjà envisagé des gazoducs vers les pays démunis, comme un pas vers une solution durable du déséquilibre en énergie.

9. **L'accès aux marchés des pays développés** : le développement de l'agriculture et sa diversification seront d'autant plus opérants que les pays développés ouvriront leurs marchés à nos produits. Les efforts visant à cette ouverture constituent une des grandes priorités du NEPAD.

10. **L'environnement** : le poids d'un environnement détérioré sur la condition des populations, surtout dans les grandes villes, est aujourd'hui établi. Ses

aspects les plus connus tels que la désertification et la sécheresse, sont des menaces très sérieuses à la vie même des populations africaines.

De plus, la dégradation rapide des côtes africaines avance comme la sentinelle inexorable de l'avancée de la mer. À cela, il faut ajouter les menaces réelles de transfert de déchets toxiques ou de farines contaminées vers l'Afrique, ce qui constitue un grand danger pour le cheptel et pour les êtres humains.

Quelques principes de participation de la société civile au NEPAD

L'avènement du NEPAD, en tant que Plan d'action de l'Union africaine (UA), est un atout sans précédent tant pour l'UA que pour le peuple africain dans son ensemble. Il est donc très important de tout faire pour assurer le plein succès de cette initiative. Ceci d'autant que l'une des grandes originalités du NEPAD est son caractère transnational. En d'autres termes, les projets NEPAD sont communs à un ensemble de pays africains, notamment, au moins à chacune des cinq régions de l'Afrique.

Les quelques principes ci-dessous esquissés sont proposés pour guider la réflexion sur la participation de la société civile africaine au NEPAD. Il s'agit des principes de partenariat, de programme autonome de la société civile, de contribution financière de la société civile, de l'accès de la société civile à un pourcentage de financement proportionnel à son programme, et, enfin, du principe de contrôle social.

Principe général de partenariat

La société civile africaine participera à la mise en œuvre du NEPAD comme partenaire des États d'une part, et du secteur privé d'autre part. Elle jouera son rôle spécifique dans cette vaste entreprise en général et dans des secteurs clairement identifiés, en particulier. Elle ne souhaite ni faire du suivisme, ni servir d'agence de sous-traitance.

Principe du double partenariat tripartite

Au nom de toute l'Afrique, le NEPAD va engager la réalisation des centaines de projets en faveur, non plus des pays spécifiques, mais de chacune des cinq sous-régions du continent. Cette réalisation se fera grâce à un double partenariat tripartite impliquant les États, le secteur privé et la société civile. Il s'agit d'un partenariat horizontal entre les États africains et leurs homologues du Nord, le secteur privé africain et son homologue du Nord, la société civile africaine et son homologue du Nord. Le partenariat tripartite proprement dit est en fait vertical en ce sens que ce sont les États qui impriment l'orientation générale à laquelle adhèrent leurs partenaires que sont le secteur privé et la société civile. Évidemment, ces derniers apportent des paramètres complémentaires déterminants aux orientations initiales des États.

Principe de programme complémentaire autonome

La société civile africaine entend exécuter, dans le cadre du NEPAD, un programme autonome en complémentarité avec les programmes des États et ceux du secteur privé. L'ossature de ce volet autonome, intitulé Plan d'action de renaissance panafricaine (PARPA) à été proposé, en août 2001, aux chefs d'État promoteurs du NEPAD et au chef de l'État camerounais. Les Organisations de la société civile (OSC) africaines sont invitées à améliorer ce document de référence et à engager sa mise en œuvre dans le cadre global du NEPAD.

Principe d'apport financier autonome de la société civile

La société civile africaine, à travers ses différentes organisations participantes, apportera sa contribution financière autonome à la mise en œuvre du NEPAD. Cet apport constituera un pourcentage du financement du volet autonome de la société civile dans le NEPAD. Les modalités de mise en œuvre de cet apport seront arrêtées de commun accord entre les OSC participantes. Chaque OSC participante a certainement un apport personnel évaluable en termes financiers. Cet apport traduit l'engagement des OSC à la réalisation d'un maillon précis d'un des chantiers du NEPAD. Par ailleurs, l'Organisation de la société civile africaine (OSCA) s'efforce de promouvoir un auto-financement global et autonome du PARPA dans le NEPAD. Les mécanismes du développement de cet auto-financement sont esquissés dans la 5e partie du document de référence PARPA.

Principe de financement proportionnel du volet de la société civile

La société civile africaine souhaite que le financement de l'autre partie de son volet autonome soit proportionnel au pourcentage de cette partie dans le NEPAD. En d'autres termes, si cette partie représente par exemple 20 % du NEPAD, alors 20 % du budget global du NEPAD devraient être alloués aux activités dudit volet. Les négociations pour ce financement se feront entre les trois partenaires, à savoir les États, la société civile africaine et le secteur privé.

Principe de contrôle social

La société civile africaine entend conduire le programme du contrôle social des chantiers du NEPAD. Il s'agira pour les OSC participantes de mettre en œuvre ce programme pour un contrôle permanent de l'exécution de ces chantiers, au nom du peuple africain. Les rapports y afférents seront rendus publics, tout au long de la durée du NEPAD. Ce programme de contrôle social fera partie intégrante du volet autonome de la société civile dans le NEPAD.

Les principes ci-dessus ne sont exhaustifs ni dans leur formulation ni dans leur nombre. Des améliorations y seront apportées ultérieurement. À ce stade, nous pouvons nous demander quel rôle peuvent jouer le PROPELCA, le BASAL et le CONAL pour assurer le succès du NEPAD.

PROPELCA

Les trois programmes illustratifs du rôle des langues africaines comme garant du succès du NEPAD seront maintenant succinctement présentés, en commençant par le tout premier, qui est aussi le plus ancien, à savoir le PROPELCA.

Aperçu historique

Le Programme PROPELCA a commencé en 1978 comme Projet de recherche opérationnelle pour l'enseignement des langues au Cameroun. Au fil des années, cette recherche opérationnelle a été menée sur le terrain par l'Université de Yaoundé de 1981 à 1995 avec la participation active de l'Enseignement privé confessionnel, des communautés linguistiques camerounaises réunies au sein de l'ANACLAC (Association nationale des comités de langues camerounaises) et grâce au soutien financier de WBT-USA, de LEAD (au Canada), de l'ACDI (Agence canadienne pour le développement international), de l'UNICEF, et des communautés bénéficiaires.

En 1995, le projet PROPELCA est devenu un programme d'enseignement bilingue identitaire « langue maternelle (L1)- première langue officielle (LO1) » (L1-LO1). Ses résultats ont été remis au ministère de l'Éducation nationale (MINEDUC) lors des États généraux de l'éducation tenus du 21 au 26 mai 1995. Un nouveau souffle a été apporté à cet enseignement, surtout dans les écoles publiques, grâce à un partenariat à la base avec des inspecteurs du MINEDUC. À tel point que, dans le cadre de la mise en pratique des résolutions issues des États généraux de l'éducation, le MINEDUC a effectivement pris en compte l'enseignement des L1. Ainsi, dans la loi 98/004 du 14 avril 1998 portant orientation de l'éducation au Cameroun, au terme de l'article 5 alinéas 1 et 4 et de l'article 11, l'enseignement des langues nationales fait désormais partie des missions du MINEDUC. Ce dernier emboîte ainsi le pas à l'Assemblée nationale qui, dans la Constitution de janvier 1996, affirme que les langues nationales font partie du paysage linguistique camerounais et que la République du Cameroun « œuvre pour la protection et la promotion des langues nationales ».

Principes et orientations opérationnelles pour la généralisation

Trois sous-modèles ont été développés pour asseoir les bases de la généralisation du PROPELCA :

- Le sous-modèle de l'instruction orale : il concerne l'usage sous la forme orale de toute langue pour l'éducation initiale. Il peut donc s'appliquer à toutes les langues camerounaises standardisées ou non.
- Le sous-modèle informel : il concerne surtout l'utilisation des syllabaires et post-syllabaires dans des classes formelles pour enseigner la lecture et l'écriture de la langue maternelle comme matière. Certains enseignants intègrent cette approche informelle dans quelques disciplines comme la Culture nationale ou l'Environnement...
- Le sous-modèle formel : il s'agit ici en fait du Modèle original du PROPELCA qui concerne l'école primaire et se base sur une pleine utilisation de la langue maternelle comme médium principal d'enseignement dès les premières années de l'école primaire. Il est bilingue identitaire L1-LO1. C'est ce modèle qui effectivement a contribué à faire du PROPELCA le programme de référence pour un nouveau système éducatif.

Quelques données statistiques

Voici, à titre indicatif, quelques données statistiques sur le PROPELCA à ce jour (août 2002), concernant les enseignants et les responsables éducatifs formés, le nombre de langues et d'écoles privées confessionnelles, publiques et communautaires actuellement impliquées dans l'enseignement bilingue identitaire sur l'ensemble du territoire national.

- Nombre de langues : 38, réparties dans les 10 provinces du pays.
- Nombre d'Inspecteurs du MINEDUC et Confessionnels formés : 60
- Nombre de Superviseurs locaux opérationnels : 40
- Nombre de Coordonnateurs scientifiques provinciaux : 15
- Nombre de centres de formation temporaires (stages PROPELCA) : 27
- Nombre d'écoles (publiques, privées confessionnelles et communautaires): 300
- Nombre d'élèves inscrits annuellement dans les écoles PROPELCA : 34 120
- Nombre de titres dans la Collection PROPELCA : 105.

Il ne fait aucun doute que le PROPELCA est aujourd'hui généralisable, sous l'un ou l'autre de ses trois sous-modèles, ou tous les trois simultanément, non seulement au Cameroun, mais aussi dans tout autre pays africain. Ce programme peut donc, naturellement, servir d'instrument pour atteindre l'objectif de la super-priorité éducative du NEPAD.

BASAL

Objectifs

Le BASAL est le projet de Standardisation de base de toutes les langues africaines non écrites (en anglais Basic Standardization of all unwritten African Languages - BASAL). C'est un projet conçu en 1998 pour faire bénéficier des langues africaines du Corps des Volontaires de l'OUA dont le projet venait d'être retenu à Ouagadougou, au Burkina Faso. Le but de ce projet est la standardisation initiale de toutes les langues africaines qui ne sont pas encore écrites. Ce but vise 2 niveaux : le niveau continental et celui national. La standardisation initiale de toutes les langues africaines passera par la standardisation de toutes les langues au niveau de chaque pays africain.

Au niveau national : l'objectif principal est de placer sur chaque langue non encore écrite au moins un linguiste volontaire qui, au bout de 2 à 3 ans, aura amené ladite langue à un niveau « minimal » de standardisation.

Au niveau de chaque langue ciblée l'objectif est de : a) réaliser au bout de 2 à 3 ans en moyenne les activités de base pour la standardisation initiale de la langue. Il s'agit notamment de publier un manuel de lecture et écriture pour les locuteurs natifs non lettrés, un manuel de transition pour les locuteurs natifs déjà lettrés en français ou en anglais, et un petit dictionnaire bilingue d'au moins 2000 mots ; b) assurer une base pour la pérennisation de l'usage écrit de la langue (en termes de capacités humaines locales et d'environnement lettré), par exemple en créant un comité de langue.

Globalement, le BASAL vise à déployer environ 3000 linguistes volontaires sur tout le continent africain, sur une période de 10 à 15 ans. Le résultat principal attendu est de sortir toutes les langues non encore écrites de leur forme exclusivement orale pour en faire des médiums écrits viables et permanents.

La plupart de ces linguistes volontaires feront partie du Corps des volontaires de l'Union africaine (CV. UA).

État d'avancement en août 2002

L'exécution du BASAL a commencé effectivement au Cameroun en octobre 2000, avec le recrutement de 3 candidats pour être déployés sur 3 langues. Au début de 2001, deux des 3 candidats sont effectivement partis sur le terrain où ils travaillent avec acharnement sur la langue bangolan dans la plaine de Ndop au Nord-Ouest, et la langue mada dans l'Extrême Nord.

Au niveau de l'ANACLAC, une coordination centrale du Projet a été mise en place avec un personnel chargé en permanence de promouvoir le projet et de le suivre sur le terrain. Cette coordination centrale du BASAL s'emploie donc à effectuer tous les contacts, les relations publiques et l'information nécessaires tant pour impliquer les autres partenaires institutionnels que pour recruter des jeunes linguistes volontaires.

Malgré des débuts difficiles et des problèmes de communication liés à la nature pionnière de cette phase du BASAL, les deux premiers volontaires se sont mis avec succès au travail, en menant des études de base pour la standardisation des deux langues. Ils ont aussi sensibilisé la communauté et créé une synergie locale pour le développement de ces langues. Aujourd'hui il y a, tant chez les Bangolan que chez les Mada, une grande appréciation du travail des volontaires BASAL. De même, des noyaux de Comités de langues résolument décidés à s'affilier à l'ANACLAC se sont créés avec l'appui de ces volontaires.

Les deux sont actuellement dans la phase délicate et capitale de la réalisation des manuscrits des manuels BASAL de référence cités plus haut.

À partir d'octobre 2002, l'ANACLAC va déployer 5 nouveaux volontaires sur 5 nouvelles langues, portant le nombre de volontaires et de langues à 7, avec une possibilité de les étendre à une dizaine au cours de 2003.

L'ANACLAC va s'investir encore plus à fond dans la réalisation du BASAL, principalement sur la standardisation des langues dites minoritaires et même des langues menacées d'extinction. Ces langues, faut-il le rappeler, ont toutes besoin autant que toute autre langue d'être mises par écrit. C'est même un devoir scientifique et moral que toute langue soit mise par écrit, afin que ses locuteurs puissent accéder véritablement à une alphabétisation durable.

Au niveau africain, et sous l'égide de la FALAA (Fédération des académies de langues africaines et associés), le Centre ANACLAC de linguistique appliquée va promouvoir le projet BASAL pour l'Afrique en recherchant des partenaires institutionnels et un financement approprié.

Dans la perspective de ce partenariat, des contacts sont en train d'être établis avec d'autres grands projets comme le Bantu Initiative, initié par la branche africaine de la SIL. De même, un effort est en cours pour établir un partenariat entre le BASAL et les projets visant à préserver les langues menacées (endangered languages) de disparition.

Ainsi, le BASAL contribuera à intégrer les locuteurs des langues africaines minoritaires et/ou menacées dans les réseaux de communication moderne. Ces populations, où qu'elles soient, deviendront des acteurs à part entière du NEPAD, entre autres.

CONAL

Le CONAL est le projet du Réseau de communication par satellite en langues africaines (en anglais Communication Network in African Languages). L'idée fondamentale de ce projet est publiée dans un récent article intitulé, « The challenge of Satellite Communication in African Languages » (*AJAL* n° 3). L'idée de ce projet est née en février 2000, à la suite d'un contact avec des responsables de

WorldSpace à Washington. WorldSpace est un système satellitaire développé par M. Noah Samara, un digne fils de l'Afrique.

C'est un projet axé sur les possibilités de développement des réseaux de communication par satellite en langues africaines. Il valorise les impacts d'un tel système sur le développement global du continent. Ce système, tel qu'il est envisagé, consistera à diffuser des informations vitales pour les populations africaines à travers des réseaux satellitaires. Ces informations seront reçues par des radios communautaires, puis traduites et retransmises aux communautés locales, dans leurs langues respectives. L'insertion des langues africaines dans ces réseaux semble opportune car elle permettra aux communautés locales d'être intégrées dans la réalité de la communication moderne, et de ce fait facilitera et accéléra leur développement. La collecte des informations essentielles sera menée par des stations de radio satellitaire, en langues ayant une capacité de communication étendue, appelées langues de liaison, à savoir : l'anglais, le français, l'arabe, le kiswahili, le fulfude, etc. L'information ainsi collectée et diffusée sera recueillie, puis traduite en langues locales et retransmise par les radios communautaires.

Ce projet représente en fait un triple défi : un défi au niveau des ressources humaines, un défi technologique ainsi qu'un défi sur le plan financier. Tout d'abord, il nécessite le développement d'un réseau institutionnel dont feront partie les spécialistes et professionnels des langues africaines. Il requiert ensuite un déploiement des technologies de communication par satellite dans le continent tout entier. Le projet nécessite enfin de nouvelles ressources financières pour gérer tout le système. Le défi en ressources humaines étant néanmoins majeur, nous y mettrons un accent particulier.

Chaque communauté cible se connectera à la station de radio communautaire la plus proche. Cette dernière sera équipée d'un receveur satellitaire approprié. Chaque Académie de langue associée à ce programme mettra sur pied une unité de communication composée d'au moins deux personnes. Celle-ci sera responsable de la réception des informations des programmes courants à partir du satellite et de leur traduction et retransmission en langue locale. Ce système d'information radiophonique par satellite pourra aussi s'associer aux journaux locaux en langues africaines et fournir ainsi les informations les plus récentes à la communauté. Ces informations porteront sur des domaines variés tels que la santé, l'éducation, l'environnement, etc.

Les Académies des langues africaines seront les principaux acteurs de ce processus. Ces académies sont des institutions locales responsables du développement des langues africaines, et de leur utilisation sous la forme écrite dans les domaines de l'éducation formelle, de l'alphabétisation des adultes et d'autres activités du développement local. Il y a plus de 300 académies de langues africaines dans le continent, avec des appellations variées. Au Cameroun, par exemple, elles sont connues sous l'appellation de comités de langues et se sont fédérées en une organisation nationale : l'ANACLAC. Sur le plan continental, les fédérations nationales des académies de langues se regroupent progressivement dans le cadre de la Fédération des académies de langues africaines et associés (FALAA).

À Lusaka, en Zambie, en juillet 2001, le sommet de l'Organisation de l'unité africaine a adopté l'Académie africaine de langues (ACALAN) comme l'une de ses institutions spécialisées. Cette récente adoption a contribué à asseoir le réseau institutionnel quasi complet pour développer un système de communication par satellite qui intégrera les langues africaines. Bien que la matérialisation de ce projet en soit encore à la phase pilote, l'enthousiasme qu'il suscite présage des jours meilleurs. Ceci d'autant que des projets similaires sont en cours d'initiation par des institutions des Nations Unies, telles que l'UNICEF, ailleurs en Afrique (par exemple au Niger). De même, des radios communautaires se multiplient à travers le continent à une vitesse porteuse de tous les espoirs.

Le projet CONAL apparaît donc comme l'un des instruments pour atteindre au moins trois des super-priorités du NEPAD dans les domaines des TIC, de l'éducation et de la santé. On pourra aussi l'étendre aux domaines de l'environnement et de la bonne gouvernance.

Financement

Les programmes illustratifs présentés ci-dessus sont, par ailleurs, en train d'être proposés comme sous-programmes du NEPAD dans les domaines super-prioritaires de l'éducation, de la santé, des TIC, de l'agriculture et éventuellement de la bonne gouvernance. Il faut toutefois reconnaître que l'intégration officielle des volets de la société civile dans le NEPAD est encore un long processus, si ce n'est une toute autre bataille. Mais le principe de cette intégration étant déjà acquis, il convient simplement de se mettre à l'œuvre et de croire fortement tant au NEPAD, qu'au rôle particulier des langues africaines.

Le financement des sous-programmes à base des langues africaines sera, en principe, une fraction du financement du NEPAD. Mais, ce qu'il faut bien comprendre, dès le départ, c'est que le financement du NEPAD, comme celui de tout projet de développement authentiquement africain, sera essentiellement d'origine africaine. Les apports extérieurs, aussi importants soient-ils, ne constitueront, à long terme, qu'un appoint. Deux processus de financement doivent donc être immédiatement engagés : d'abord une évaluation claire du coût financier à long terme de chaque programme. Par exemple, au terme de beaucoup de recherches, de réflexion et de calcul, il est aujourd'hui clairement établi que le programme BASAL, pour l'ensemble du continent, coûtera approximativement cinquante millions de dollars US en une quinzaine d'années. Ce montant, comparativement à d'autres programmes et à l'impact global attendu sur le développement du continent, n'est vraiment pas élevé.

Après une évaluation objective du coût à long terme, il faut déterminer les ressources de démarrage. Et c'est ici qu'il faut faire preuve d'engagement patriotique de la part des promoteurs à tous les niveaux. Car, en réalité, les ressources du démarrage doivent impérativement être locales, c'est-à-dire provenir des finances des institutions et organisations dans lesquelles travaillent lesdits promoteurs. Ceci est valable pour le NEPAD comme pour les OSC qui veulent y participer. Il s'agit de réorienter nos priorités, par exemple en redéployant une partie de notre personnel dans les nouveaux programmes. Il s'agit plus particulièrement pour les Départements des langues africaines et/ou de linguistique, de mettre davantage l'accent sur la linguistique appliquée au développement et à l'enseignement des langues africaines. Nos partenaires ne nous croiront et ne nous apporteront un financement extérieur complémentaire que lorsqu'ils nous verront déjà profondément impliqués dans la réalisation de notre vision. Ceci est déjà valable pour le NEPAD lui-même.

Il faut rappeler ici, pour le déplorer, que très souvent, ce n'est pas le financement qui manque, mais des personnes ayant une vision, une intégrité morale, et désireuses de développer l'Afrique. Pour ce qui concerne les linguistes, il faut rappeler qu'ils ont souvent constitué des obstacles au développement des langues africaines que les non-linguistes. L'Afrique étant maintenant entrée dans un grand processus de changement, les professionnels de nos langues doivent s'inscrire sur la ligne de front.

Aucun pays du monde ne s'est développé en utilisant exclusivement des langues étrangères. L'Afrique, qui est aujourd'hui plus pauvre qu'en 1960 (et même qu'en 1990), ne pouvait pas constituer une exception. La vérité est qu'aucune communauté linguistique africaine n'est trop pauvre pour développer sa propre langue. Ce qui leur manque le plus, c'est le savoir et le savoir-faire. Nous, linguistes et professionnels des langues africaines, nous détenons précisément ce savoir et ce savoir-faire. Et l'Histoire nous attend au coin pour nous demander de rendre compte de ce que nous aurons fait d'un si grand pouvoir.

Conclusion

L'objectif visé ici est de faire prendre conscience à tout linguiste africain, à toute institution chargée de développer les langues africaines, de l'appel historique que le NEPAD, implicitement, lance à leur endroit. Les illustrations données tout au long de cet article ne constituent que la partie visible de l'iceberg. Car, c'est une nouvelle ère qui s'ouvre pour nos langues, grâce aux nouveaux développements technologiques. La communication satellitaire, combinée avec les programmes des radios communautaires en langues locales, jouera un rôle sans précédent dans ce processus. Le champ d'action est très vaste.

Chaque linguiste africain devrait se faire l'honneur d'inscrire son nom en lettres d'or dans cette nouvelle page de l'histoire africaine.

2

African Development: Focus on the Nigerian Milieu

Adeyemi Adegoju

Sometimes when we do not see what we are looking for, it is because we are looking for it in the wrong place.

Lucinder Baker Greiner

Introduction

The need for the so-called Third World countries to break the jinx of underdevelopment in the twenty-first century should be a cause for concern to academics, administrators, political leaders, policy makers and executors, cultural activists, and, in particular, the youth who long for an enabling environment to compete with their contemporaries in the developed nations. The Third World, according to Gambari (1981:60), refers to:

> ...the large group of developing countries in the continents of Africa, Asia, and Latin America relatively united in their awareness of being dependent on the more industrially advanced countries and in their determination to change these unequal relations with them. Common colonial experience or experience of alien exploitation and subjugation provide additional raisons d'etre for the membership in and existence of, the Third World.

It is rather regrettable that two decades after the above assertion was made by Gambari, no significant measure of success has been recorded by African countries in the bid to change the 'unequal relations' with the industrially advanced countries, whereas some other countries in this group in Asia and Latin America have made remarkable and enviable strides on the global development scene.

Why then do African countries find it difficult to make steady progress towards realistic development? What is the missing link between Africa and its development? These questions have been asked in diverse ways by Anya (1981:73):

> What then are the factors responsible for this dismal picture in the midst of otherwise not so dismal possibilities given our natural resources? ... How is it that despite its vast resources, Africa, as a continent, remains the poorest in terms of the standards of living and the quality of life of its citizens?

Anya cites Thomas Odhiambo who has argued that the reasons may be as much cultural as economic. For Gambari (1981:65-8), there are certain general constraints on 'Third World Power/Influence': dependence on industrialized powers for military weapons; adverse international economic order; ideological diffusions and problem of leadership in the Third World; poor representation in United Nations Security Council and UN specialized agencies. Others include the dominance of western media over dissemination of news; global politics of food; and boundary disputes and political animosity among Third World nations.

These constraints have, no doubt, stood between Third World countries and their development. But in the African context, a major constraint which has impeded and, in fact, delayed African development is Africa's over-reliance on foreign languages, especially English and French. In the twenty-first century, therefore, it behoves African linguistic studies to look inwards and explore the enormous and latent potentials of African indigenous languages as a veritable tool for sustainable development.

This is the question this chapter seeks to address, focusing on the Nigerian milieu. After this introduction, we will attempt to establish the place of local languages in national development processes. We will then go ahead to identify and discuss certain fields that require the instrumentality of Nigerian indigenous languages for radical transformations. Finally, we will discuss the constraints that must be tackled urgently to make the dream of African development and, in particular, that of Nigeria, become realistic.

The Place of Local Languages in National Development Processes

Every nation, according to Roberto Michels, has two dominant myths—the myth of origin and the myth of mission (see Mazrui 1981:6). For a nation to break away from the former and actualize the latter, it has to take off the 'borrowed robes' of foreign languages which are almost always tied to the former, and exploit its own indigenous languages for innovative purposes. This must have informed American rebellion against European ideals manifested in part through the evolution of 'American English' which has significant import for the American identity and, in effect, its development.

It is also compelling to underscore the Renaissance movement of seventeenth-century England and the underlying tool for its sustainability. Renaissance, in the main, means rebirth or renewal. Beyond this interpretation, it is a spirit, a climate and an environment that encourages people not to look only to the past but also at themselves in the present. For seventeenth-century England to break away from the past and sustain the various facets of development recorded during the Renaissance movement, there were the gradual displacement and eventual demise of Latin as 'the language of knowledge' and the empowerment of English (a language hitherto considered a 'vernacular tongue').

When we leave the European scene and come to Asia, one country that particularly strikes us as outstanding in development, relative to its ranking as a Third World country barely two decades ago, is Malaysia, which is now one of the newly industrialized nations of the world. Citing Dr Idris Bugaje, a Nigerian who lectured in the University of Malaysia, Lawal (2002) identifies certain areas of development where Nigeria is no match for Malaysia.

In terms of power generation, the last time Malaysia had a major blackout was in 1993; something that is a daily occurrence in Nigeria. The telephone services of the two countries show that more Malaysians have access to telephone and at cheaper rates. As to the health sector, Malaysia has excellent health facilities; and they are affordable. Their leaders do not have to go outside the country for medical treatment, unlike Nigeria. Lawal (2002:2) also invites attention to the agricultural sector, especially the production of palm oil, where Malaysia is a world leader, controlling about 51 per cent of the world's traded palm oil. This would sound rather appalling when we recall that Malaysia got its palm seedlings from Nigeria in the 1960s.

Judging from the above, one is bound to wonder about the secret behind Malaysia's success given that both Nigeria and Malaysia were ranked among the Third World countries barely two decades ago. Lawal (2002:2) observes:

> The advantage of using local language as an official language has contributed in making Malaysia what it is today. Malaysia does not use English, they use Malay language and we know that no nation develops by using a foreign language....

It then stands to reason that a nation striving towards development must sever its link with a 'foreign tongue' and connect to the umbilical cord of its 'local tongue(s)' for a natural source of development.

With close reference to the African situation, a major and recent call for transformation in which the instrumentality of local languages could be explored is the historic conference held in Johannesburg on 28 and 29 September 1998 to discuss and debate Thabo Mbeki's heralded African Renaissance initiative. The renewal motif underlying the African Renaissance, according to Dalamba (2000:40):

> ... will ensure Africa's participation and competitiveness in the global arena, validating Africa's progress and development in economic, cultural, technological, spiritual, communications and political spheres. This renewal will also legitimize and celebrate Africa's almost forgotten, if not ignored, historical contributions to global development in areas such as civilization, state formations, religious worship, science, engineering, agriculture, technology, astronomy and communications.

We need to stress here that a major gap in the discourse of the conference, as pointed out by Dalamba (2000:43), is that 'the question of how an African renaissance was going to be realized was never sufficiently critically addressed except through a general realization that it somehow had to be implemented'. Consequently, she posits, among other things, 'the development and implementation of Afrocentric curricula and schools that are aimed at working with an Afrocentric programme ...' (2000:43). How else can we successfully implement an Afrocentric programme other than empowering our local languages? In the present discourse, we contend that until the African languages are made the pivot for propelling the African Renaissance initiative, the concept may turn out to be a mere phraseology coined and noised about just for propaganda without any concrete plan to usher in African development as a means of making meaningful contributions to global development.

In this respect, the agricultural sector is one of the major areas of development in which the use of local languages would be a big boost. It is interesting that there is hardly any higher institution in Nigeria that does not have a faculty or school of agriculture. Some of these institutions are wholly devoted to agriculture. Besides these, there are research institutes, including Cocoa Research Institute of Nigeria (CRIN), Nigerian Institute for Oil palm Research (NIFOR), and International Institute for Tropical Agriculture (IITA). In spite of these resources, Nigeria's agricultural sector has not witnessed any remarkable turn-around.

The fact remains that most of the research breakthroughs recorded by these institutes over the years have not gone beyond the pages of long essays, theses and log books; their impact and practical utilization at the grassroots level where the rural dwellers do the real planting and harvesting is poor. Agricultural researchers in Nigeria have turned out to be what some people satirically refer to as 'farmers who hoe with the pen'. How could research carried out in English optimally benefit the local farmer who does not understand English? How much of the literature on research breakthroughs is available in the local languages? How many orientation and enlightenment programmes in the local languages have been organized for the local farmers? All of these must have been responsible for the failure of past agricultural blueprints in Nigeria, such as Operation Feed the Nation of the Olusegun Obasanjo military administration and the Green Revolution of the Shehu Shagari civilian administration. This, in fact, remains one of key setbacks to the development of Nigeria's agricultural sector.

Another area of development that needs to be transformed is food technology. There are certain communities in Nigeria that are historically known for producing certain types of food. For instance, in Yoruba land, we have 'dodo Ikire' and 'akara Ogbomoso' that are known beyond the boundaries of their areas of production. Besides, there are food drinks such as *kunu*, *fura dai nonu* and *zobo*, which are common among the Hausa people. Food technologists in the tertiary institutions conduct research (for academic purposes) on such food (drinks) only in the medium of English. And their research findings do not go beyond the four walls of the laboratory because the language of research is alien to that spoken by the local producers of such food (drinks). How then can the local producers learn how to better preserve, package and market their products beyond the borders of the local environment?

This is why a lot of agricultural produce go to waste in Nigeria, thereby making virtual destitutes of the local farmers. A large percentage of the cashew, mango, pineapple, orange and other wild fruits produced in Nigeria rot away and are fed on by animals because the farmers lack an effective means of storing, processing and packaging them for export. This is an area in which an aggressive communication drive in the local languages would yield fruitful results. For instance, it would be helpful to have magazines published in the indigenous languages on food processing and how to properly harness African resources for improved food technology. If widely circulated, people would learn to appreciate the rich natural sources of vitality in the African menu which are lacking in the exotic ones they crave for on the shelves of supermarkets across the country.

Finally, the empowerment of local languages would enhance the practice of traditional medicine in Nigeria. According to Tella (1992:115):

> ...Traditional medicine is the sum total of all knowledge and practices whether explicable or not, used in diagnosis, imbalance and relying exclusively on practical experience and observations, handed down from generation to generation, whether verbally or in writing.

For our purposes, we will focus on two forms of treatment, namely herbal medicine and bone setting. Herbal medicine could be in the form of concoction made from plants or incinerated ingredients, infusion of herbs in cold water or alcohol, or medicated soap from local materials and herbs (Tella 1992:117). As regards bone setting, Ogunbodede (2000:313) points out that the effectiveness and prowess of traditional healers have been particularly recognized in this area. Tella, however, remarks that the healing system could be physical or metaphysical and that in the treatment of diseases, either system could be used alone or in combination.

One aspect in which the local languages could be used to improve on the practice of traditional medicine in Nigeria is in the area of proper documentation. To this end, Agbebi (1992:125) writes:

> The proper documentation of traditional herbal therapies is an invaluable instrument towards ensuring the preservation of this vital aspect of the Nigerian culture. This is because the Nigerian society is at crossroads between the old traditional beliefs and the realities of the modern age.

This becomes imperative in view of people's heavy skepticism about the administration of trado-medicare due to its lack of formal structure and organization. However, there are certain ailments that defy the treatment of orthodox medicine but are cured by traditional medicine. For instance, a number of typhoid fever patients have found out that the disease is sometimes resistant to the treatment of orthodox medicine. Interestingly, this is one disease against which herbal medicine has turned out to be a veritable antidote. There are also some skin diseases that dermatologists have treated only to find out that they are drug-resistant. Such diseases are known, however, to have disappeared with the application of such traditional medicated soap as Dudu Osun and cream. Practitioners of orthodox medicine find it difficult to accept this reality—not because they cannot appreciate it—but because they have to uphold the ethics of their own profession.

We find it rather compelling to commend the therapeutic feats recorded in trado-medicare. Many accident victims with serious bone fractures who have escaped outright amputation in orthopaedic hospitals did so thanks to the healing genius and artistry of traditional bone setters.

In view of the foregoing, there is need for a proper and systematic documentation of traditional therapies in health care magazines produced under the close supervision of the National Agency for Food and Drugs Administration and Control (NAFDAC), which would validate such therapies. By so doing, people would gradually be able to erase the prejudice they have about the administration and efficacy of traditional medicine, thus making the practice to improve.

We have so far considered three major areas of development that need the exploration of local languages for reconstruction. But we may begin to wonder if certain prevalent conditions in Nigeria give any glimmer of hope. In this light, we seek to address the handling of some issues that can make or mar Nigerian development.

Nuts to Crack

Attitude Towards Indigenous Values

The first constraint to the development of Nigeria is the attitude of the people to their indigenous values. We tend to place so much emphasis on what is foreign and neglect that which is ours. This is what has culminated in the obsessive love for English. Writing on the neglect of indigenous languages and the over-reliance on English as the bane of Nigeria's development, Osundare (1982:102) points out that:

> The system takes for granted that everybody must have an aptitude for a second language and whichever learner does not, is faced with frustration even though he shows remarkable promise in other areas of study. Thus, the country has lost countless potential technologists, engineers, accountants, etc., whose professional hopes have been shattered by lack of flair for the master's language.

Therefore, when we look forward to heralding African development, using the tool of African linguistics, are we anticipating the deployment of the local languages that are now 'alien tongues' to most homes and 'mere cosmetic subjects' in our school curricula? I have noted elsewhere that 'there is practically no relevance that the Yoruba language has in our educational system, notwithstanding the paper policies and lip-service paid ... [to] the entrenchment of indigenous languages in Nigeria' (Adegoju 2002a:5).

Besides, when the developmental efforts begin to yeild results, shall we still be using the quality of the products of the western world as yardsticks to measure ours? For instance, Nigerians value imported products more than theirs. Although we do not dispute the dubious character of some Nigerians to make money by producing fake products, the pejorative term 'Aba-made' used by Nigerians to denigrate the industrial ingenuity of the Igbo of south-eastern Nigeria is unhealthy for national development. Osofisan's (2000:3) observation in this regard is apt. he says:

> We will never climb onto the podium of developed nations until we understand that what we need is not just the appetite to consume, but rather, the ability to liberate our own creative energies. What we need is to free and empower our people's immense imaginative powers, to turn them into fearless and adventurous explorers in every sphere of activity.

Besides, it is now a status symbol in certain elitist circles in Nigeria to serve imported fruit juice at parties and state functions. With this attitude of the cream of the Nigerian society, what fate awaits the indigenous food drinks like *fura dai nonu, kunu, zobo* and others that could as well be preserved and packaged for such occasions?

The situation of Nigeria is at variance with what obtains in Malaysia. Citing Idris Bugaje, Lawal (2002: 2) says:

> Malaysia's belief in itself is one of the reasons why it left Nigeria behind. You see they have one notion called 'Malaysia Boley' which means Malaysia is the best. So psychologically and orientation wise their minds are prepared that their own products should be better than foreign products and that is why quality standard is maintained . . .

From the foregoing, we can conclude that unless there is a radical change in people's attitude to the indigenous languages and homemade goods, we may wander for long in the doldrums of underdevelopment.

Media's Responsiveness

The orientation of the print and electronic media in Nigeria is not auspicious for a realistic African development. The electronic media, for instance, need to shed the bulk of their programmes aired in English and incorporate more programmes in the local languages. This would help to propagate the local technological breakthroughs recorded by the people from time to time. The Lagos State Government took a commendable step when it established a radio station that broadcasts predominantly in Yoruba language. The radio station is christened 'Radio Lagos 107.5 FM *Tiwantiwa*'. *Tiwantiwa* means 'what is ours is ours, and, therefore, has to be so appreciated'. The identification of the radio station with the *self* and not the *other* is an attempt to break away from the stifling posture of English in Nigeria's media broadcast. This trail blazed by the government of Lagos State is worthy of emulation.

In the case of the print media, a number of newspapers are currently published in indigenous languages. What is worrisome about them is that by their present orientation, they cannot help to advance the cause of a healthy and enduring development. For instance, newspapers and magazines published in Yoruba propagate mainly the politics of identity and self-determination. This is analysed in greater detail by Odeyemi (2002). But such ideological underpinning needs to be curtailed to make the print media supportive of the envisioned African development. Moreover, they need to highlight local technological breakthroughs in their columns as a way of stimulating public interest in their own creativity.

Apart from the media approach to this problem, the National Institute for Nigerian Languages (NINLAN) in conjunction with the National Orientation Agency (NOA) and the National Productivity Centre (NPC) should develop language materials that would be suitable for use in print and the broadcast media. By so doing, they will be propagating breakthrough research findings in agriculture and local technology. This collaborative effort would also include organizing workshops in local languages in order to educate the local end-users on research findings from our higher institutions and research centres. In addition, the government should set specific and measurable targets for its institutions and research centres. That is the only way to guarantee the continued relevance of such institutions.

The 'Nigerian Factor' Syndrome

The cliché 'Nigerian factor' encapsulates some peculiar socio-cultural and political constraints and forces that tend to pull Nigeria down when and where other countries are reaching for greater heights. For instance, so many policies have been formulated to transform Nigeria's agricultural, economic, educational, technological, as well as oil and gas sectors, but the set targets have never been met. Such policies fizzle out as soon as they are formulated. Apparently, Nigerians know that the high level of corruption—one of the ugliest faces of the 'Nigerian factor' syndrome—among those entrusted with the 'destiny' of the nation at whatever level is responsible for Nigeria's backwardness. Osofisan's (2000:2) comment on this is quite instructive:

> We have built our values around the pillar of cash, forgetting that such a pillar cannot endure because it has no room for any soul within it. That is why ours is the age of buccaneers, of predators without conscience or dignity. Whether in the banking halls, on the open streets or in the closets of parliament, the heroes are those with the sharpest teeth. It is one of the reasons, surely, why development among us continues to be tragically thwarted.

Following the thrust of the present discourse, it often happens that when research centres are instituted to execute, fine-tune and finance research breakthroughs in local languages, those saddled with the responsibilities first think of ways of satisfying their own selfish needs before ever thinking of the rest of the society. Generally, the problem of leadership in Africa also impacts negatively on development efforts on the continent. In Osuntokun's (2001:106) view:

> What Africa lacks in modern times are leaders that are aware of the present predicament of the black people and are determined to overcome them (sic). The leaders of modern Africa are people whose mental and political horizon are (sic) so restricted that they do not distinguish between self-interest and group interest...Africa's problems are both managerial and political. Therefore, until either the right leaders emerge or the people are prepared to take their destiny into their own hands, the continent may continue to vegetate at a low level of human existence.

Given this situation, would one sound so cynical to say that our envisioned African development is far beyond the horizon? In any case, we believe that the evolution of the Nigerian state and its ideals is in progress. This is why the National Orientation Agency needs to be far more aggressive in the bid to re-orientate the Nigerian people and make them sincerely think of building rather than ruining the country.

Concluding Comments

In this discussion we have touched on four main variables that are pivotal to the discourse: the tool (local languages), the site (Nigeria/Africa), the supposed artisans (Nigerians/Africans) and the anticipated goal (development). To have a balanced treatment of our discussion, we juxtapose the enormous potentials that abound in Nigeria for landmark reconstruction with some very fundamental issues that need to be addressed with every sense of urgency, obligation and patriotism they deserve. This is imperative so that we do not end up romanticizing the whole idea of African development, for in such a slippery discourse as this it is very easy to slide from a critical and scholarly posture to an emotional one. Therefore, our posture in the contribution is not to run Nigeria down but to set it free by setting the truth free!

References

Adegoju, A., 2002a, 'Towards Re-engineering Indigenous Nigerian Languages for Sanctity: The Yoruba Experience', paper delivered at the 2nd University of Uyo Conference on Languages and Literature, February 13-5.

Agbebi, E. A., 1992, 'Bridging the Communication Gap between Traditional and Modern Medical Practitioners: A First Step towards Valid Documentation', in *Popular Traditions of Nigeria*, Lagos, Nelson Publishers Limited, pp. 125-27.

Anya, A. O., 1981, 'Science Policy, Development and Geopolitics: A Nigerian Case Study', in *Ibadan Journal of Humanistic Studies*, No. 2 October, pp. 72-91.

Dalamba, Yolisa, 2000, 'Towards an African Renaissance: Identity, Race and Representation in Post-Apartheid South Africa', in *Journal of Cultural Studies*, Vol. 2, No. 1, pp. 40-61.

Gambari, Ibrahim A., 1981, 'The Third World as a Centre of Influence or Power', in *Ibadan Journal of Humanistic Studies*, No. 2 October, pp. 60-71.

Lawal, Muhammad S., 2002, *Nigeria vs Malaysia: The Palm Oil Miracle* . Available online at http://www.allafrica.com.html, pp. 1-4.

Mazrui, Ali A., 1981, 'Political Nostalgia', in *Ibadan Journal of Humanistic Studies*, No. 2 October, pp. 1-17.

Odeyemi, Femi, 2002, 'Language and Grassroots Democracy: The Use of Yoruba for Political Mobilization via the Print Media', paper presented at the 2nd University of Uyo Conference on Languages and Literature, February 13-5.

Ogunbodede, E. O., 2000, 'The Possible Applications of African Traditional Methods of Bone-Setting in Orthodox Dentistry: A Preliminary Exploration', in *Journal of Cultural Studies*, Vol. 2 No. 1, pp 313-17.

Osofisan, Femi, 2000, *The Intellectual Deficit in Nigeria's Quest for Development*. Available online at http://www.allafrica.com.html, pp.1-4.

Osundare, Niyi, 1982, 'Caliban's Curse: The English Language and Nigeria's Underdevelopment', in *Ufahamu*: Journal of the African Activist Association, Vol. X No. 2, pp. 96-107.

Osuntokun, Jide, 2001, 'Some Thoughts on African Idea of Management', in *Journal of Cultural Studies*, Vol. 3 No. 1, pp. 99-107.

Tella, Ayodele, 1992, 'The Practice of Traditional Medicine in Nigeria', in *Popular Traditions of Nigeria*, Lagos, Nelson Publishers Limited, pp. 115-124.

3

Langues et intégration sociale

**Engelbert Teko Domche
& Lem Lilian Atanga**

Introduction
La problématique linguistique et spécifiquement la question de la promotion des langues nationales est un problème latent dans le cœur des citoyens de toute nation. Cette question trouve différentes réponses suivant les États et leurs politiques. Pour ce qui est des États africains, ce problème se pose en terme de l'intégration des langues nationales dans le développement socio-économique, car l'un des éléments qui permet de définir une nation précisément est la langue. Et comme on le dit souvent, un peuple s'instruit, se cultive et s'éduque plus vite s'il s'instruit, se cultive et s'éduque dans la langue qu'il parle. Il est donc important, pour qu'une nation puisse se construire sereinement, qu'elle puisse intégrer toutes ses composantes ethniques. Pour cela, il faut un environnement politique susceptible de favoriser le choix d'une ou des langues nationales comme véhicule de la pensée et de la culture nationale, résoudre des problèmes sociopsychologiques liés à la pratique et l'enseignement des langues nationales, bref, définir clairement la politique linguistique nationale. Celle-ci devra concilier trois exigences :

- Généraliser les langues véhiculaires comme langues de travail.
- Maintenir l'ouverture culturelle.
- Intégrer à la vie nationale et faire participer à la culture d'aujourd'hui toutes autres langues parlées dans le pays.

On le constate donc, la question linguistique n'est pas à mettre entre parenthèses; elle fait partie intégrante et inaliénable de l'histoire du développement d'une nation. Cette dimension, pourtant très importante et décisive, est paradoxalement sous-estimée par les planificateurs du développement national. En cela ils oublient une dimension capitale de la linguistique que souligne Calvet (1974:169) lorsqu'il affirme que : « les révolutionnaires français considèrent que le plus sûr ciment de la nation est l'unité linguistique ». C'est-à-dire que la langue est l'instrument par lequel vit et s'exprime toute une nation.

Et sans la résolution de la question linguistique, aucun État ne peut se sentir en sécurité tant sur le plan interne que sur le plan externe.

En effet, produits et patrimoines d'une nation, les langues participent comme véhicules de la pensée au développement du pays et contribuent ainsi à faciliter l'assimilation par les peuples des idées et des techniques nouvelles. Aussi la dimension nationale repose-t-elle sur sa fonction dans la société.

Voilà pourquoi nous croyons ici que la langue est l'instrument par excellence de l'union des composantes de la société. Elle est supra ethnique et se situe juridiquement au-dessus de toutes les pratiques sectaires. La relation entre langue et nation peut-être établie aussi bien dans ses dimensions politique, idéologique, socioculturelle, qu'économique. Pour qu'une intégration sociale se fasse sans heurt dans une nation, il est important que celle-ci mette en place des conditions objectives et subjectives qui permettraient de détruire les bases erronées et anachroniques du tribalisme et du régionalisme.

Dans les lignes qui suivent, nous essayons d'analyser ces conditions dans le but de trouver une solution à ce problème séculaire qu'est l'intégration sociale.

Le groupe ethnique comme une identité

Il est important de noter que les principes d'une politique concernant les problèmes du tribalisme, du régionalisme, de l'unité nationale, de l'intégration sociale, etc. dépendent de la manière d'aborder, les questions de tribus, d'ethnies, de langues nationales, de suppressions des inégalités économiques, sociales et culturelles (désenclavement, développement, etc.) des questions de structures administratives et territoriales de l'État (décentralisation, responsabilisation, etc.).

Il existe un certain nombre de données qui permettent d'engager les processus de construction d'une nation.

La question qui se pose maintenant est celle de la politique linguistique à mener dans le cadre d'une stratégie autogestionnaire, et d'une révolution culturelle démocratique ; pour ce faire, le principe directeur est que dans une nation, toutes les langues, qu'elles soient véhiculaires (à notre sens supra ethniques) ou maternelles (à notre sens ethniques) constituent tout le patrimoine de la nation. Il ne saurait par conséquent exister une politique de la « réserve », de la « hiérarchisation » ou « d'apartheid » entre elles. La prise en compte de ce patrimoine, tel que nous venons de le définir, laisse voir que toutes les langues d'une nation ont les mêmes possibilités de développement, car comme l'observent Madrat et Marcellesi (1981), « la diversité linguistique dans la mesure où elle ne conduit pas à la non-compréhension, est un capital inestimable pour une nation ». C'est pourquoi, après les études scientifiques faites par les linguistes, il revient aux gouvernements, aux décideurs de définir une politique linguiste claire et objective, basée sur l'égalité de toutes les langues de la nation. Il serait aussi intéressant que les décideurs utilisent la décentralisation dans le sens du renforcement des échanges au niveau des ressources humaines entre régions pour provoquer, créer et cimenter l'esprit de fraternité entre les régions et, au-delà, entre les hommes. Ils doivent introduire les langues nationales comme matière dans le système éducatif national, intéresser et associer la population au débat linguistique, car il n'y a qu'une politique linguistique clairement définie par les textes officiels et suivie d'une application effective pour aider les chercheurs à orienter et à coordonner leurs travaux dans ce domaine. C'est ce qu'on appelle en langue technique « génie linguistique » c'est-à-dire toute la méthodologie nécessaire à l'aménagement de l'espace linguistique.

Vu sous cet angle, le groupe ethnique constitue une identité remarquable, une force qui doit être endiguée et orientée vers la cause nationale pour la nation. Le groupe ethnique peut ainsi être vu sous cinq dimensions : le fonctionnel, le symbolique, le social, le sociopolitique et le linguistique.

Le fonctionnel renvoie aux attributs du groupe, c'est ici que toutes les décisions importantes se prennent, que la morale s'inculque, que la prise de conscience s'éveille, que tout fonctionnement s'organise autour d'un pilier central, qu'il est ou qui représente le chef de la communauté. Toutes les décisions, tant administratives que traditionnelles y sont commentées, analysées puis exécutées.

Le symbolique renvoie aux représentations sociales qui y ont cours. Les coutumes, les usages y sont enseignés, vulgarisés, encouragés. Il est important de souligner que c'est à ce niveau que l'identité du groupe se soude et se prémunit contre toutes attaques internes et externes. La vertu ici prend une place importante car l'image du groupe doit être sauvegardée, d'où l'accent mis sur le social.

Le social : le groupe occupe un site, un espace social au milieu ou à côté d'autres groupes sociaux. Comme le distinguent les sociologues, le groupe ethnique entretient trois types de relations :

a) Les relations dites primaires qui concernent les rapports avec les membres de la famille ou des amis proches.

b) Les relations dites secondaires qui englobent les voisins, les personnes que l'on rencontre régulièrement lors des activités champêtres, sportives ou dans les associations, etc.

c) Les relations dites tertiaires pour désigner des contacts plus épisodiques et anonymes qui se passent dans les lieux publics.

Quel que soit le type de relation, la langue dans le social constitue un important marqueur d'identité des lieux et du mode dominant d'être en public.

Le politique ici renvoie aux processus de mobilisation du groupe pour faire triompher ses droits, ses idéaux, pour se prémunir contre des menaces éventuelles (problèmes de sécurité, de bien-être, etc.). De telles mobilisations constituent des temps forts de la construction de l'identité du groupe, donc de sa dimension symbolique. Il est important de savoir analyser cette force pour éviter tout débordement.

Le linguistique renvoie à ce qu'il y a de non annihilable dans un groupe qui sort de l'anonymat et le distingue des autres. Le linguistique met tous les membres au même pied d'égalité, alors personne n'est minoritaire dans le groupe. La langue étant le véhicule séculier de la culture ancestrale.

Ces cinq dimensions, telles que présentées, soulignent l'importance du groupe ethnique dans la consolidation de l'intégration sociale et de l'unité nationale.

La langue comme facteur d'intégration sociale

La variable déterminante

Comme l'affirme Cyr (1998) : « le pouvoir des mots va bien au-delà de leurs simples propriétés descriptives, une dimension du langage que même les linguistes sont parfois portés à oublier ».

En effet, le code d'une langue sert non seulement à décrire, mais aussi à construire, à entretenir, à transformer la réalité quotidienne des acteurs en cause, à rapporter, à sceller des liens au niveau des relations primaires, secondaires et tertiaires. Le code représente ainsi comme la variable déterminante de toute intégration sociale. Les traités de paix, par exemple, sont souvent des vues de l'esprit matérialisées par le langage, sans rapport avec la réalité physique, mais ils ne sont cependant pas moins « réels » pour autant, surtout lorsque l'on considère leur impact sur le comportement des acteurs, leur interprétation des réalités quotidiennes et leur prise de position par rapport aux us et coutumes de la société où ils vivent.

Le problème de l'émigration/immigration

Tous les pays du monde, dans leurs constitutions, reprennent en préambule l'article des Droits de l'Homme qui stipule que les hommes naissent égaux en droits, en devoir et tout homme a le droit de jouir de la liberté d'aller et venir... Cet exemple illustre bien comment la langue sert non seulement à décrire la réalité, mais aussi à la construire, à l'aménager et à la transformer. Et comme le remarque Foucault, les « évidences » les plus apparentes sont souvent des préconstruits partages en vertu d'un processus dit de « naturalisation », lequel consiste à attribuer une valeur universelle à des intérêts particuliers.

Dans cette optique, la langue se présente comme l'instrument de construction de la réalité qui permet d'établir des points d'amarrage ou des balises cognitives qui permettent aux acteurs de la société d'adopter des comportements convergents avec les finalités nationales. C'est donc une activité essentiellement langagière. Le langage et, au-delà le discours, est donc le principal instrument du ciment social. Vu sous cet angle, le développement et la consolidation de l'unité sociale est, dans une large mesure, un phénomène discursif, car le discours est le principal instrument utilisé pour définir, entretenir et transformer le patrimoine d'une nation. Il donne aux acteurs la capacité à s'intégrer dans un environnement déterminé en observant ses conventions et règles souvent inconscientes ; ce qui présuppose leur application « correcte » plutôt que mécanique.

Il est vrai que la langue possède des facettes qu'on pourrait qualifier de « néga- tives », par exemple l'ambiguïté que plusieurs utilisent souvent à des fins stratégiques. D'aucuns qualifient cette pratique d'avantageuse parce qu'elle permet la diversité sous une apparence d'unité, amplifie les sources de pouvoir existantes et réserve la position privilégiée des acteurs dominants. Notons aussi que l'ambiguïté stratégique permet au locuteur d'établir un moyen-terme entre le besoin de se faire comprendre et celui de ne pas offenser les autres ouvertement. Elle sert aussi à préserver la base de pouvoir du locuteur en lui permettant de revenir sur ses positions au besoin.

L'occupation d'un habitat

Cependant il nous faut prendre conscience de ces différentes facettes de la langue pour bien saisir le rôle délicat qu'elle joue et peut jouer au sein d'une société, d'autant plus que les relations entre les langues et leur environnement s'inscrivent dans des temps de durée variable. La langue réfère à la fois à une entité linguistique, la langue comme système, et à une entité politique, la langue comme institution.

Par ailleurs, devant le dysfonctionnement des capacités culturelles, il s'agit de tout système culturel normatif d'intégration d'un milieu — il apparaît vital d'instaurer des dispositifs de remise en fonctionnement de l'individu et du territoire— car il faut éviter les processus ségrégationnels en cours, qui renferment une partie de plus en plus importante de la population non pas dans un *no man's land* social, mais bien dans un espace social de second ordre, une sorte d'infra société qui est « Centrée sur un marché secondaire de l'emploi, moulée sur une culture de la pauvreté assujettie à un corps institutionnel différencié et précarisé, chargé de gérer en douceur la pauvreté ».

La langue se présente alors comme une approche insertive qui vise à reconstruire la prise en charge par l'individu de sa vie, à établir des parallèles entre le social, le culturel, le politique et l'économique en fonction des besoins portés par l'individu. L'outil d'intervention mis en place doit donc reposer sur une approche globale et intégrée désignée sous le nom de parcours d'insertion.

Et pour paraphraser Gendron (1990), parler la même langue c'est accepter d'en faire un bien commun et sa valeur sociologique change. En effet, elle n'est plus seulement alors un facteur primordial d'identité collective pour les seuls locuteurs, mais elle devient le facteur premier d'une nouvelle appartenance, qui engloberait l'ensemble de la nation. Des résistances surgissent, des oppositions continuent de se manifester, mais la voie est tracée qui paraît conduire à une forme d'appartenance nationale dont ce lien premier, indispensable, sera la langue.

Le rôle de la langue dans les structures sociales

La stabilité et la paix sociale

Elle permet, entre autres, de s'affirmer et dans une certaine mesure de rapprocher des gens de la diaspora, de créer un espace identitaire—la langue renferme un champ publicitaire inestimable. C'est elle qui permet d'accueillir, de faire fonctionner les services. C'est elle qui permet de travailler, d'intégrer toutes les structures propres à une communauté.

En ce début du XXIe siècle en pleine mondialisation des échanges, la langue, en tant qu'instrument de communication, a davantage de chances de se maintenir et de se développer. Les locuteurs natifs et non natifs doivent s'intéresser à leurs langues, doivent la maîtriser et la renforcer soit par l'entremise de l'école, soit par celle de la famille ou autre structure appropriée. À ce niveau, les médias (presse écrite et parlée) doivent jouer un rôle primordial en émettant une langue correcte, une langue culturelle, une langue multidimensionnelle et plurielle.

Nous devons travailler à rechercher toujours de nouvelles approches ou de nouvelles façons de faire qui permettraient d'assurer que la pérennité de la langue progresse et débouche toujours sur du concret en matière de valorisation linguistique.

Les organisations sociales

La situation socio-économique a beaucoup évolué depuis les années 1970 : le phénomène de la mondialisation est sur la lancée. On parle même aujourd'hui de « dimension planétaire ». Le besoin de rationalisation embrasse tous les secteurs de l'activité économique (même le secteur de la pharmacopée jadis considéré comme la chasse gardée des tradi-praticiens est maintenant touché). L'information est passée dans le vécu quotidien des entreprises, des familles, des individus, les moyens de communication comme l'e-mail, l'Internet, l'Intranet, l'Extranet ont des retombées de plus en plus maîtrisées sur la vie des organisations en particulier, des travailleurs et de la population en général. Tout cela ne peut qu'avoir un certain impact sur le développement de la langue. Cette situation pourrait ouvrir de nouvelles perspectives et favoriser de nouvelles formules dans le cadre d'un statut et d'un aménagement linguistique. Dès lors, il devient intéressant de prendre en compte les bouleversements qui surviennent et qui surviendront dans les organisations sociales, de prendre en compte le rôle des changements du contexte pédagogique qui vont aussi influencer le devenir de la communauté linguistique, l'impact de la communication puisque la langue y détient une place très importante comme l'héliotrope, nous devons être analogiquement parlant, des « langues tropes» c'est-à-dire des gens portés naturellement vers le développement, la vulgarisation et l'assimilation de nos langues.

L'utilité de la langue dans un monde en pleine mutation

La globalisation de plusieurs aspects du langage a été déterminée par les récents développements linguistiques. Ainsi, la terminologie de la nouvelle technologie s'avère globale et l'on trouve le même ensemble de mots qui s'emploient sans modifications lexicales dans plusieurs langues. Tel est le cas du contexte camerounais où les langues nationales ne sont pas encore bien développées. Ainsi, les lingua franca servent comme moyen d'atteindre les masses. Le pidgin s'étend sur le territoire national, et constitue pour la plupart des ONG tels que Helvetas, WADES formation, Ballotiral, la langue de communication. Le pidgin s'emploie également dans les zones francophones, c'est le langage populaire.

Il va sans dire que le développement est plus rapide dans les pays où les langues nationales sont également développées. Fasold (1996) atteste que l'homogénéité linguistique est étroitement liée au développement économique. Il n'est pas question de simple homogénéité mais en réalité, le développement économique des pays tels que le Nigeria, la Tanzanie et l'Afrique du Sud, pays dans lesquels les langues nationales sont bien développées est le résultat d'une certaine maîtrise linguistique. Or, il n'en est pas de même pour les pays qui ne disposent pas de politique des langues nationales. Ce développement est possible dans les pays à développer parce que les informations parviennent à toutes les populations, même si elles sont illettrées. Cette dernière a l'économie avancée, occasion de suivre les informations, soit à la radio soit à la télévision dans leurs langues nationales. Ainsi, les développements les plus récents sont mieux suivis.

La situation économique du monde a beaucoup évolué surtout avec l'épanouissement de l'Internet. La communication est une partie essentielle de la vie, et pour faciliter cette communication, il faut la langue qui est le meilleur et le plus fondamental des outils.

Dans cette ère de mondialisation, il faut à tout prix parvenir à toucher les différents aspects de la vie humaine. Le moyen le plus sûr pour atteindre ce but serait la langue. C'est pour cette raison qu'il est absolument nécessaire de développer les différentes langues du monde. Ceci facilitera les moyens de communication dans le cas d'une communauté morale où la langue la plus maîtrisée est la langue locale.

D'autre part, des campagnes de santé, de mobilisation politique, et sur des nouvelles technologies agricoles nécessitent également l'utilisation d'une langue mieux maîtrisée par la population locale. Dans ces circonstances, la langue devient un outil. La langue peut être plus importante que la technologie, car sans la langue, l'on ne pourrait même pas transférer la technologie. Tel était le but des premiers missionnaires lorsqu'ils sont arrivés dans notre pays. Ils ont dû apprendre les langues locales afin de pouvoir mieux remplir leur mission évangélisatrice. C'est pourquoi des langues telles que le douala, le mungaka et le bulu ont été développées très tôt. Il reste à savoir si le développement de ces langues locales a joué un grand rôle dans l'évolution de ces sociétés.

Aujourd'hui, l'Église catholique s'est engagée dans un processus d'inculturation dont l'outil principal est la langue. L'identité culturelle d'un peuple est renforcée par l'emploi de sa langue locale ou nationale ; ceci a abouti à l'évolution des langues locales à tel point que la messe est maintenant célébrée dans ces langues.

Conclusion

La politique sur la linguistique joue un rôle important et est en même temps inséparable de l'histoire du développement d'une nation. Pour assurer l'intégrité nationale et sociale de notre société, toutes les langues nationales, qu'elles soient locales ou lingua franca, devraient être valorisées de la même manière. Elles font toutes partie de notre patrimoine.

C'est pourquoi les linguistes ont toujours proposé que le gouvernement introduise l'enseignement des langues nationales dans le système éducatif camerounais. Ceci renforcera d'avantage l'esprit de nationalisme. Cette démarche permettra aussi l'élaboration d'une politique nationale de la linguistique, chose qui facilitera l'intégration nationale.

Nous avons aussi relevé que la langue aide à maintenir des relations sociales, ce qui rapproche les citoyens les uns des autres. Le développement linguistique signifie dans ce cas l'intégration nationale.

Ainsi, la linguistique est aussi une question politique, c'est pourquoi celle-ci conditionne celle-là. Le comportement de l'homme ou d'un groupe social en dépend : sa réaction face aux problèmes de la nation, ses intérêts dans la vie, l'idéal qu'il s'est fixé. Mais encore se dresse le destin de l'homme face à son éducation, à l'orientation politique de son pays, à la structure sociale de son environnement. À ce niveau, notre philosophie en matière de langue comme le dit Ossete (1994) « partirait du principe qu'une langue correspond à une vision du monde et une forme de vie sociale qui finissent par imposer une structure mentale à ceux qui la pratiquent ».

Pour le Cameroun, le problème est entre les mains des décideurs, les scientifiques ayant fait leur devoir d'inventaire, d'analyse et de propositions. Chaque peuple a le devoir d'étudier, de vulgariser et de moderniser sa ou ses langues qui contiennent le principe actif de toute culture. Chaque peuple a l'impérieux devoir de hisser sa ou ses langues au plus haut sommet de ses structures car linguistique et nation sont étroitement liées au développement social. C'est pourquoi l'interaction qui fonctionne entre la linguistique, l'économique et le social prend une forme dialectique et la résolution de l'un de ces problèmes, pour être efficace, requiert une solution globale.

Références

Calvet, L.J., 1974, *Linguistique et colonialisme*, Paris.

Cyr, André, 1998, « Le discours en tant qu'instrument de construction de la réalité organisationnelle » dans *Langue et société* n° 38, p.77, Québec, Canada.

Fasold, R., 1996, *The sociolinguistics of Society*, Blackwell Publishers Inc.

Foucault, M., 1969, *Les mots et les choses*, Paris, Gallimard.

Gendron, J.D., 1990, « Conscience linguistique des Franco-québécois depuis la Révolution tranquille » dans *Langue et identité*, Québec, PU de Laval.

Madray F. et Marcellesi J.B., 1981, « Langues de France et Nation » dans *La pensée*, n° 221.

Ossete, E.A., « Questions de politique et de Génie linguistique en République du Congo », dactylographie inédite.

4

What Can Linguists Do to Counteract the Spread of AIDS?

Ngessimo Mutaka & Swiri Roseta Ade

Introduction
The central theme of the 23rd WALS Conference, 'Linguistics as a Tool for African Development', is significant, coming, as it were, at a time when many linguists doing fieldwork in Africa are concerned with trying to use the knowledge of applied linguistics as a real tool for development. Africa is one of the regions of the world with a crying need for development, but there is no other region that experiences a greater danger to its development, a danger that humanity still has no answer to—AIDS. The AIDS pandemic is wiping off the able-bodied people the continent relies on to work for its development. Many experts die suddenly and it is becoming more and more difficult to replace them. As linguists, the challenge before us is, what can we do to counteract AIDS and help prevent the spread of the HIV virus? In this chapter, we unveil a possible successful strategy using a case study on the ethnography of communication of the Mankon community.

Why Should the Linguist Also Do Something about the AIDS Pandemic?
Referring to the book, *Research Mate in African Linguistics* (Mutaka & Chumbow 2001), Larry Hyman (to whom this book is dedicated), makes the following observation about the work of linguists doing fieldwork:

> The second quality of the fieldwork mental state is what I would call a dedication to 'whole language'... One can arrive in the field with the intention of working on tone, but to study tone, one has to study utterances; but, when one studies utterances, other issues come up. While this happens in non-field situ-

ations as well, the pull to act on things outside one's original purpose is a typical feature of the fieldworker's state of mind.... It is thus interesting to me that most Africanists I know, whether theoretically inclined or not, have published on phonological, morphological, syntactic and semantic issues arising from the study of their languages (Larry Hyman 2001).

The key phrase in this quotation is 'dedication to whole language'. And by extension, it so happens that one becomes dedicated to the people who speak the language and may thus discover other aspects of the culture of the speakers of the language and feel excited about writing on that culture. To illustrate, we would like to mention that in response to the AIDS pandemic the first author has written a novel entitled *The Fruit of Love* (Mutaka 2001). The writing of such a book was primarily motivated by what he perceived as the need for Africans to change their sexual behaviour in order to better protect themselves against venereal diseases and AIDS.

A Possible Strategy for Fighting the AIDS Pandemic

Despite the huge efforts by various African governments to fight the spread of AIDS, it is still increasing at an alarming rate. The challenge is to design suitable materials on AIDS prevention that can motivate people to develop responsible sexual behaviours.

We would like now to briefly present a book entitled *Wish I Had Known*, by Mutaka and Bolima (2003). The book was prepared by a group of linguists and medical doctors in Cameroon to provide the type of material that should be widely disseminated to fight the spread of AIDS.

The book consists of:

1) Testimonies by AIDS victims: to let people learn from their unfortunate experiences and avoid risky sexual behaviours.

2) Basic information about AIDS: this is official information obtained from the Ministry of Public Health in Cameroon which includes wise sayings from African proverbs and biblical injunctions that encourage people to avoid HIV.

3) Special messages disseminated to various audiences to make them adopt responsible sexual behaviours, thereby arresting the spread of the AIDS virus.

4) Fighting the evils inherited from tradition against the African woman: It has been shown, for example, that widowhood rites are one of the causes of the spread of AIDS.

5) Further messages to help people have a stable family life and thus avoid risky behaviours.

The book appeals to the basic instincts of the common people and encourages them to adopt responsible sexual behaviours. It addresses their specific needs. For instance, it forces people to reflect on their lives as individuals, on what will happen to them and their families if they die (especially of AIDS). It invites them to ponder the misfortunes of the AIDS victims to make them learn from their mistakes.

Being fully aware that people do not like to read about AIDS, the authors include a section that addresses the sexual problems of individuals. They also provide answers obtained from medical doctors and pharmacists for some of the questions individuals may feel reluctant to ask their doctors, especially questions about their sexual behaviour and the problems thay face in their their sexual activities.

To make the message conveyed in the book reach the largest number of people, NACALCO, a local NGO in Cameroon, intends to translate the book into numerous Cameroonian languages and make broadcast materials from it for use in community radios. The book will also be proposed to various organized communities and industrial agencies who have signed a contract of fighting the spread of AIDS with the Ministry of Public Health in Cameroon. The following section presents a study that can be replicated in other African communities by linguists and the results of which can immediately be used as the type of AIDS-related problems that should be addressed by the various communities using this book in a bid to find local solutions to such problems.

AIDS Prevention and the Ethnography of Communication in the Mankon Community

The ethnography of communication is best described by the different components of the acronym SPEAKING, as proposed by Dell Hymes (1964) and Wardhaugh (1992). This acronym stands for setting and scenes, participants, ends, act sequences, keys, instrumentality, norms of interaction and interpretation, genre. This section of the chapter is organized around these different points, focusing only on the aspects of the Mankon community that can help understand their sexuality. In other words, the acronym SPEAKING offers the best sociolinguistic framework through which the sexual activities of a community can be observed. We believe that once we understand the sexual behaviour of a community in its social context, we can propose effective means of AIDS prevention that would be acceptable to these communities.

The Setting and Scene (S)

Social Occasions

Social occasions, more specifically, birthday celebrations and birth ceremonies, in the Mankon community serve as a setting where sexual relations are negotiated. In celebrating these occasions, there is what is commonly known as the 'moonlight dance'. This is a dance organized in the moonlight—hence, its name, and it attracts a lot of people, young and old. It offers the best opportunity for individuals to make new friends, and in the case of a boy who has always planned to make love to a girl; it offers him the opportunity of talking to such a girl face to face.

During the moonlight dance, as some people are dancing and relaxing after lot of eating and drinking, others are in shaded corners, caressing, making love, or making plans to meet some other day. If you want to know why all this is happening, there are standard replies: 'We want to have another moonlight dance nine months from now'; 'we want to have a successor to this man/woman (if it is burial ceremony); or 'we just want to be remembering this night.'

One of the boys had this to say when interviewed by the second author:

> You know, the songs that we sing and dance arouse me. They are so emotional. I am here alone. My girlfriend went back to school yesterday. I cannot wait for her to relieve myself that is why I had to "urinate" in that girl behind the house. It took me just a few seconds. I wish it happens again.

The boyfriend of the girl who was 'urinated' into was the one playing the big drum. After the dance, on my way home, I discovered that some of the dancers were by the roadsides either kissing or just conversing. One of the girls told me:

> After all, my parents know I will not be coming home early. I will take advantage of this to spend some time with my boyfriend in his room.

The crucial issue is this: the boy 'urinated' in the girl just for a few seconds. But how sure was he or she that the other was safe from HIV/AIDS? What happened in that rush? What fate awaited the 'real' boyfriend, the drummer? Or the girlfriend who had gone back to school? Answers to such questions certainly point to the fact that the moonlight dance setting is a terrain in which the spread of AIDS is culturally promoted.

Cultural Occasions

Cultural occasions in Mankon are similar to social occasions. Cases include the famous Mankon annual dance (*abíñ mfo*) funeral ceremonies, and some family ritual ceremonies having a variety of cultural activities (traditional dances, choral music, drama, just to name a few). The annual dance will be considered because it involves people of all ages, from all walks of life, in and out of the village.

At the end of each dance day, the Fon, that is, the traditional ruler, advises his subjects on topics such as responsible parenthood, the need to avoid abortions, why boys should get married, and how people should protect themselves against STDS and AIDS. To put these instructions into practice, the Fon's listeners begin to negotiate. Some of them get into these relationships out of drunkenness, or excitement. Because the Fon says, 'don't throw away the babies or kill them, bring them to me', a boy tells a girl 'let's go and make a baby for the Fon'. Mankon and non-Mankon people who come from urban areas to commune with those at home, succeed in sleeping with these girls easily because they have money and flashy cars. The whole atmosphere reeks of commercial sex. Some of the men promise to take these girls to towns. A village girl who has never dreamt of going to the big city will easily fall prey to such promise.

Thus, sexual exchange in Mankon has a monetary component, but it would be quite inappropriate culturally to define it as prostitution. The Mankon people do not consider this prostitution but a feature of their cultural life to which everybody is invited participate, whether educated or not.

Political and Economic Settings

The Mankon economy is small, with an inheritance system where the lineage or clan retains control of property. The lineage system stresses loyalty not to the individual family but to the lineage, thus preventing the development of conjugal bonds. Polygamy, in this community, has similar effects. Within a polygamous marriage, the economic unit is the woman and her children. Divorce or separation, even in contemporary times, is not a disaster. This is because women have unfettered access to land and enjoy rights to pursue legitimate economic activities. If not, the idea of divorce would have been catastrophic. Furthermore, practices such as the long postpartum sexual abstinence, the freedom that young men and women enjoy by living separately, as well as divorce and sexual transactions encourage pre-marital sex and extra-marital affairs.

Relationships may last from a few hours to several years. They always involve some level of material transactions. Men and women of different classes have different stakes in their sexual and marital relationships. For men, the stakes may be paternity, provision of housekeeping services, sexual adventure or the quest for an educated and well turned out companion and business front. For women, it is likely to be economic security, motherhood and sexual desire. These multiple forms of non-marital relationship can be seen to reflect processes of widening socio-economic differentiation in Mankon.

Sex is an important currency for cementing these non-marital relationships. For the very poorest women, it is one of the few ways of gaining access to social wages. The socially specific link between sex and the exchange of cash, clothing, gifts, and domestic services in this community renders the use of the term 'prostitution' extremely problematic.

Understanding the bases of these exchanges is a pre-requisite for understanding the degree to which those involved in them have the capacity of changing or modifying their sexual behaviour. Poor women depending on 'lover' relationships for part of their economic survival may have very little leverage around issues such as 'safer sex' and condom use. This may equally be true of women in monogamous marriages who lack other means of economic support. There was, therefore, an urgent need to devise interventions to reach this population of men and women whose sexual relationships and networks render them highly vulnerable to HIV/AIDS transmission. Because this community sets sexual exchanges within their context, it points to a different conceptualisation of risk. Prostitutes may not in fact be at risk to the same degree as women who depend on 'lover' relationships for maintaining household survival, while married women who do not have affairs themselves can be at high risk from husbands who maintain extra-marital relationships and refuse condom use.

It should be noted, for instance, that the current Fon of Mankon has eight wives and the question is, does he satisfy these women sexually? Or, rather, does each of these women feel sexually satisfied by a single man who has eight different wives? If he does not, one understands why these women may be easily tempted to seek sexual satisfaction outside their marriage. As will be pointed out later, the Fon felt the necessity of forbidding 'the bottle dance' around the palace presumably because he knew that his wives could see in such a dance a way to have casual sex with strangers as is common during such occasions.

Participants (P)

Boys and Girls

Each society has different age groups, each one differentiated usually by their language features. Because of social pressure and in order to be free from constraints at home, the Mankon youths learn the characteristics of their age group and conform to them. They discuss sexuality among themselves, but, as would be seen in the following conversations, there are differences in their language use and that of the 'adults'.

John: Good morning Jane

Jane: Are you sure the morning is good?

John: Of course, yes. I had a sweet night with my 'sharper'. She took me to heaven.

Jane: Who was the one this night? I hope it is the same one you 'sucked' two days ago?

John: I rarely repeat these 'ndiems' except when she is exceptional. The one I had last night is from Bambui. I met her last evening at pa Adangwa's funeral ceremony.

Jane: John, you should be very careful. Have you not heard there is 'seven plus one' (AIDS). You will die oh oh ...

John: My friend, AIDS does not exist. It is an American idea to discourage sex. I no de play oh. I go for business, and when the opportunity comes I don't let it go. I really work for nigh na why dat my skin sweet this morning. I go full contact to suck the honey.

Jane: Bye bye. Enjoy yourself but try to sleep with one girl and also protect yourself else your parents will bury you soon.

As shown in this conversation, the boy is direct in expressing his intentions. He makes it clear to the girl that he prefers 'full contact', that is, he does not like the idea of using a condom when having sex. He considers AIDS as an invention of the American people to discourage sex.

Adults: Women/Men

Mama: ...Adzong did you sleep? You look exhausted.

Baba: Nimó, true, my wife travelled. She has gone to wash Mambo's baby. You know Mambo is married to one of the mbanga's and they are in the South West province. She had a baby a week ago.

Mama: So where did you sleep? Was there an aliye nívo (wake-keeping) some where?

Baba: No! (Smiles). You like to know everything. I will not tell you this one. It is somebody who gives me warm water to wash my legs and very cold water to drink when my wife is away.

Mama: (exclaims) At your age! You don't think you should resign from that habit? This sickness that eats bones (AIDS), you are not afraid of it? That woman lost the husband two months ago and it is that thing that killed her. Today you go and sleep there. When my sister comes back I will tell her.

Baba: Nímo, I know how I do it. I am not fast, hard or using any force. I have Vaseline in my bag, when it is difficult I use it so that I will not have a wound. You think I don't have sense. I have been doing this thing for so long, I don't know why you think it is only now that I will develop a sudden sickness?

Mama: It is for your health and that of your wife and children. If you die, they will suffer, I am just advising you to be careful. That woman's husband died of AIDS and you go and sleep with her (moves away).

Baba: (Shouting) He did not die of AIDS, the brother gave him into a nyongo house to have more money. He is somewhere working for the brother.

This conversation shows how the man is reluctant to tell the woman about his extra-marital relationship. He does it in a roundabout way. But the woman gets the message and is more direct. She warns him about the danger of the HIV/AIDS virus. But, as is clear from the conversation, the man does not believe in the existence of AIDS. Rather, he believes the husband of the woman he is having an extra-marital relationship with died because he was offered to a 'nyongo' house, in other words, he was killed by witchcraft. From the two conversations above, one can already see that it is imperative to educate the Mankon people, young and old, about the danger of AIDS. And the first thing to do is to convince them that AIDS is real, and that it kills people.

Opinion Leaders

Church Leaders (Christianity)

Paradoxically, while the missionaries have been trying to suppress Mankon sexual practices in the name of Christianity, they themselves have failed to live according to the virtues they preach. For example, I know a young Mankon girl who is nursing the daughter of a Reverend Pastor who has a wife and kids. The missionaries' servants and taxi drivers help them to look for women. It seems public morality can only make sense in Mankon when its maintenance mechanisms operate effectively.

The missionaries aim at converting individual natives. Expectedly, the degree of conversion is measured by the extent to which these natives abandon their customs. Using this yardstick, most Mankon natives are converts; but most live double lives: they assume one type of behaviour in the mission station and another outside. As a result, moral issues cannot be discussed openly at a level that would reflect or reveal the tensions.

The major contention in the Mankon independent church movements is not Christian morality, nor is it a result of stubbornness of their sexuality; rather, it is the oppressive form in which Christianity is introduced

A Moslem leader had this to say:

> Our tradition holds that girls should get married as early as ten, eleven, twelve, and thirteen. It is accepted and it is a good method to fight HIV/AIDS.

He does not seem to see or realize that there are a lot of disadvantages when a young girl or an adolescent gets married to an elderly man.

It should be clear that if there is to be any success in the control of HIV/AIDS and other sexually transmitted diseases, there is need to address this problem of early marriages, especially in the permissive Mankon community.

Traditional Leaders

These will include the Fon, the traditional councillors, and the quarter heads. Unknown to them, they are a major role in the spread of the AIDS pandemic. Yet, paradoxically, they also fight to prevent it. Most of these leaders encourage polygamy. The Fon inherits wives added to his harem, but he cannot satisfy them sexually. As a result, some of them go out with other men. In addition, some of the girls get married to the Fon not because they love him but because they are forced to become his wives. Therefore, since there is no love for such a woman, *ab initio*, she is most likely to look elsewhere for love, notwithstanding the attendant dangers.

The traditional leaders believe that gods and ancestral sprits punish wrongdoing. Yet they assign to the gods and ancestral spirits a peripheral role in the control of sexual activity without providing any cogent reason. The leaders represent scholars who admit that, in the Mankon society, right behaviour is mystically rewarded and wrongdoing mystically punished.

We would also like to point out that the high rate of land disputes in the Mankon community contribute its own share to the spread of AIDS. Some leaders receive young girls as bribe to render judgment in favour of the guilty. Soon enough, these young girls become widows as their husbands tend to die shortly after. As a result, the young widows visit bars, bottle dance halls and end up in multiple relationships.

Ends (E)

This refers to the conventionally recognized and expected outcomes of an exchange as well as to the personal goals that participants seek to accomplish on particular occasions. Take, for example, the case of Awa who got married to Sammy not out of love, but so that, with the support of his rich parents, he could take her to places she loved to go, live in a good home and bribe her way into a good professional school. She got all she wanted—even more! While in school, many other boys much better off than Sammy approached her for love. She finally fell in love with one Nde, and, as a result, decided to end the relationship with Sammy. Nde, the son of an ex-parliamentarian had just returned from Germany where doctors confirmed that he was HIV positive. After being together with Awa for four years, he died. Awa fell seriously ill later but her parents believed that Sammy and his family had bewitched her.

Meanwhile Sammy's love for Awa was still burning. He did everything he could and finally got her back. He believed that it was because of his curse that Nde had died. He did not accept what others told him. Awa continued living him. His parents disowned him after they had struggled in vain to make him understand that Awa had AIDS.

The Mankon society strongly believes in witchcraft ('nyongo'). Many mysterious deaths have been blamed on it because it is a convenient peg on which to hang the people's ignorance. Such erroneous beliefs as these always lead to the doom of gullible individuals. The sooner people abandon such beliefs, the better they stand to fight the spread of AIDS.

Acts and Sequences (A)

This implies the actual form and content of what is said: the precise words used, how they are used, and the relationship of what is said to the actual issue in the discussion. Linguists have long shown interest in this aspect of speaking.

The 'bottle dance' scene offers a good opportunity for illustrating acts and sequences. 'Bottle Dance', with the bottle as the main instrument, is a very popular dance in the Mankon community. During this dance, people practice a lot of promiscuity. This usually leads to unsafe sexual acts. Girls indulge in sexual relationships with men in exchange for something (a bottle of beer, money, etc). Most of these relationships end with the dance.

Key: Language of Love (K)

This refers to the tone or manner of conveying a particular message. Is the message light-hearted, serious, precise, pedantic, mocking, sarcastic or pompous? It can equally be non-verbal. Listeners, most often pay much more attention to the key than to the actual content. Consider the following examples:

1. If a man shakes a girl's hand and one of the fingers scratches the girl's palm, this implies that the man admires the girl and is telling her 'I love you'.
2. If the tip of the tongue is protruded and one of the eyes blinks, this is indirectly telling the girl 'I would like to make love to you'.
3. When a female sits in front of a male, plays with her hair, adjusting her dress, crossing her legs, it means that she admires the man and would want him to ask her out.
4. If in a crowd, a man looks at a girl and 'cuts eye' (blinks one of the eyes), moves outside or aside, this implies that he wishes to converse with her confidentially. The discussion could be on any issue, but, most often, it is on the topic of love and sex.
5. Hissing (whistling) is another gesture for calling someone from a distance. Most often, boys do this to girls.

Instrumentality (I)

This is one of the key factors for achieving the objectives of this study. Instrumentality refers to the choice of the channel—for example, whether it is oral or written. It also refers to the actual forms of speech employed, such as the language, code or register that is chosen.

In the course of a conversation between two lovers, an expression from a different language can be used either because one of the lovers cannot find a suitable word for a joke, or does not wish to use a particular word. There is an instance in a story where the friend of Adeline's father admires her and wants to go to bed with her. Adeline's father is very strict and does not allow her daughter to go out. She is beautiful, so he thinks that boys will run after her and impregnate her. But his friend keeps frequenting the house because he wants Adeline badly. Whenever he is around he tries as much as he can to converse with her. When her father is around the topic changes. He would talk to his friend in parables. Presently, he starts dating Adeline without the knowledge of her father even though all the arrangements were made in his house.

Norms of Interaction and Interpretation (N)
This refers to specific behaviours and proprieties that attach to 'speaking' and also to how these may be viewed by someone who does not share them. For instance, loudness, silence and gaze return. An example of this can be seen in a conversation between two strangers. These norms, however, vary between social groups.

One partner can refuse what the other says by shouting down on him/her. Just a gaze return (change of eyes) answers a question either negatively or positively. It can also express surprise.

Consider the following example.

Mother: (Shouts) where are you going?

Son: (going without uttering a word)

Mother: I ask where you are going? You think you are now big and you can go wherever you wish without telling me.

Son: (Looks back sternly) To see a friend.

Mother: (To herself) Those your numerous girlfriends who come to this compound and you do not listen to my advice. (Aloud) I hope you are aware of what you are doing. There are a lot of illnesses now especially HIV/AIDS. When you die, you will not be buried with me. I have done my own part.

This conversation shows that there is tension between the mother and his son when they talk about sex. The son cannot tell his mother that he is going to see his girlfriend. He simply refers to her as a friend. But the mother suspects that he is going to see one of his numerous girlfriends and she warns him about the danger of AIDS. However, the circumstances in which she tries to advise her child against this danger of AIDS does not seem to be the right atmosphere where her son would readily agree with her and change his behaviour. Maybe, parents should think about different norms of interacting with their children, for example, by accepting to talk to them about sex, when these children relax or do something where they do not feel threatened by their parents' probe into their privacy.

Genre (G)
This is the final term, and it refers to clearly demarcated types of utterances: poems, proverbs, riddles, sermons, prayers, lectures, and editorials. They are all 'marked' in specific ways in contrast to casual speech. Given the topic under study, we can find common instances in the Mankon community where lovers express their emotions using the above-mentioned forums.

What Hymes offers us in his Speaking formula is a very necessary reminder that talking is a complex activity, and that any particular bit of it is actually a piece of 'skilled work'. It is skilled in the sense that, if it is to be successful, the speaker must reveal a sensitivity to, and awareness of, each of the eight factors outlined above. This formula helps linguists discover realities about the behaviour of people as it occurs in their social contexts. Probably, one might be shocked that promiscuity is allowed during 'bottle dance' in the Mankon community. But it is a reality that we cannot ignore. Even educated people are involved in this kind of promiscuity because it is part of their culture. The challenge for linguists who like to propose means of fighting the spread of AIDS in such community is to reckon with this reality. Using this Speaking formula to probe the sexual behaviour of other sub-Saharan African communities will surely reveal similar factors that may be specific to such communities and which are usually hidden because talking about sex is always considered a taboo in most African cultures. Therefore, unveiling the real motivations of the sexual behaviour of various African communities would certainly help in the devising of appropriate startegies for the prevention of AIDS in sub-Saharan Africa.

Conclusion
We wish to make two points. First, we would like to point out that the problems raised in this chapter are part of the bigger problem of the effective means of AIDS prevention. As pointed out in Paul Farmer (1996), AIDS in Africa is closely related to poverty and gender inequality. Although these problems will not find immediate solutions, we believe that, if people can be made aware of alternatives to better manage their lives, they will make better choices as far as their sexual behaviour is concerned. Hopefully, such educated choices will drastically reduce the spread of AIDS.

Secondly, we would like to draw the reader's attention to the fact that findings, such as those revealed about the sexual behaviour in the Mankon community, easily fit into the kinds of follow-up discussions advocated in *Wish I Had Known*. There is a section in the book entitled 'Ask your question: difficult issues related to the fight against AIDS' in which the users of this book are encouraged to discuss issues that are of interest to their own communities in a bid to find solutions to their peculiar problems. It is our hope that linguists and any related professional who is interested in the ethnography of communication will encourage the replication of similar studies in other parts of sub-Saharan Africa that are likely to help understand better the sexual behaviour of the African people and use the findings for discussing the best ways of helping the people involved in such studies to avoid HIV/AIDS. We strongly recommend the use of *Wish I Had Known* as it gives the right framework for discussing AIDS-related problems specific to any African community, as reflected, for example, in the instances of the ethnography of communication of the Mankon community.

References

Farmer, Paul, Connors, M. & Simmons, J., eds., 1996, *Violence, Poverty and AIDS: Sex, Drugs, and Structural Violence*, Monroe, Maine: Common Courage Press.

Hyman, Larry M., 2001, 'Fieldwork as a State of Mind', in Paul Newman and Martha Ratliff, eds., *Linguistic Fieldwork*, Cambridge: Cambridge University Press.

Hymes, Dell, 1964, 'Towards Ethnographies of Communication: The Analysis of Communicative Events', *American Anthropologist*, 66:1-34.

Mutaka, N. & Chumbow, S. B., eds., 2001, 'Research Mate in African Linguistics: Focus on Cameroon'. A Fieldworker's Tool for Deciphering the Stories Cameroonian Languages Have to Tell. In Honour of Professor Larry M. Hyman, Cologne: Rudiger Koppe Verlag, pp. 55-77.

Mutaka, Philip, 2001, *The Fruit of Love*, Yaounde, Editions SHERPA.

Mutaka, Philip and Bolima, Flora A., eds, 2003, *Wish I Had Known*, Yaounde: Editions SHERPA.

Wardhaugh, R., 1992, *An Introduction to Sociolinguistics*, Oxford, UK: Blackwell.

5

Les enjeux de la traduction en langues africaines : le cas du Cameroun

Moïse Ateba Ngoa

Introduction

Le continent africain est resté pendant longtemps marginalisé dans le domaine de la science à cause de son histoire. En effet, ce continent aura connu successivement l'esclavage, la colonisation, puis le néocolonialisme. Même la jeune science de la traduction appelée la traductologie et surtout sa pratique vont aussi ostraciser le continent africain, sous le fallacieux prétexte que les sujets africains parlent déjà les langues occidentales héritées de la colonisation.

Aujourd'hui encore, très peu de langues africaines font l'objet d'un quelconque intérêt en matière de traduction en dépit de ce que la traduction de ces langues pourrait apporter comme richesse au patrimoine linguistique de l'humanité.

Notre propos a pour objectif de montrer le bien-fondé de la traduction en langues africaines dans le cadre de la dissémination du savoir et dans la perspective du développement des langues africaines ainsi que de la diffusion des cultures africaines. Nous nous proposons enfin de démontrer qu'aucun choix de traduction n'est innocent et de montrer ainsi l'enjeu idéologique que cachent les choix de traduction, qui jusqu'à présent, excluent les langues africaines de cet espace d'échanges culturels. Pour des raisons de méthodologie, nous allons focaliser notre attention sur le Cameroun, pays considéré comme l'Afrique en miniature grâce à sa diversité linguistique et culturelle.

Aspects historiques

Notre propos commencera par la paraphrase d'un dicton populaire : « Dis-moi quelles langue(s) tu parles et je te dirai qui tu es ».

Les problèmes de traduction en langues camerounaises sont à l'image de la situation linguistique du Cameroun—pays multiculturel par excellence où se pratiquent plusieurs langues locales et pour lequel le terme de mosaïque linguistique est souvent utilisé—depuis les premiers contacts avec le monde occidental. De l'avis de Essono (2000:10), auteur de l'ouvrage *L'Ewondo, langue bantu du Cameroun : phonologie-morphologie-syntaxe* publié en janvier 2000, « En plus des deux langues officielles que sont l'anglais et le français imposées lors de la réunification du Cameroun occidental anglais et du Cameroun oriental français le 1er octobre 1961, l'Atlas linguistique (1983) inventorie près de 247 langues nationales... ».

En fait, pendant la colonisation, deux tendances s'affrontent au Cameroun : les partisans de l'enseignement des langues nationales et ceux qui, apparemment plus nombreux ou alors plus influents, soutiennent l'enseignement des langues occidentales. C'est la raison pour laquelle Stumpf (1977:13), auteur de *La politique linguistique au Cameroun de 1884 à 1960, comparaison entre les administrations coloniales allemande, française et britannique et du rôle joué par les sociétés missionnaires,* indique dans son introduction « la préférence des Camerounais pour la langue coloniale au détriment du vernaculaire ». Les missionnaires étaient en faveur des langues dites indigènes comme le démontrent les travaux du missionnaire Alfred Saker en duala avec au bout du compte une réalisation majeure qui est la traduction de la Bible. Un autre missionnaire, le Révérend Père Nekes écrit une grammaire ewondo et le tout premier manuel de la même langue en 1911. Dans le même ordre d'idées, il proposera l'ewondo comme langue territoriale du Cameroun.

Les administrations coloniales quant à elles n'étaient pas entièrement disposées à encourager cet essor des langues nationales. Les partisans de ce refus de l'introduction de langues nationales seront soutenus par certains Camerounais qui, à cause des rivalités ethniques ou des ambitions culturelles, s'opposeront à l'émergence des langues nationales. Stumpf (1977) révèle par exemple que les habitants de Victoria (actuel Limbé) se sentaient supérieurs aux peuples de l'arrière-pays, c'est-à-dire la région du Mont Cameroun, actuellement dénommée Buéa. C'est à ce titre qu'ils se considéraient comme des gens civilisés tandis que les villageois éloignés de la Côte de quelques kilomètres n'étaient que des «bushmen». Ainsi, lorsque le duala fut introduit, cet auteur écrit que :

> Pour les Victoriens [les habitants de Victoria] le duala ressemblait trop à la langue des bakweris[sic], considérés comme des Bushmen arriérés. Donc comment auraient-ils pu accepter la langue de ces broussards alors qu'eux les Victoriens étaient des civilisés[sic] christianisés et instruits dans une langue européenne ? Les parents exigeaient pour leurs enfants une éducation civilisée. Dans une lettre rédigée en anglais à la direction de la mission de Bâle en Suisse (1889) ils contestèrent l'introduction du duala, langue barbare, qui est contre raison (...it is quite against reason...). L'anglais ou l'allemand seraient les bienvenus car ce sont deux langues civilisées (Stumpf 1977:33).

Ils concluaient en évoquant le fait que le duala n'est pas leur langue maternelle et que sans connaissance de l'allemand ou de l'anglais, on ne pouvait entrer au service du gouvernement ou d'une personne civilisée.

Lors de la réunion du « Board of Education » tenue en octobre 1956 à Buéa, personne—pas même les Camerounais, les représentants baptistes, ni les catholiques—ne prit la défense des langues locales. Le rapport sur la conférence de Brazzaville du 30 janvier au 8 novembre 1944 stipule que seul le français est la langue d'instruction et que les dialectes locaux sont interdits dans les écoles.

Par ailleurs, certains Camerounais considéraient l'apprentissage d'une langue locale comme une entreprise inutile et peu profitable, préférant ainsi les langues occidentales qui conféraient le prestige social et la possibilité d'obtenir un emploi, ainsi que des avantages financiers.

Cette situation de marginalisation des langues africaines va planter le décor et explique les difficultés auxquelles est confrontée la traduction en langues africaines aujourd'hui. L'on peut donc comprendre le peu d'engouement qui caractérise encore de nos jours la traduction en langues camerounaises.

Notre préoccupation est de savoir s'il ne faut pas repenser tout le problème linguistique camerounais aujourd'hui et encourager la traduction en langues camerounaises dans le but de favoriser la dissémination des connaissances, le développement des langues camerounaises et leur prise en compte dans la confection d'ouvrages lexicographiques.

La traduction en langues camerounaises pourrait offrir la possibilité de s'approprier de nouvelles connaissances et de permettre leur dissémination. En effet, tout texte qui fait l'objet d'une traduction en langue locale suscite plus d'intérêt de la part du lectorat cible qui s'y reconnaît. Il y a dans l'œuvre de traduction un réel désir de briser les barrières linguistiques. C'est dire combien il est urgent de traduire dans les langues camerounaises pour une compréhension effective de certaines informations par l'ensemble de la population. Nous disons bien « comprendre » dans son acception première synonyme de « prendre avec soi » et donc intégrer.

C'est ce qui explique l'effort des missionnaires en faveur des langues nationales et l'immense succès connu par ces traductions dans les campagnes. La Bible est parfois le seul livre connu dans certaines régions de l'arrière-pays parce que celui-ci a fait l'objet d'une traduction. Le lecteur d'un tel texte se sent non seulement intégré dans la communauté du savoir, mais également interpellé parce que toute bonne traduction prend en compte les éléments culturels de la langue d'arrivée.

En procédant ainsi, le lecteur a l'impression que sa communauté est intégrée dans le grand ensemble et il devient plus réceptif à un tel message. En revanche, l'exclusion d'un groupe linguistique de cette grande chaîne interactive ne favorise pas la communication. Car quiconque se sent étranger à la langue intègre avec moins d'enthousiasme les informations que véhicule le texte écrit dans cette langue, surtout si ladite langue est considérée comme celle du maître.

Le paradoxe relevé au Cameroun est que les langues officielles sont principalement utilisées dans les zones urbaines, alors que les campagnes se servent de langues locales pour communiquer. Cette situation linguistique devrait favoriser la traduction en langues camerounaises dans le but de permettre à ce grand nombre d'avoir accès à l'information. Il est par exemple étonnant de constater que les informations relatives à la pandémie du SIDA ne soient disponibles que dans les langues officielles, ce qui contribue à laisser les campagnes en marge de la lutte contre le VIH-SIDA. C'est à croire que les campagnes de sensibilisation en question ne s'adressent qu'aux populations des zones urbaines. Il y a là un cas d'abandon d'une bonne frange de la population camerounaise qui a autant besoin d'être informée que les populations qui peuplent les villes. Nous sommes d'ailleurs persuadés que le premier groupe sus-évoqué a beaucoup plus besoin d'informations que le second, eu égard à la rareté de la documentation en zone rurale.

Il s'avère par conséquent important de traduire en langues camerounaises pour rendre l'information accessible à tous et particulièrement à ceux qui n'ont pas été à l'école occidentale.

La traduction en langues camerounaises s'impose aussi comme une nécessité dans le développement desdites langues. En effet, les langues camerounaises qui ont fait l'objet d'une traduction ont connu un développement réel. C'est le cas de l'ewondo qui a servi comme langue véhiculaire dans les provinces du Centre, du Sud et de l'Est. La même langue a été utilisée par l'administration coloniale pour des contacts avec les indigènes et les missionnaires dans le cadre de l'évangélisation.

Il va sans dire que la traduction permet, à travers la quête des équivalents dynamiques dans le travail de restitution du sens, de déployer une activité créatrice susceptible d'enrichir la langue par des mécanismes à la fois conscients et inconscients auxquels recourt le traducteur. C'est ainsi que l'on peut évoquer des cas de néologismes, et des procédés techniques tels que l'emprunt, le calque, la paraphrase et l'analogie qui permettent, grâce à la traduction, d'enrichir les langues en contact. Dans le cas de la traduction de et vers les langues camerounaises, le problème fondamental est l'établissement des équivalents dynamiques. Car les traductologues s'accordent sur un principe, c'est que l'on ne traduit pas les langues, mais des messages. Dans la quête des équivalents dynamiques, le traducteur qui travaille de ou vers une langue camerounaise peut recourir à un moyen astucieux pour résoudre les problèmes d'absence d'un concept dans l'un ou l'autre univers culturel en recourant à l'emprunt qui enrichit ainsi la langue d'arrivée. Beaucoup de langues camerounaises ont ainsi vu leur lexique s'enrichir grâce à la traduction.

En parcourant les traductions en ewondo, nous avons relevé de nombreux cas d'emprunts avec des approches qui sont fondées sur le degré d'intégration à la langue camerounaise.

La première approche consiste à reproduire le mot tel qu'il s'écrit et se prononce dans la langue de départ. Il s'agit d'une absence d'intégration morphologique et phonétique. L'on peut citer le cas du vocable « Vatican » qui, traduit en ewondo, reste tel quel.

Langue de départ (français)	Langue d'arrivée (ewondo)
Vatican	*Vatican*

C'est ainsi que l'on peut lire : « Vatican II, voie tracée par le pape Jean XXIII et poursuivie par son successeur Paul VI... »[1] devient « Esok nnen mfufub tara yoannes XXIII angatogëlan, Paulus VI akë ai dzo osu, 'Vatican II'... ».[2]

Dans son ouvrage intitulé *Ongola*, l'abbé Mvogo (Wenceslas) recourt aux emprunts tels que « ministère, garage, poste centrale, quartier, etc. » pour traduire des réalités inconnues dans l'univers culturel d'arrivée. Tous ces mots restent inchangés sur les plans morphologique et phonétique. Toutefois, la présence d'une marque orthographique, les guillemets en l'occurrence, confirme le fait qu'il s'agit d'un mot nouveau dans la langue emprunteuse. Il arrive parfois aussi que dans la traduction d'un terme, la prononciation reste inchangée mais que l'orthographe soit différente. Ainsi, voit-on l'expression « Ebug grèk » apparaître dans le texte de l'abbé Mvogo. Le terme « grèk », bien que prononcé comme en français, ne s'écrit pas comme dans la langue de départ.

À côté de ce type d'emprunts, l'on peut également relever ceux dont l'intégration morphologique et phonétique est presque totale. C'est ainsi que dans sa préface à la traduction en ewondo du *Missel du dimanche* ; Mgr Jean Zoa opère les choix suivants :

Texte de départ (français)	Texte d'arrivée (ewondo)
Jean XXIII	*Yoannes XXIII*
Paul VI	*Paulus VI*

Dans la traduction de L'Ancien Testament par l'abbé Lucien Anya Noa, « Psaume de David 'devient' Salm David ». C'est dire que grâce à l'emprunt, le vocabulaire s'enrichit davantage dans la langue d'arrivée. En dehors du phénomène de l'emprunt, les traducteurs recourent parfois à la paraphrase.

Le vocable paraphrase vient du latin *paraphrasis* qui veut dire *phrase à côté*. La paraphrase est en réalité un développement explicatif d'un énoncé. *Le Dictionnaire de linguistique* de Dubois (1973:355) définit la paraphrase en ces termes : « Un énoncé A est dit paraphrase d'un énoncé B si A contient la même information que B, tout en étant plus long que lui ». Ce procédé est très récurrent dans les traductions vers les langues camerounaises, notamment l'ewondo. En règle générale, le traducteur s'en sert pour combler une lacune d'ordre conceptuel dans la langue d'arrivée. Ainsi, chaque fois qu'une réalité x exprimée dans une langue A n'a pas d'équivalent conceptuel y dans la langue B, le traducteur se sert d'une tournure explicative, c'est-à-dire d'une paraphrase en vue de permettre au lecteur du texte d'arrivée de ne pas perdre l'intégralité du message. Dans la préface de *Kalara mes me amos Nti*, Mgr Jean Zoa, l'ex archevêque de Yaoundé utilise un terme nouveau dans l'univers conceptuel beti, « Vatican II ». Pour le rendre, le traducteur recourt d'abord à l'emprunt comme nous l'avons relevé précédemment. Mais le fait que ce concept est loin d'être compris comme tel par le lecteur ewondo qui ne connaît pas la langue de départ, le français ici, pousse le traducteur à recourir à une paraphrase, *esok nnen* qui signifie littéralement la grande réunion à huis clos qui est susceptible d'être mieux comprise par le locuteur ewondo. En effet, ce terme provient de l'univers culturel beti et s'utilise dans le cadre des grandes rencontres entre les sages d'un groupe social déterminé pour décider de l'avenir de la communauté. C'est le forum dans lequel se prennent les grandes décisions. En effet, l'esok intervient lors des grandes crises.

Un autre avantage que pourrait offrir la traduction en langues camerounaises est la prise en compte de ces langues dans la confection des ouvrages lexicographiques.

Le fait que les langues africaines ne fassent pas l'objet de traduction est à l'origine de plusieurs lacunes d'ordre lexicologique. En effet, plusieurs réalités de cet espace culturel sont purement ignorées dans les dictionnaires. Une telle situation met alors le traducteur africain en face de difficultés qui ressemblent parfois à des apories. Ainsi en est-il de certains termes courants en agriculture mais absents des dictionnaires qui ne tiennent pas compte de ces réalités. Le mot « tarot », une culture locale bien connue au Cameroun renvoie à une autre réalité dans un dictionnaire français. Il en est de même pour le terme « prune ». L'urgence de la prise en compte des langues africaines dans la conception de ces ouvrages lexicographiques n'est donc plus à démontrer.

En dépit de l'existence de tant de langues africaines, celles-ci sont rarement prises en considération dans les choix de traduction. L'on peut donc se poser la question de savoir qu'est-ce qui oriente lesdits choix de traduction. Car, il est évident que toutes les langues ne bénéficient pas de la même attention auprès des instances de traduction. L'œuvre de traduction implique nécessairement l'ambition de mettre à la disposition d'une communauté culturelle le mode de pensée de la culture de départ. Une telle entreprise traduit parfois un désir d'hégémonie culturelle. Or pour exporter sa culture, il faut avoir les moyens économiques pour le faire. Ce n'est pas un pur hasard si les pays pauvres sont ceux-là qui n'offrent que des langues de moindre diffusion. L'on comprend donc le manque d'intérêt qui entoure la traduction vers ces langues.

Les langues africaines sont donc victimes aujourd'hui de ce que Stumpf (1977:91) appelle « la langue comme ARGENT linguistique ».

Les langues africaines font les frais des difficultés économiques auxquels sont confrontés les pays africains et l'hégémonie culturelle de ceux qui n'ont pas cessé de penser que « les langues locales seraient incapables de traduire les termes abstraits européens ».

Conclusion

La traduction en langues africaines est à l'image du statut desdites langues pendant la période coloniale.

Toutefois, ces langues ont besoin de l'apport de la traduction pour leur développement et leur survie ; car la traduction permet à une langue de s'enrichir davantage au contact des autres et lui permet ainsi de ne pas mourir. Les langues humaines tireraient ainsi profit de cet enrichissement mutuel que favorise la traduction.

La traduction en langues africaines favoriserait par ailleurs l'enrichissement des ouvrages lexicographiques qui prendraient ainsi en compte l'univers culturel africain dans un monde désormais interdépendant.

L'entreprise de traduction ne devrait par ailleurs plus être à l'origine d'une marginalisation liée à l'économie et à la pseudo-suprématie de certaines cultures. Elle devrait plutôt permettre à toutes les langues de s'exprimer dans une symphonie culturelle qui engloberait toutes les tendances linguistiques universelles.

Notes

1. Mgr Jean Zoa, préface à *Kalara mes me amos Nti*.
2. Mgr Jean Zoa, préface à *Kalara mes me amos Nti*.

Références

Alexandre, P. et J. Binet., 1958, *Le groupe dit pahouin, (Fang- Bulu- Beti)*, Paris, PUF, (Monog. Eth.n. Africaines).
Amara, F. X., 1987, *Kalara mes me amos Nti*, Yaoundé, Archidiocèse de Yaoundé.
Anya Noa, L., 1992, *Mfufub Bibel. A nkobo ewondo (nnom amvoe)*, Milan, impr. Tino Allegri.
Auwens *et al.*, 1975, *Missel dominical de l'assemblée*, Paris, Éditions Brepols.
Auwens *et al.*, 1992, *Ngogelan besalmen*, Milan, impr. Tino Allegri.
Bilongo, P., 2000, Petit catéchisme familial à l'usage des jeunes des lycées et collèges de l'aumônerie catholiques du diocèse de Mbalmayo. D'après les Traditions monastiques de l'Abbaye Saint-Joseph de Clairva.
Dubois, J., *et al.*, 1973, *Dictionnaire de linguistique*, Paris, Librairie Larousse.
Essono, Jean-J. M., 2000, *L'Ewondo langue Bantu du Cameroun: phonologie-morphologie-syntaxe,*. Presse de l'UCAC, Yaoundé.
Graffin, R. et Pichon, F., 1930, *Grammaire ewondo*, Paris, Didot et Cie.

Graffin, R. et Pichon, F., 1940, *Dictionnaire: 1- Kalara afelan bibuk ewondo ai fulansi 2- Lexique ewondo-français,* Yaoundé, VIII.

Haarpainter, W., 1909, « Grammatik der Jaundesprache » (Kamerun) [Grammaire de la langue ewondo (Cameroun)], in *Anthropos 4,* (1-2). pp.684-701, 919-930.

Heepe, M., 1919, *Jaunde-Texte von K. Atangana und P. Messi, nebst experimentalphonetischen Untersuchungen überdie Tonhöhen in Jaunde einer Einführung in die Jaundesprache,* [Textes ewondo de K. Atangana et P. Messi, accompagnés d'une enquête phonétique expérimentale sur les tons en ewondo et d'une introduction à la langue ewondo], Hamburg, L. Friederschen (Abhandlungen des Hamburgischen Kolonialinstituts 24), XVI.

Laburthe-Tolra, P., 1970, « Yaoundé d'après Zenker » in *Annales de la faculté des lettres et sciences humaines de Yaoundé,* vol. n°2, P.3-113.

Laburthe-Tolra, P., 1981, *Les seigneurs de la forêt,* Paris, La Sorbonne,

Laburthe-Tolra, P., 1985, *Initiations et sociétés secrètes au Cameroun. Essai sur la religion beti,* Paris, Karthala,.

Mvogo, W., 1998, *Man diksionèr ewondo-fulansi,* Yaoundé, impr. AMA.

Mvogo, W., 1998, *A moe, yeege ewondo mbembe nkobo/ Mon ami, apprends la belle langue ewondo* (Ms).

Mvogo, W., *Le Cameroun catholique en images: 1890-1961* (Ms).

Mvogo, W., 2001, *Le grand jubilé de l'an 2000 et les 110 ans du Cameroun catholique* (Ms).

Mvogo, W. 2001, *Ebon be Kamerun bengabed befada ataregi mbu 1935 akui a ....* (Ms).

Ndongo, Semengue A., 1981, « Traduction : de la théorie à la pratique. Traduction technico-scientifique vers une langue exempte de concepts correspondants. Exemples de l'ewondo, Paris, Université de la Sorbonne Nouvelle ». Thèse de 3e cycle.

Nekes, H., 1910, *Fibel für Schulen in Jaunde* [Manuel pour les écoles de Yaoundé], Lumburg, Pallotiner Verlag.

Nekes, H., 1913, *Die Sprache der Jaunde in Kamerun* [La langue des Ewondo au Cameroun], Berlin, D. Reimer (Deustche Kolonialsprachen 5).

Nekes, H., 1927, «Zur Entwicklung der Jaunde-Sprache unter den Einfluí der europäischen Kultur », [Le développement de la langue ewondo sous l'influence de la culture européenne], in *Festschrift Meinhof: Sprachwissenschaftliche und andere Studien,* Hamburg.

Ossama, N., 1980, *Feg beti, Contes et proverbes ewondo pour l'enseignement,* Douala, Collège Libermann, Coll. Langues et Littératures nationales 8.

Segond, L., 1992, *La Sainte Bible,* Alliance biblique universelle.

Stumpf, Rudolf, 1977, *La politique linguistique au Cameroun de 1884 à 1960,* Berne, Peter Lang.

Tsala, T. 1957, *Dictionnaire ewondo-français,* Lyon, impr. Vitte, XXXI.

Vinay, J.P. et Darbelnet, J., 1958, *Stylistique comparée du français et de l'anglais,* Montréal, Beauchemin.

6

Développement des langues gabonaises : état des lieux et perspectives

Daniel Franck Idiata

Introduction

La présente contribution porte sur les langues gabonaises. À l'heure de la mondialisation et au moment où le pays prend conscience de l'intérêt de l'intégration de ces langues dans l'éducation scolaire, il s'agit d'esquisser un bilan des travaux portant sur le développement des langues, processus préalable à tout programme scolaire impliquant les langues vernaculaires. Le bilan que nous proposons ici va s'articuler autour de deux grands axes. Les exigences méthodologiques imposent une présentation générale des langues du Gabon. C'est l'objet de la seconde section qui va concerner l'inventaire, la classification linguistique et l'état des connaissances sur l'ensemble des langues. La troisième section, quant à elle, propose un historique du développement des langues gabonaises, c'est-à-dire toutes les étapes visant à leur adaptation à l'univers de l'écrit. Cet historique va concerner l'écriture, la standardisation, la place des langues dans l'alphabétisation et l'enseignement scolaire et leur statut dans le cadre général du développement du pays.

Les langues du Gabon : aperçu général

Point sur l'inventaire des langues

Le nombre exact des langues vernaculaires[1] gabonaises n'est pas connu avec certitude à ce jour (Idiata 2002). Cependant, une approche objective du terrain pourrait situer ce nombre autour de la quarantaine. Cette idée s'appuie sur les sources (plus ou moins) récentes : 37 langues pour Jacquot (1978) et 40 langues pour Grimes (1996).

La configuration linguistique du Gabon est caractéristique de la plupart des pays africains subsahariens, où les langues vernaculaires cohabitent avec les langues héritées de la colonisation. Dans le cas du Gabon, cet héritage colonial est la langue française, élevée au statut de langue officielle dès l'accession du pays à l'indépendance en 1960. Cette langue est devenue au fil des années la principale langue de communication intercommunautaire et la seule langue véhiculaire du pays à l'échelle nationale, en plus de son statut de langue officielle.

Les langues vernaculaires appartiennent presque essentiellement à la grande famille bantu, respectivement aux zones A, B et H de Guthrie (1967-1971). À ces langues s'ajoutent quelques parlers pygmées (l'exemple du baka ou du bakoya), mais qui demeurent très mal connus aujourd'hui, parce que très peu documentés.

Une synthèse des travaux réalisés sur l'inventaire des langues gabonaises (Guthrie 1953 ; Raponda-Walker 1960 ; Jacquot 1978 ; Grimes 1996 ; Kwenzi Mikala 1998), mais aussi les informations publiées dans le cadre du dernier recensement de la population gabonaise permettent d'esquisser la liste des langues gabonaises ainsi qu'on le voit en (1) ci-dessous :

(1) Aduma (liduma)
    Akele
    apindji (gepinzipinzi)
    bekwil (bakwele)
    benga
    civili (vili)
    fang
    gevia (evia)
    gisir (gisir)
    ikota (kota)
    imwele
    lekaningi
    (bakaningi)
    lisigu
    mahongwe

isangu
mbangwe (mbaouin)
mbaouin
myene (omyene)
ndambomo
ndasa (mindasa)
ndumu (lindumu)
ngubi
inzebi
obamba
(lembaama)
okande (kande)
pove (gevove)
seki (sekyani)
shake (shake)

shiwa, (makina)
simba
latege (teke)
itsengi (tsengi)
tsogo
varama
ivili
vungu
wanzi (liwanzi)
wumvu (wumbu)
yesa (mwesa)
yilumbu (lumbu)
yipunu

A (liduma) Il est important de relever deux choses. Tout d'abord le fait que cette liste ne tienne pas compte des langues non bantu, c'est-à-dire les langues pygmées (telles que le bakola ou le baka) ou les langues d'origine étrangère (par exemple le haoussa) ; ensuite, le fait que cette liste ne comporte pas nécessairement des langues différentes. En fait, tout dépend de la perspective dans laquelle on se situe, sociopolitique ou scientifique (linguistique). D'un point de vue sociopolitique, tout parler humain est une langue à part entière. De ce point de vue donc, la différenciation entre « langue » et « dialecte » tient uniquement au statut sociopolitique des parlers. À l'opposé, c'est-à-dire du point de vue scientifique, une étude sérieuse sur les relations entre les parlers en présence peut amener à effectuer des regroupements qui orienteraient sans doute le débat autour d'une quarantaine de langues. Cette hypothèse est beaucoup plus évidente pour les parlers fang et myene qui représentent respectivement des dialectes de la langue fang et de la langue myene (ou omyene).

La plupart des travaux linguistiques gabonais (Moussirou-Mouyama 2000 ; Kwenzi Mikala 1998 ; Voltz 1990) localisent les différents groupes ethnolinguistiques gabonais à des endroits précis du territoire. Mais, il est crucial que l'on distingue une localisation qui concerne les sites historiques des populations de celle qui les localise aujourd'hui en tenant compte de leurs nouveaux « habitats». Pour prendre un exemple précis, on peut s'appuyer sur la province de l'Estuaire, à l'intérieur de laquelle seulement cinq parlers sont localisés dans cette carte (okak, seki, meke, benga et mpongwe). Il est évident que quiconque a une idée même vague de cette province arrivera à la conclusion que l'on peut identifier plus de cinq peuples, donc plus de cinq langues dans cette province. Ce que nous disons de la province de l'Estuaire peut s'appliquer à d'autres provinces, pourvu que l'on accepte le truisme d'un véritable travail de terrain pour réactualiser[2] les paradigmes traditionnels.

Par rapport à cette idée, les données officielles publiées dans le cadre du recensement de la population (1993) montrent que la plupart des groupes ethnolinguistiques recensés se retrouvent, en réalité, dans plusieurs localités du pays et que chacun des groupes compte un nombre plus ou moins important d'individus[3]. Il serait donc totalement illusoire, aujourd'hui, de limiter une communauté donnée à une partie spécifique du territoire national, même si on continue de « coller » à chaque ethnie une étiquette régionale spécifique. À partir de ce moment, toute étude qui se veut sérieuse et qui traite de la localisation des langues gabonaises se doit de tenir compte de cette évidence.

Point sur la classification des langues

La classification linguistique, rappelons-le, pour bien comprendre l'objet de cette partie, est une opération qui consiste à répartir les langues en familles linguistiques. Il existe deux grands types de classification, à savoir la classification génétique et la classification typologique.

D'après Dubois *et al.* (1994), la classification génétique ou historique consiste à classer les langues en leur assignant une parenté plus ou moins grande fondée sur une communauté d'origine plus ou moins ancienne et des points de ressemblances plus ou moins nombreux. Ce type de classification permet d'établir des familles de langues (par exemple les langues bantu, les langues latines, les langues germaniques, etc.). La classification typologique (ou typologie) consiste, quant à elle, à classer les langues selon des listes de critères linguistiques préétablis (syntaxiques, morphologiques), sans se préoccuper d'autres ressemblances ni d'une possible communauté d'origine (par exemple les langues isolantes, les langues agglutinantes, les langues à classes, les langues à tons, etc.).

La classification des langues gabonaises, comme d'ailleurs leur identification, est l'un des domaines qui demandent le plus de recherches si l'on veut aboutir à une meilleure connaissance des rapports réels entre les différentes langues. On peut cependant, d'après les données dont on dispose aujourd'hui (Guthrie 1953; Raponda Walker 1960 ; Jacquot 1978 ; Kwenzi Mikala 1987 et 1998)[4], répartir les langues gabonaises en huit groupes tels que décrits ci-dessous.

Le Groupe Fang

Nous parlons de groupe fang, à la suite de Medjo Mve (1997), pour référer à la langue fang. Celle-ci est parlée non seulement au Gabon, mais aussi en Guinée équatoriale, au Cameroun (groupe Bulu-Beti-Fang) et, semble-t-il au Congo et en République centrafricaine. Pour ce qui est de la variété gabonaise, elle comprend les six dialectes présentés en (2) ci-dessous :

(2) meke   mvai
     okak   nzaman
     ntumu   atsi

Le groupe myene

Le groupe myene réfère à la langue omyene (d'après les locuteurs). Contrairement à la langue fang, l'omyene est parlé uniquement au Gabon. Cette langue comprend aussi six dialectes répartis à différents endroits du territoire, essentiellement entre les provinces de l'Estuaire, du Moyen Ogooué et l'Ogooué Maritime. Ces différentes variétés de la langue omyene sont présentées en (3) ci-dessous :

(3) galwa   mpongwe
     enenga   ajumba
     nkomi   orungu

Le groupe kota-kele

L'étiquette kota-kele désigne, en fait, un ensemble de langues (et / ou parlers) diverses. Il est nécessaire de préciser que ce groupe appelé aussi groupe B.20 dans la classification des langues bantu de Guthrie (par exemple), est l'un des plus complexes et des moins connus au Gabon. En effet, très peu de langues de ce groupe disposent d'une documentation linguistique suffisante. Ce groupe est composé des entités présentées en (4) ci-dessous :

(4) akele   ungom
     lisigu   mbangwe
     metombolo   seki
     tumbidi   shake
     wumbu   lendambomo
     ikota   shamayi
     benga   mahongwe
     ndasa

Le groupe tsogo-apindji

Ce groupe, identifié sous l'étiquette B.30 dans les classifications des langues bantu (d'après Guthrie), comprend environ six langues que nous présentons en (5) ci-dessous :

(5) tsogo   apindji
     okande   pove
     simba   geviya

Le groupe sira-punu

Le groupe sira-punu est normalement désigné par l'étiquette B.40 dans la classification des langues bantu de Guthrie. Une synthèse des propositions d'inventaires montre que ce groupe comprend huit langues (et/ou parlers), même si le statut de certaines d'entre elles reste à confirmer (précisément le yirimba et le yigama, qui n'ont été inventoriés que par un seul chercheur). Les composantes du groupe sira-punu sont présentées en (6) ci-dessous :

(6) gisir   isangu
     varama   vungu[2]
     yipunu   yilumbu
     ngubi   yirimba
     yigama

Le groupe nzebi-duma

Le groupe nzebi-duma est aussi appelé groupe B.50 dans la classification des langues bantu (par Guthrie, notamment). Il comprend six langues dont la plus importante, en termes démographiques, est le inzebi parlé aussi au Congo voisin. Ce groupe est composé comme on le voit en (7) ci-dessous :

(7) inzebi   liduma
     itsengi   liwanzi
     imwele   ivili

Le groupe mbede-teke

Ce groupe comprend les langues des groupes linguistiques B.60 et B.70 de Guthrie. Il est constitué d'au moins cinq entités telles que citées en (8) ci-dessous :

(8) lembaama   lekaningi
     lindumu   teke
     latsitsege

Nous ne disposons pas d'informations d'ordre lexicostatistique (ou autre) sur le degré de proximité des langues de ce groupe.

Les autres langues bantu

Il s'agit ici de langues que l'on ne peut intégrer dans les catégories précédentes du fait de différences notables à divers niveaux. Ce sont le civili classé par Guthrie (1967-1971) en H.12 et qui est parlé au Gabon et en République du Congo ; le benga (A.30) parlé en Guinée équatoriale et au Gabon ; le shiwa et le bekwil qui sont en fait des langues du groupe A.80 de Guthrie.

Les langues pygmées

Il s'agit, sans aucun doute, du groupe de langues les moins connues au Gabon. Il n'existe pas, en effet, d'informations précises sur le nombre de ces langues à ce jour, ni de documentation linguistique qui permette de les caractériser. La liste que nous présentons ci-dessous se limite donc aux noms récurrents.

(9) baka   bakoya
     bakola   babongo

Pour terminer cette partie qui concerne la classification des langues gabonaises, il est important de retenir que nous ne prétendons pas avoir réglé la question. Les regroupements que nous avons opérés s'appuient sur les propositions de classification existantes. Il faut, bien sûr, garder à l'esprit que si certains groupes paraissent homogènes (l'exemple des groupes fang et myene), dans d'autres groupes, les langues (et / ou parlers) présentent une hétérogénéité plus ou moins importante, selon les cas, et cela peut amener à remettre en cause, au moins en partie, les propositions existantes. Cet argument est principalement illustré par le groupe kota-kele (Bastin et Piron 1999 ; Van Der Veen 1999).

Pour espérer arriver à une meilleure connaissance des réalités de terrain, et donc à une composition beaucoup plus fiable au niveau des groupes, Hombert (1990) propose d'orienter la recherche dans deux directions, celle de l'uniformisation des degrés d'homogénéité des groupes et celle de l'établissement du degré de proximité linguistique entre les différents groupes.

Point sur la recherche linguistique

La recherche linguistique sur les langues gabonaises s'est développée et s'est diversifiée ces vingt dernières années. On référera, pour une vue d'ensemble, à Hombert (1990) ; Hombert et Mortier (1990 ou, plus récemment, à Medjo Mve (2001). Pour la majorité des groupes, on a une idée à peu près claire de la situation de la plupart des langues vernaculaires gabonaises sur les plans phonétique, phonologique et morphologique. Les travaux de syntaxes sont assez rares et sont limités à quelques langues, notamment celles qui ont fait l'objet d'études doctorales (comme le fang ou le isangu). Il en est de même pour la recherche en sociolinguistique qui est orientée presque essentiellement autour de la langue française. Concernant les études de psycholinguistique, il faut relever que moins de cinq langues ont été sollicitées à ce jour (seule la langue isangu bénéficie d'études sérieuses publiées). Comme on le voit donc, l'étude des langues vernaculaires gabonaises reste un vaste chantier, à peine exploré.

À propos du développement des langues

Considérations théoriques

Le projet actuel de l'intégration des langues gabonaises dans le système éducatif impose, comme préalable, que ces langues soient développées. Nous utilisons le concept de développement des langues dans le sens de Fergusson (1968) ou Cooper (1982), c'est-à-dire le processus de changement et d'adaptation de ces langues aux nouvelles exigences afin qu'elles servent aux nouveaux besoins. Ces exigences nécessitent tout le processus de modernisation des langues, processus qui couvre, dans le sens de Nikiema (2001), la normalisation et la standardisation, l'instrumentalisation et l'assignation de statuts et de fonctions aux langues.

À propos de l'écriture des langues gabonaises

Les tentatives d'écriture des langues gabonaises remontent à l'arrivée des premiers colons. Dans son article sur l'histoire de l'écriture des langues du Gabon, Mayer (1990) propose trois grandes phases ou périodes : (1) l'écriture des premiers Européens (écriture exploratoire) ; (2) l'écriture des missionnaires (écriture pédagogique), et (3) l'écriture scientifique.

La première période se situe entre 1500 et 1850. Elle commence avec l'arrivée des Portugais sur le littoral. Au cours de cette période, tous les écrits sur les langues gabonaises sont faits sur la base de l'alphabet de la langue des colonisateurs. Les écrits hérités de cette période concernent des listes de noms de peuples, de lieux, de personnes et des noms communs. La seconde période débute à partir de 1850, jusqu'à l'inauguration des travaux ayant adopté une écriture scientifique, c'est-à-dire Raponda Walker (1932). Cette période est caractérisée par un changement de mentalités chez les colons. Ces derniers, pour reprendre les termes de Mayer (1990:73), « ne vont plus seulement s'intéresser à leur communication avec ceux qu'ils appellent les indigènes, mais passent à l'apprentissage de la langue, et même, avec l'œuvre de la scolarisation missionnaire, enseignent la lecture et l'écriture des langues aux locuteurs natifs ». Mais, comme pour l'époque précédente, c'est encore l'alphabet latin de la langue des colons qui sert pour l'écriture des langues gabonaises. La troisième période est caractérisée par l'utilisation des systèmes d'écriture spécifiques aux langues vernaculaires gabonaises. Ces systèmes d'écriture résultent des études linguistiques (Alphabet scientifique des langues gabonaises ; Voltz et Dechangy 1990).

Il existe, à ce jour, quatre propositions de systèmes d'écriture des langues gabonaises : (a) la proposition de Raponda Walker (1932), (b) l'Alphabet scientifique des langues du Gabon publié par le LUTO (1990), (c) le nouvel alphabet des langues gabonaises adopté en 1999, et (d) le système utilisé pour la méthode Rapidolangue (Guérineau 1996, 1998 & 1999). Ci-dessous, quelques détails sur chacune de ces contributions. Une comparaison de ces différentes propositions montre que l'on a évolué de systèmes calqués des langues occidentales, notamment le français, vers un système plus adapté aux propriétés structurelles des langues gabonaises, en fonction de leurs caractéristiques phonétiques, phonologiques et morphologiques (Idiata 2002).

À propos de la standardisation des langues gabonaises

La standardisation d'une langue réfère au processus de codification et d'acceptation par une communauté d'usagers d'une série de règles formelles définissant le « bon usage » de leur langue (Steward 1968). C'est donc le processus par lequel une variété spécifique d'une langue émerge comme la variété préférée d'une communauté linguistique (Ansre 1971) et celle à partir de laquelle seront réalisés tous les projets d'écritures. Aucune des langues gabonaises ne dispose d'une étude relative à la standardisation ou à la codification. L'exception porte uniquement sur le fang et sur le isangu pour lesquels des projets de recherche sur la standardisation sont en cours (Nzang-Bie (2001), sur le fang, et Idiata (2002), pour le isangu).

La place des langues gabonaises dans l'enseignement et l'alphabétisation

Le constat que l'on peut faire aujourd'hui par rapport à la place des langues gabonaises dans l'enseignement et l'alphabétisation est, de manière générale, très insignifiant, contrairement à l'époque coloniale où une certaine dynamique par rapport à une prise en compte de ces langues était attestée. La seule exception concerne les religieux, notamment les protestants qui ont traduit nombre de textes, dont la Bible et le Nouveau Testament dans plusieurs langues gabonaises. Bien entendu, nous ne passerons pas sous silence la place des langues gabonaises dans l'éducation populaire par le biais des médias (notamment la radio). On mentionnera aussi quelques actions d'associations communautaires qui entreprennent l'enseignement de leur langue à l'intérieur de la communauté avec pour objectif d'essayer de la conserver. Depuis six années, une expérience d'enseignement de six langues gabonaises est menée dans les établissements confessionnels de Libreville. En effet, sur la base de la méthode (Rapidolangue) proposée par la Fondation Raponda-Walker, les élèves des classes de sixième et troisième reçoivent, en moyenne une heure par semaine, l'enseignement d'une langue de leur choix sur la base des six langues proposées (Idiata, sous presse).

À propos de l'assignation de statuts et de fonctions aux langues vernaculaires gabonaises

Lorsque l'on parle de statut des langues, on fait référence à leur reconnaissance, et donc à leur accès à un certain nombre de fonctions qui sont presque exclusivement occupées par ce que l'on appelle aujourd'hui « langue partenaire » (pour faire du politiquement correct). S'agissant des fonctions d'une langue, nous envisageons ce concept dans le sens de Fishman (1991), c'est-à-dire les divers rôles que l'on assigne à une langue (à quoi elle sert ?).

Comme le précise encore Nikiéma (2001), le relèvement des statuts des langues africaines et leur utilisation dans les fonctions valorisantes (langue officielle, langue de l'enseignement formel, langue de communication, etc.) restent un défi majeur.

Depuis l'Indépendance, le pays a opté pour le français comme langue officielle et unique langue d'enseignement. Malgré un article de la dernière constitution qui prône la sauvegarde du patrimoine linguistique, aucune langue n'a le statut de langue officielle. Il n'existe aucune langue locale véhiculaire à l'échelle nationale, cette fonction étant aussi assumée par le français. De plus, la plus grande part des langues gabonaises comptent moins de 10 000 locuteurs. Si le nombre de locuteurs est un critère important pour la vitalité d'une langue, on peut considérer que les langues vernaculaires gabonaises sont vouées à l'extinction à très court terme (Grimes 1996), excepté peut-être le fang (30 % de la population), et peut-être le ipunu et le inzebi. Il faut ajouter, sur la base de deux enquêtes respectivement réalisées par Power-Lapointe (1994) et Idiata (2001 et 2002), que l'utilisation des langues gabonaises connaît un recul qui s'explique principalement par le fait que le français occupe toutes les fonctions de prestige et que l'usage des langues gabonaises est normalement réservé aux activités familiales, religieuses, interpersonnelles, etc. à l'intérieur de la communauté.

Conclusion et perspectives

Nous avons esquissé un bilan du développement des langues gabonaises depuis l'époque pré-indépendance jusqu'à ce jour. Cette esquisse a porté sur l'inventaire des langues, leur classification, l'état des connaissances et la situation des projets de valorisation de ces langues dans l'optique de leur intégration dans l'éducation scolaire.

Depuis de nombreuses années, la valorisation des langues vernaculaires africaines est un sujet à la mode. Aujourd'hui encore, avec la naissance de l'Union africaine, se développe une théorie de la « Renaissance africaine par les langues ». Cette théorie consiste à affirmer que les langues vernaculaires peuvent et doivent, pour reprendre les termes de Bearth (2000:5-6), servir de dispositif d'apprentissage pour l'acquisition des contenus essentiels d'un programme scolaire qui soit fonctionnel sans être aliénant. L'accès aux savoirs de base, médiatisé par nos langues vernaculaires, est la clef de voûte d'un système éducatif qui, tout en étant le reflet des rapports socioculturels dont émane et dont s'inscrit le vécu quotidien, assurera du même coup une ouverture plus large des esprits vers d'autres horizons ; un modèle scolaire qui, plutôt que de provoquer une rupture intellectuelle et psychologique au nom d'un développement déconnecté du milieu d'origine, ancrera dans la connaissance de ce dernier l'éveil de capacités innovatrices qui, en retour, y trouveront leur terrain d'application privilégié.

Mais, aussi intéressante que soit cette théorie, elle ne saurait se développer dans un contexte comme celui du Gabon, sans un certain nombre de préalables qui sont, de notre point de vue, des conditions nécessaires et indispensables. Le premier de ces préalables concerne la perception négative que l'on a des langues vernaculaires. En effet, dans le subconscient et même le conscient de beaucoup de Gabonais (Africains, de manière générale), les langues européennes— le français dans le cas qui nous concerne au Gabon—sont les seules considérées comme courroies de transmission exclusives des savoirs conduisant au progrès. Seules ces langues sont supposées offrir, aux yeux des gouvernements et des populations concernées, les meilleures garanties d'un développement équilibré ainsi que la promesse d'assurer, à moyen terme, à chaque citoyen, des chances de départ égales. Changer ce vieux paradigme, c'est s'éloigner de cette idéologie coloniale et accepter l'évidence que les langues vernaculaires africaines ne sont pas des sous-langues et qu'elles peuvent parfaitement être modernisées pour assumer des rôles de prestige dans l'optique de développement d'un pays. Le second préalable concerne le principe que toutes les langues vernaculaires sont importantes et qu'elles méritent toutes d'être développées, pourvu que ceux qui les pratiquent au quotidien y voient un intérêt. Le troisième préalable à la réussite du projet de modernisation des langues gabonaises en vue de leur intégration dans l'éducation scolaire impose que l'on s'éloigne de la perception populaire qui voudrait que seuls les linguistes soient interpellés par la question du développement des langues. La situation devient même totalement absurde quand ce sont des linguistes professionnels qui soutiennent une telle idée. Bien sûr, le travail de modernisation d'une langue nécessite, en amont, la description de la langue, qui est faite par le linguiste. Mais le processus dans son ensemble doit impliquer tout le monde, en commençant par les communautés elles-mêmes. Un tel projet doit ensuite faire l'objet d'une approche multidisciplinaire entre la linguistique descriptive, la sociolinguistique, la psycholinguistique, la didactique, la psychopédagogie, etc. Le dernier préalable concerne l'illusion qu'au Gabon on va réinventer le concept de modernisation des langues. Des pays, en Afrique ou ailleurs, ont entrepris depuis de nombreuses années le processus de développement de leurs langues. Ces pays ont aujourd'hui des programmes opérationnels. Il est simplement souhaitable que l'on s'inspire des expériences des autres, aussi bien en ce qui concerne les échecs que les réussites.

Enfin, et c'est la proposition forte que nous formulons ici pour orienter le débat relatif à la modernisation des langues vernaculaires gabonaises, la réussite d'un tel projet nécessite la création d'un institut spécialisé. En effet, seule une structure spécialisée pourra mener à bien la mission de valorisation des langues gabonaises dans l'optique de leur promotion et leur utilisation réelle dans le processus de développement du pays. Une telle structure pourrait œuvrer, entre autres, à l'impulsion de la recherche appliquée, la valorisation et la diffusion de cette recherche, l'élaboration et l'application des normes linguistiques, l'appui technique pour la formulation et la mise en œuvre de la politique linguistique du pays, l'appui des chercheurs en linguistique appliquée, la modernisation des outils linguistiques par l'utilisation des nouvelles technologies de l'information et de la communication, l'harmonisation des curricula d'enseignement des langues aux normes, l'archivage de documents et la constitution de banques de données sur les langues gabonaises et assurer l'interface entre l'État, les communautés linguistiques, les organisations gouvernementales et non gouvernementales, aux niveaux national et international.

Notes

1. Une langue vernaculaire est un système linguistique spécifique employé dans la région et la communauté d'origine.
2. C'est l'objet d'au moins deux projets en cours, à savoir celui portant sur l'Atlas linguistique du Gabon (ALGAB) et celui sur l'Acquisition et le développement des langues gabonaises (ADELAG).
3. On constate d'ailleurs, sur le plan politique, une réelle prise en compte de ce fait puisque des individus appartenant à des communautés diverses sont candidats, pour une élection locale, dans une circonscription qui appartient historiquement à une communauté différente de la leur.
4. Idiata (2002) pour plus d'amples détails sur les propositions de classification de ces différents auteurs.

Références

Ansre, G., 1971, « Language Standardization in Sub-Sahara Africa », in *Advances in Language Planning*, Paris, Mouton.

Bastin, Yvone et Pascale Piron, 1999, « Classification lexicostatistiques », dans Hombert, Jean-Marie and Lary Hyman (eds.), *Bantu Historical Linguistics, Theorical and Empirical Perspectives*, pp.149-163, CSLI Publications.

Bearth, T., 2000, « Introduction », *Tranel*, 26:5-13.

Carpentier de Changy, H. et Michel Voltz, 1990, « Alphabet scientifique des langues du Gabon : liste alphabétique », *Revue gabonaise des sciences de l'homme*, 2:113-115.

Cooper, R., 1982, *Language Planning and Social Change*, Cambridge, Cambridge University Press.

Dubois, J. L. *et al.*, 1994, *Dictionnaire de linguistique et des sciences du langage*, Paris, Larousse.

Fergusson, J., 1968, « Language Development », in Fishman, J. (ed.), *Language Problems of Developing Nations*, pp.27-36, New York, Willey.

Fishman, J., 1991, *Reversing Language Shift*, Clevedon, Avon, Multilingual Matters, Ltd.

Grimes, Barbara, 1996, *Ethnologue*, Languages of the world 13th Edition Dallas, Summer Institute of Linguistics, Inc.

Guérineau, Hubert, 1996, *Rapidolangue*, Libreville, Editions Raponda Walker (réédité en 1998 et 1999).

Guthrie, Malcolm, 1953, *The Bantu Languages of Western Equatorial Africa*, Oxford University Press.

Guthrie, Malcolm, 1967-1971, *Contribution from Comparative Bantu Studies to the Prehistory of Africa*, Dalby D, New York.

Hombert, Jean-Marie, 1990, « Les langues du Gabon : état des connaissances », *Revue gabonaise des sciences de l'homme*, 2:29-36.

Hombert, Jean Marie et Anne Marie Mortier, 1990, « Bibliographie des langues du Gabon », *Revue gabonaise des sciences de l'homme*, 2, p.335-358.

Idiata, Daniel Franck, en préparation, *Les langues vernaculaires africaines sont-elles aptes à réussir le pari d'une entrée dans l'univers de l'école ? Essai sur le projet gabonais d'intégration des langues gabonaises dans l'éducation scolaire*, à paraître chez l'Harmattan.

Idiata, Daniel Franck, 2001, « Diversité ethnolinguistique et vitalité des langues au Gabon », Communication présentée au Symposium International « Langue en contexte : l'oralité africaine face à l'écrit », Université de Zurich, Suisse, 18-20 octobre.

Idiata, Daniel Franck, 2002, *Il était une fois les langues gabonaises*, Libreville, Éditions Raponda-Walker.

Jacquot, André, 1978, « Le Gabon », in D. Barreteau (éd.), *Inventaire des études linguistiques sur les pays d'Afrique noire d'expression française et sur Madagascar*, pp.493-503, Paris, CLIF.

Kwenzi Mikala, Jérôme, 1998, « Parlers du Gabon : classification du 11-12-97 », in Raponda-Walker, *Les langues du Gabon*, 1998, pp.217-221, Libreville, Éditions Raponda-Walker.

Mayer, Raymond, 1990, « Histoire de l'écriture des langues du Gabon », *Revue gabonaise des sciences de l'homme*, 2:65-92.

Medjo Mve, P., 1997, *Essai sur la phonologie panchronique des parlers fang du Gabon et ses implications historiques,* NR, Université Lumière Lyon 2.

Medjo Mve, P., 2001, « Bibliographie revisitée des langues gabonaises », *Revue africaine d'études francophones,* publication de l'École normale supérieure du Gabon, n° 11, pp. 67-82.

Moussirou-Mouyama, Auguste, 2000, « Libreville, ancien village d'esclaves libérés : des contraintes de la langue à la liberté des citoyens », in Louis-Jean Calvet & Auguste Moussirou-Mouyama (éds.), *Le plurilinguisme urbain* — Actes du colloque de Libreville sur les villes plurilingues, 25-29 septembre 2000, pp.31-51, Institut de la francophonie, Didier Érudition.

Nikiema, Norbert, 2001, « La modernisation des langues africaines, communication présentée à la Consultation africaine pour la création d'une Académie africaine des langues », Bamako, 25-27 mai.

Power-Lapointe, C., 1994, « Enquête sur la situation linguistique au Gabon », étude non publiée.

Raponda Walker, André, 1932, « L'alphabet des idiomes gabonais », *Journal de la société des africanistes,* 2 (2):139-146.

Raponda Walker, André, 1960, « Notes d'histoire du Gabon », Mémoire IEC 9.

Voltz, Michel, 1990, « Carte linguistique du Gabon », *Revue gabonaise des sciences de l'homme,* 2:53-54.

Wiesemann, Ursulla, 1987, « Standardisation d'une langue », *Journal of West African Languages* XVII - 1:74-80.

7

L'identification d'une unité-langue par l'auto-évaluation : cas du giziga, langue tchadique, dans l'Extrême-Nord Cameroun

Etienne Sadembouo

Introduction

La région de Maroua dans l'Extrême-Nord du Cameroun et ses principales localités dont la présente étude a pour but d'évaluer l'intercompréhension dans l'aire géo-ethnolinguistique giziga par l'approche sociolinguistique, en privilégiant les attitudes des locuteurs natifs, afin de délimiter le nombre d'unités-langues qu'on devrait compter dans cet ensemble de variétés linguistiques.

Le peuple giziga a pour site d'origine : Maroua-gayak, Gazawa-Perpere, Loulou, Ndoukoula, Moutourwa et Midjivin. Ils cohabitent sur les mêmes sites avec les Fulbe qui se réclament aussi autochtones comme eux. Le mélange des deux populations dans certaines localités est tel qu'il est difficile de distinguer clairement les villages ou les quartiers giziga des villages ou des quartiers exclusivement fulbe. Dans tous les cas, les deux peuples vivent paisiblement.

Les Giziga, aujourd'hui, sont de parfaits bilingues en fulfulde et en giziga. Mais la langue exclusivement employée dans ce qui touche leur culture ancestrale, à l'instar des danses, des chants et des rites traditionnels est le giziga. C'est aussi la langue parlée en famille, que ce soit à Loulou, à Ndoukoula, à Foumou, à Moutourwa, à Midjiving ou à Perpere. À Gayak, tout près du périmètre urbain de Maroua, où la population foulbé prédomine, même en famille, le giziga n'est pas absent, chez les adultes au moins, même si chez les jeunes et les enfants, le remplacement du giziga par le fulfulde s'installe fortement.

Le giziga est connu dans la littérature linguistique comme une langue tchadique du phylum afro-asiatique de Greeberg (1963), tandis que Barreteau (1987), dans ses études sur les langues tchadiques de cette région, raffine cette classification dans sa branche centrale, et l'ALCAM attribue à cette entité linguistique deux (2) numéros de code pour signifier la répartition du giziga en deux unités-langues Nord et Sud. Notre question de départ est de savoir, à la suite des tergiversations que rencontrent les agents de standardisation soucieux de promouvoir la littérature en langue locale dans cette aire, si l'on devrait y distinguer 2 (deux) unités-langues comme le considérait l'Atlas Linguistique du Cameroun en 1983 et en 1993 (Dieu et Renaud 1983 ; Breton et Fothung 1991) à partir des premières études lexico-statistiques réalisées auparavant (Barreteau 1981) ; et si ce groupe parle une seule langue comportant des dialectes plus ou moins rapprochés, ne devrait-on pas de ce fait y développer une seule forme standard pour la communication écrite ?

Notre étude veut clarifier cette situation en l'observant non de l'extérieur, mais de l'intérieur, c'est-à-dire du point de vue des locuteurs utilisateurs des 4 à 5 grandes variétés linguistiques en présence.

Résoudre une telle question nous semble important si l'on doit envisager, au-delà de l'inventaire des unités-langues, le développement du système d'écriture de ladite ou desdites unité(s)-langue(s) et, surtout, le développement et la promotion d'une littérature viable dans cette (ces) langue(s), au moment où s'ouvrent au Cameroun, pour les langues locales sans exclusive et considérées toutes comme les langues nationales, les portes de l'école.

Schéma 1 : Schéma topologique de l'aire d'enquête giziga

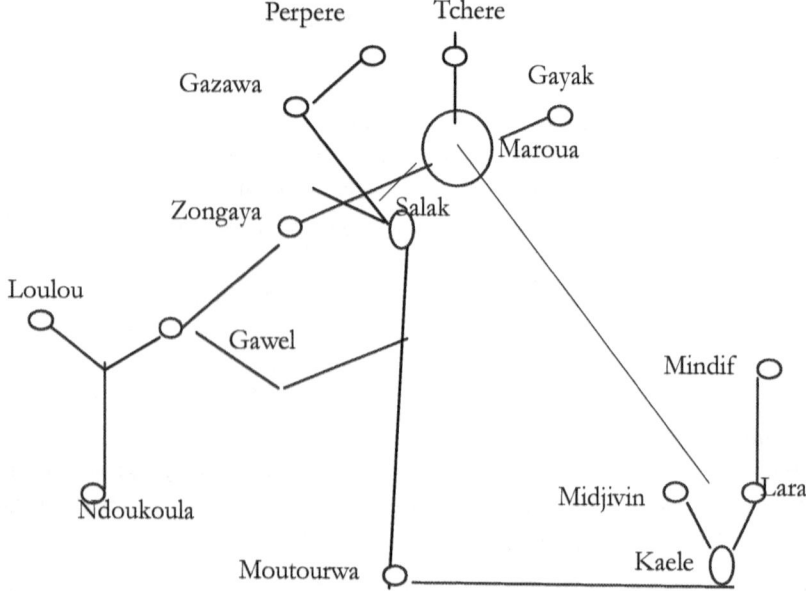

Schéma 2 : Arbre de classification génétique du giziga

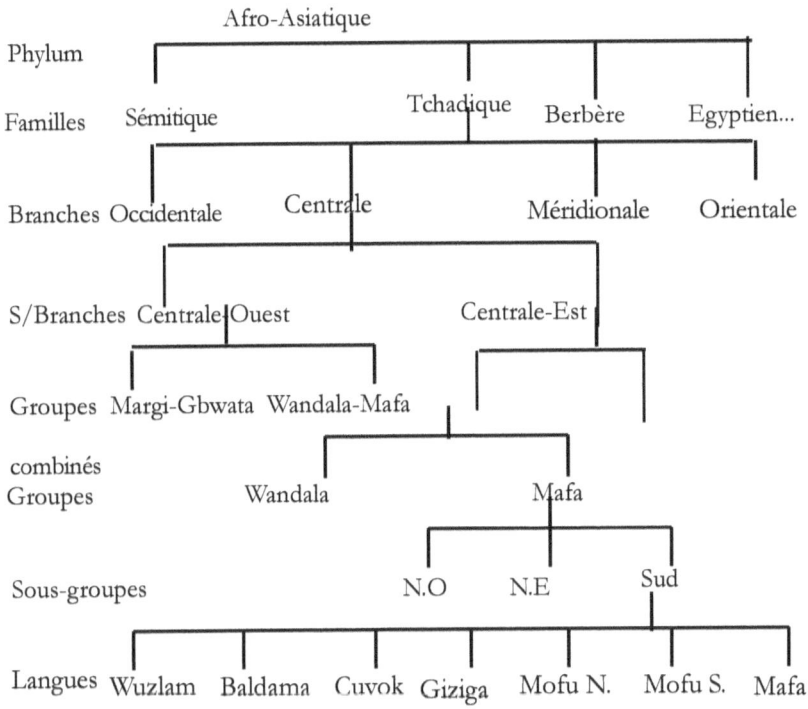

Avant de décrire notre procédure d'enquêtes et nos résultats, nous présentons ci-dessous le schéma topologique de l'aire linguistique du giziga et sa classification génétique.

Procédure d'enquête et méthode

Nous avons réalisé nos enquêtes chez les Giziga à l'aide d'un questionnaire élaboré à partir de celui proposé par Dieu *et al.* (1983). Les questions posées ont porté principalement sur :

- l'identification des variétés linguistiques parlées dans la zone et l'aire d'extension géographique de chaque variété répertoriée ;
- l'évaluation de la compréhension de ces parlers par les locuteurs natifs à différents sites d'enquête, un site étant le point de référence d'une variété spécifique ;
- la description des unités-langues distinctes éventuelles de l'aire à travers le groupement, par les locuteurs, des variétés mutuellement intelligibles de manière acceptable et satisfaisante ;
- l'identification du dialecte de référence préféré par les locuteurs en vue de la standardisation de l'écriture des unités-langues identifiées.

L'usage oral des langues et éventuellement leur usage écrit dans la vie courante de la communauté constituaient un autre aspect de notre enquête, secondaire certes, mais permettant d'évaluer la dynamique et la vitalité des langues présentes au sein du groupe.

Le choix des points d'enquête a été orienté par les données d'observation, des indications bibliographiques et au fur et à mesure que l'enquête avançait, c'est-à-dire en tenant compte des indications fournies par les enquêtés et les notabilités du site précédent. C'est pourquoi notre enquête s'est limitée à cinq sites principaux : Perpere-Gazawa, Gayak-Maroua, Loulou, Midjiving et Moutourwa. Nous nous sommes rendus à d'autres localités telles que Tchere, Mindif et Lara, ainsi que dans les quartiers du faubourg de Maroua vers Salak, pour vérifier rapidement nos données sans passer systématiquement en revue tout notre questionnaire.

L'enquête à chaque point était une interview faite de questions-réponses orales entre le chercheur et les locuteurs natifs originaires du site, hommes et femmes, adultes et jeunes. Ceux-ci étaient généralement au moins une quinzaine, paysans pour la plupart, rassemblés au point d'enquête par le chef de canton ou son représentant, et en présence duquel l'enquête se déroulait. Une lettre d'introduction signée du Préfet du Diamaré et du sous-préfet de Maroua avait facilité nos contacts avec les populations visitées (à l'époque de cette enquête, Kaélé n'était pas une préfecture, et Moutourwa, Ndoukoula et Gazawa n'étaient pas non plus des chefs-lieux d'arrondissement.) L'enquête durait environ trois heures de temps, même quand une foule de curieux ou de personnes oisives se formait, grossissant le nombre d'enquêtés de départ que l'autorité traditionnelle avait convoqués. Les réponses consignées étaient celles résultant d'un consensus général obtenu parfois après un long débat entre les locuteurs. Et si le groupe n'arrivait pas à un consensus, nous relevions alors les différents points de vue exprimés avec le nombre de participants qui se sont accordés sur un point de vue spécifique, afin d'en tenir compte lors du dépouillement des données, c'est-à-dire pour établir les pourcentages favorables à chaque réponse et retenir l'opinion de la majorité comme celle de l'ensemble du groupe. C'est surtout lorsqu'il s'agissait du choix d'une variante comme dialecte de référence, une fois la délimitation de l'aire de l'unité-langue établie, que des divergences survenaient au sein du groupe.

Résultats

Nous distinguerons trois aspects dans la présentation des résultats de nos enquêtes, résultats qui découlent des déclarations des locuteurs natifs groupés à différents sites et interrogés sur leur situation sociolinguistique. C'est ainsi que notre analyse portera sur : la description de l'aire d'extension géographique de l'unité-langue, conformément à la vision que les locuteurs s'en donnent en y vivant et en y communiquant les uns avec les autres quotidiennement ; l'évaluation de la compréhension des différentes variétés linguistiques identifiées et citées par les enquêtés comme appartenant à l'aire concernée ; la description du groupement de ces variétés intercompréhensibles en une ou plusieurs unités-langues devant avoir un système d'écriture autonome, à partir des propositions faites par les locuteurs interviewés à chaque site d'enquête.

L'aire d'extension des unités-langues

Pour faciliter cette description de l'aire d'extension des parlers, nous nous sommes servis d'une carte géographique de Maroua à l'échelle de 1/500 000 et d'une autre à l'échelle de 1/200 000. Nous avions aussi à notre portée le « Dictionnaire des villages du Diamaré ». Des aide-mémoire nous permettaient de rappeler aux interviewés des noms de localités qu'ils avaient éventuellement oubliés de citer spontanément en délimitant l'aire d'extension de leur variété linguistique et celle des autres variétés plus ou moins proches.

Nous avons récapitulé dans un tableau cette description de l'aire d'extension des unités-langues faite par les locuteurs à travers leurs réponses à la question : « où parle-t-on votre 'langue' ? », reformulée circonstanciellement de plusieurs manières telles que : « où parle-t-on aussi approximativement comme vous mais de façon encore compréhensible sans aucun problème pour vous ? », « où parle-t-on de manière un peu semblable mais difficile à comprendre à l'immédiat ? », etc.

Dans le tableau ci-dessous, les noms des sites d'enquête sont placés verticalement et les noms des localités citées sont placés horizontalement. Dans cette liste, nous n'avons retenu que les localités importantes sur le plan administratif, les chefs-lieux de canton et surtout les localités représentant une variété linguistique spécifique. C'est pourquoi la liste des localités citées est bien restreinte et est presque égale à celle des sites.

Dans le tableau 1 le signe ±indique une localité considérée et citée par les enquêtés d'un site d'enquête comme faisant partie de l'aire d'extension de l'unité-langue à laquelle ledit site appartient ; indique une localité retenue par les uns et exclue par les autres membres d'un site, de l'aire de l'unité-langue dans laquelle les gens du site se placent.

Tableau 1 : Aire d'extension des unités-langues

Aires d'extension		M	MJ	MT	LL
Sites d'enquête		V			
Perpère-Gazawa (=MV)		+	+	+	+
Gayak-Maroua (=MV)		+	+	+	+
Midjiving (MJ)		±	+	+	+
Moutourw-/Roumou (=MT)		+	+	+	+
Loulou-Massif (=LL)		+	+	+	+

Commentaires

Pour les locuteurs natifs interviewés, à quelques exceptions près, l'aire d'extension du giziga ne présente aucune ambiguïté. Au regard des résultats du tableau ci-dessus, les locuteurs sont unanimes sur l'aire de leur unité-langue : les descriptions qu'ils en ont donné à chaque site distinct coïncident, avec une petite exception à Midjiving, plus influencé par le Mundang voisin que les autres, où les locuteurs sont partagés au sujet du giziga de Maroua : certains pensent que ces derniers font partie de leur unité-langue, mais d'autres estiment que l'on devrait les séparer. Mais les Giziga de Maroua, les Marva, incluent les Midjiving dans leur aire d'enquête.

Nous allons voir à présent comment ces mêmes gens évaluent, à chaque site, leur compréhension les uns des autres lors des rencontres et des situations de communication avec les originaires des autres sites.

Évaluation de la compréhension dans l'aire

Dans tous les sites, les locuteurs sont conscients du manque d'homogénéité qu'il y a au sein de leur communauté linguistique. Ils sont aussi conscients des particularités linguistiques qui les distinguent les uns des autres, en même temps qu'ils le sont de leur unité en tant que groupe culturel face à d'autres groupes. Ainsi, à la question de savoir quelle langue ils parlent, ils répondent tantôt qu'ils parlent la langue giziga ou qu'ils parlent, selon le groupe interrogé, la langue « Marva », « Lulu », « Midjiving » ou « Muturwa ».

À la question de savoir : à quel point vous comprenez vos voisins, notamment ceux cités comme appartenant à l'aire d'extension de l'unité-langue où vous vous situez, les enquêtés ont établi une évaluation de la compréhension globale qu'ils ont les uns des autres, en spécifiant le degré de compréhension de manière qualitative, c'est-à-dire en indiquant si elle était : très bonne (=5), bonne (=4), assez bonne (=3), insuffisante (=2) ou limitée à quelques expressions (=1), voire nulle (= 0). Le tableau 2 présente cette évaluation :

Tableau 2 : Évaluation de la compréhension

Groupes /compris Sites/Zones d'enquête	MV	MJ	MT	LL
Perpère-Gazawa (=MV)	5	4~3	5	5
Gayak-Maroua (=MV)	5	3~2	4	3~2
Midjiving (MJ)	3~2	5	4	4
Moutourwa/Roumou (=MT)	3~2	5	5	5
Loulou-Massif (=LL)	3	4	5	5

Interprétation

Au regard de ce tableau, si l'on établit le seuil de compréhension satisfaisante au niveau « assez bien » (=3), alors l'on peut dire qu'à certains points de l'aire, la compréhension de certaines variantes est tangente, c'est-à-dire à la limite d'une compréhension globale satisfaisante : c'est le cas à Moutourwa et à Midjiving vis-à-vis de la variante « Mi marva » (=mv) parlée à Gayak-Maroua et à Perpere-Gazawa, localités situées au Nord de l'aire, alors que dans l'un de ces deux sites, la compréhension de toutes les variantes est au moins assez bonne, tandis que dans l'autre site (Gayak-Maroua), c'est la compréhension des variantes de Loulou et de Midjiving qui est à la limite de la satisfaction.

Les locuteurs des 3 variantes majeures, à savoir celles de Moutourwa, de Midjiving et de Loulou comprennent la variante « mi marva » de Gayak-Maroua et de Perpere-Gazawa au niveau « assez-bien » (3) ou passable (3~2). La variante la mieux et la plus comprise est celle de Moutourwa : tous la comprennent au niveau « Très Bien » ou « Bien ».

Cette auto-évaluation met en relief les quatre principales variantes de l'aire, c'est-à-dire sa diversité linguistique, une diversité au sein de laquelle il y a une forte tendance à l'unité et à l'intégration et non à la séparation et à l'exclusion.

Pour compléter cette auto-évaluation et permettre de bien l'apprécier, les enquêtés ont été invités à classer dans un ordre décroissant, cette compréhension qu'ils ont de leurs voisins parlant d'autres variantes, soit de la mieux comprise à la moins comprise. Le résultat obtenu est présenté dans le tableau 3 qui suit.

Tableau 3 : Ordre de compréhension

Groupes compris Zones/sites d'enquêtes	MV	MJ	MT	LL
Perpère-Gazawa (=MV)	1er	3e	2e	4e
Gayak-Maroua (=MV)	1er	3e	2e	4e
Midjiving (MJ)	4e	1e	2e	3e
Moutourw-/Roumou (=MT)	3e	2e	1er	1er
Loulou-Massif (=LL)	4e	3e	2e	1er

Ce classement montre que les locuteurs du Nord de l'aire sont plus à l'aise avec le parler de Moutourwa qu'avec les autres qu'ils comprennent aussi bien. Puis ceux du Sud de l'aire sont plus à l'aise entre eux (LL, MT, MJ) qu'avec ceux du Nord (MV). Mais ce classement ne donne pas lieu de conclure que l'aire comprend deux (2) unités-langues. Si l'on schématise cette auto-évaluation de la compréhension, l'on obtient les groupements présentés dans le schéma 3.

Schéma 3

a) Pour les Marva (MV)   b) Pour les Midjiving (MJ)

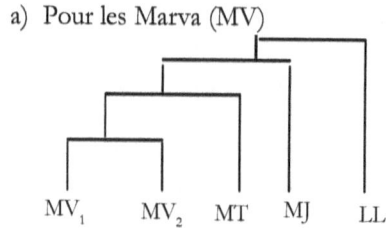
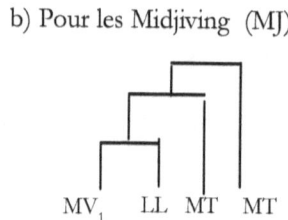

c) Pour les Moutourwa (MT)   d) Pour les Loulou (LL)

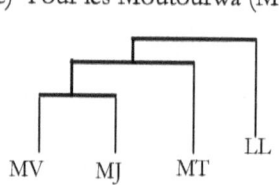
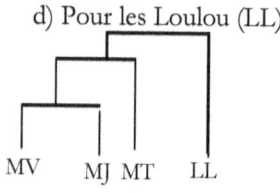

Il y a une constance dans le classement de la compréhension au sein de l'aire : la variante Marva (MV) est moins bien comprise des autres qui se comprennent mieux entre elles. Et quand les locuteurs du Marva placent le parler de Moutourwa au second rang de compréhension, c'est une preuve que l'aire, en dépit de sa diversité, garde une unité appréciable.

Groupement des variantes

Au-delà de la classification des parlers dans l'ordre de compréhension, les locuteurs regroupés par site et interviewés devaient répondre à une question relative au regroupement des variétés répertoriées et déclarées comme comprises en ensembles et en sous-ensembles, en fonction du degré de cette compréhension, tout en pensant à la possibilité de donner une forme écrite unique aux variétés qui constituent une seule entité, un seul ensemble. Question difficile, certes, mais qui permet de vérifier les groupements effectués à partir des déclarations fournies à travers les questions précédentes.

Tableau 4 : Auto-groupement des variantes

Variantes regroupées Zones/Sites d'enquêtes	MV	MJ	MT	LL
Perpere-Gazawa (=MV)	1	2	2	2
Gayak-Maroua (=MV)	1	2a	2b	2c
Midjiving (MJ)	1	2	3	4
Mouturwa-/Roumou (=MT)	1	2	3	3
Loulou-Massif (=LL)	1	2	3	3

Dans ce tableau, les variantes regroupées en un même sous-ensemble ont le même chiffre. Ces regroupements peuvent être schématisés de la manière suivante :

Schéma 4

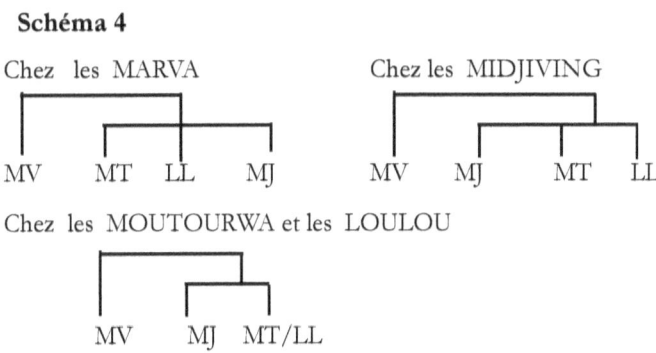

Commentaires

Ces groupements sont semblables à ceux dégagés du classement des niveaux de compréhension. Il y a une constance permanente dans les jugements des locuteurs. Pour les uns, l'aire est constituée de deux (2) sous-ensembles : le Marva d'une part et les autres d'autre part ; pour les autres, l'aire est constituée de 3 sous-ensembles, à savoir : le Marva, le Mijving et le Muturwa-Lulu ; tandis que pour les gens de Midjiving, elle est formée de quatre variantes que l'on peut regrouper ainsi : Lulu et Muturwa, Lulu-Muturwa et Mijiving, puis Lulu-Muturwa-Mijiving et Marva.

Ces groupements permettent de tirer la conclusion suivante : l'aire est constituée d'une unité-langue qui comprend plusieurs variantes dont 4 principales ont été identifiées et regroupées en un ensemble. Ces variantes se répartissent en deux (2) principaux dialectes : le dialecte Mi-Marva d'une part au Nord de l'aire, et d'autre part le dialecte de Muturwa-Lulu-Mijiving, situé dans la partie globalement Sud de l'aire par rapport au « Mi-marva » ; ce deuxième dialecte se subdivise en deux (2) sous-dialectes : le Mijiving et le Muturwa-Lulu. C'est ce que montre le dernier des 3 schémas ci-dessus qui d'ailleurs n'est pas contradictoire par rapport aux autres, car le premier reconnaît les deux dialectes et le deuxième reconnaît les 2 sous-dialectes de la deuxième grande variante.

Conclusion

Les évaluations successives réalisées par les locuteurs natifs regroupés et interviewés à plusieurs sites de l'aire giziga révèlent une vision uniforme de la variation linguistique vécue par eux-mêmes dans leur aire géo-linguistique. Elles permettent de tracer pour le giziga l'arbre classificatoire suivant de l'unité-langue et de ses variantes.

Schéma 5

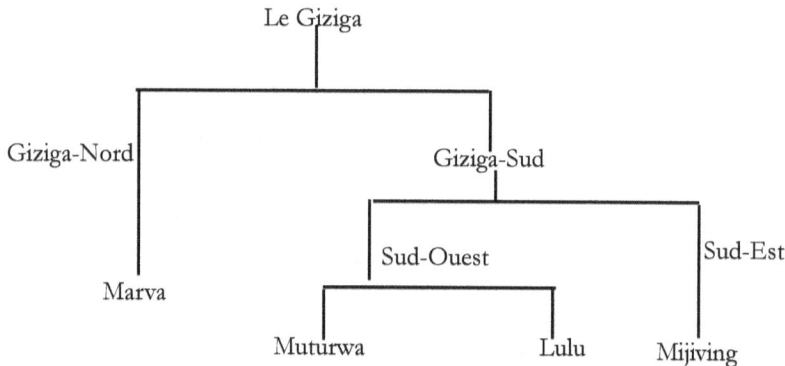

L'unité-langue Giziga établie à travers cette auto-évaluation globale des locuteurs est constituée d'un dialecte Nord le « Mi-marva » et d'un dialecte Sud qui est subdivisé en sous-dialectes S-Est, le « Mi Mijiving » et un sous-ensemble S-Ouest qui comprend le « Mi Lulu » et le « Mi muturwa » (mi- signifie la bouche, le parler).

L'évaluation de la variation linguistique au sein de l'aire giziga est faite à partir des opinions exprimées par les locuteurs natifs eux-mêmes qui vivent dans l'aire et expérimentent toutes sortes de situation de communication langagière au sein du groupe. Cette évaluation, disions-nous, constitue une étape importante des études pour le développement de cette langue et mérite d'avoir toute la considération qui se doit dans le processus de standardisation du giziga.

Références

Barreteau, Daniel, 1981, « Un essai de classification lexicostatistique des langues de la famille tchadique parlées au Cameroun » in *Langues et cultures dans le bassin du Lac Tchad*, Paris, ORSTOM, pp. 43-77.

Breton, Roland et Fortung, Bikia, 1991, *Atlas Administratif des langues nationales du*

Cameroun MESIRES, CERDOTOLA, ACCT Yaoundé / Paris.

Dieu Michel et Renaud Patrick, 1983, *Atlas Linguistique du Cameroun : Inventaires préliminaires*, CERDOTOLA, ACCT, DGRST Yaoundé / Paris.

Greenberg, Joseph, 1963, *Languages of Africa*, The Hague, The Netherlands, Mouton et Co.

Sadembouo, Etienne, 1995, « Controverse autour d'un standard Fali » *Journal of West African languages*, N° XXV.1 pp.107-120.

Tadadjeu Maurice et Sadembouo Etienne, 1984, *Alphabet général des langues camerounaises*, Collection PROPELCA N° 1, édition bilingue, Université de Yaoundé.

Wiesemann U., Sadembouo E. and Tadadjeu M., 1983, *Guide pour le développement des systèmes d'écriture des langues africaines*, Collection PROPELCA N° 2 Université de Yaoundé.

8

Critères de généralisation de l'enseignement des langues maternelles dans le système éducatif

Gabriel Mba

Introduction

L'introduction des langues maternelles dans les systèmes éducatifs a été pendant longtemps encore, sujette à controverses, à polémiques et à joutes oratoires. Cependant, des expériences conduites çà et là en Afrique et ailleurs (PROPELCA au Cameroun, Projet Ife au Nigeria, Projet-Nord en Côte d'Ivoire, etc.) ont démontré, si besoin en était encore, que les langues maternelles en général, et africaines en particulier, appelées « à servir de dispositif d'apprentissage pour l'acquisition des contenus essentiels d'un programme scolaire qui soit fonctionnel sans être aliénant » (Bearth 1997:5) ont permis une réconciliation entre l'école et la communauté (Tadadjeu et Mba 1997), un changement profond des attitudes et une flexibilité des systèmes éducatifs en contextes multilingues (Gfeller 1997, 2000).

Notre conviction profonde est que seule une généralisation de la pratique de l'usage, à l'oral et à l'écrit des langues maternelles dans les systèmes éducatifs peut véritablement être le moteur du développement attendu de chaque communauté, de tout État ou de toute nation. Il n'y a pas meilleures stratégies de partage du discours de développement que le recours aux langues maternelles qui doivent fonctionner non pas dans l'exclusivité qui sans nul doute serait suicidaire, mais dans un esprit d'ouverture plus large au monde extérieur et à des horizons nouveaux. Autrement dit, l'introduction des langues maternelles dans le système éducatif doit s'effectuer à la fois dans le souci de maintien et de promotion des identités particulières des locuteurs de ces différentes langues, mais aussi, dans un processus de découverte d'autres identités véhiculées par d'autres langues déjà présentes dans le système ou susceptibles de s'y insérer.

C'est en raison de ce qui précède, que nous nous proposons, dans le cadre de cet article, de présenter des critères qui puissent permettre une généralisation de l'enseignement de ces langues, qui soit rationnelle, permanente, et hautement bénéfique tant pour les agences de développement des langues, les décideurs politiques, que les sujets réels embarqués dans une pareille action. Les scénarios de généralisation sont multiples et s'appliquent selon les niveaux de développement écrit des langues, les politiques linguistiques et options des États en matière d'éducation nationale.

Types de généralisation

Dans une étude antérieure (Mba 2002), nous avons émis l'hypothèse de 4 types de généralisation de l'enseignement des langues maternelles qui épousent le niveau écrit de chaque langue et les politiques éducatives. Il s'agit de la généralisation orale (GO), de la généralisation informelle (GI), de la généralisation zonale (GZ) et de la généralisation nationale (GN). Toute langue maternelle non écrite peut être introduite immédiatement à l'école, de manière orale, dans les disciplines scientifiques (mathématiques, etc.) et les disciplines à dominante culturelle (chants, dessins, contes, peinture, etc.). Cette pratique, élargie à toutes les langues, constitue la généralisation orale (GO). Il s'agit ici d'une pratique consciente, systématisée, organisée et non un simple recours aux langues maternelles aux fins de traduction des concepts rencontrés dans les disciplines scolaires et dont la compréhension immédiate dans les langues étrangères qui les véhiculent pose problème.

La généralisation informelle (GI) consiste à considérer la langue maternelle comme sujet ou matière à l'école et à la pratiquer à une heure précise et à des jours précis de l'emploi du temps hebdomadaire. Cette pratique, qui très souvent a lieu dans les classes supérieures de l'école primaire (CE II-CM II), prive les langues maternelles de révéler leur côté stratégies didactiques, co-vecteurs d'acquisition et de manipulation du savoir et du savoir-faire.

La généralisation zonale allie le modèle oral et le modèle informel, c'est-à-dire qu'elle combine la pratique orale et la pratique écrite de la langue maternelle dès les premières années du primaire. Ainsi, la langue maternelle est utilisée à la fois comme co-vecteur d'acquisition des connaissances et sujet d'apprentissage. Mieux encore, elle est utilisée comme moyen de communication orale et écrite dans la transmission des savoirs et comme sujet d'introspection. Si la pratique d'un tel enseignement s'effectue sur toute l'étendue de l'aire naturelle d'une langue, c'est-à-dire dans toutes les écoles de la zone linguistique considérée, alors, nous parlons de la généralisation zonale.

La généralisation nationale (GN) qui constitue le bouquet final est la somme des généralisations zonales spécifiques par langue. Ainsi, petit à petit, l'enseignement généralisé des langues maternelles couvrira tout le territoire d'un État ou d'une nation. Il faut souligner ici, que la généralisation nationale est un idéal qui doit être atteint de manière progressive avec en prime, la mise à contribution de tous, de toutes les bonnes volontés, de tous les décideurs à des degrés divers.

Les critères de généralisation

La généralisation de l'enseignement des langues maternelles obéit à un ensemble de critères et de procédures. Les critères se puisent dans les domaines scientifique, politique, psychosocial, technique et enfin économique.

Les critères scientifiques et techniques participent de la mise en œuvre dans le système éducatif, de l'enseignement des langues avec tout ce que cela englobe en termes de matériel, de programme, de formation des maîtres, de description et de standardisation des langues.

Les critères sociopsychologiques reposent sur l'imagination quotidienne que se font les individus ou les groupes sociaux des langues locales qu'ils utilisent et du statut social à elles réservé. Sont-ce uniquement des moyens de communication interpersonnelle, familiale ou ethnique ? Sont-ce aussi des instruments de communication orale susceptibles d'être mis à l'écrit pour des besoins d'éducation et de développement ? Mieux, quelle valeur réelle est accordée aux langues maternelles ?

Les critères politiques sont ceux relatifs aux actes gouvernementaux (textes de lois, arrêtés, décrets, discours officiels) qui traitent des statuts des langues et de leur utilisation effective dans le cursus scolaire.

Les critères économiques s'intéressent au prix à payer pour cet enseignement, au bénéfice palpable et non palpable, au gain tangible ou intangible que l'utilisation des langues maternelles peut offrir. C'est aussi ici le domaine de l'analyse des coûts et bénéfices culturels, scientifiques, développementaux et autres.

Présentation des critères

Critères scientifiques

    Sc1 : études scientifiques théoriques sur la langue

    Sc2 : identification du parler de référence et élaboration du système d'écriture

    Sc3 : élaboration des principes de reconnaissance des frontières de mots

    Sc4 : existence d'ouvrages d'orientation théorique pour l'élaboration des manuels didactiques

    Sc5 : niveau de développement écrit de la langue

Critères techniques
    T1 : définition des objectifs et programmes d'enseignement
    T2 : existence des manuels d'enseignement
    T3 : formation du personnel
    T4 : mise en place d'un appareil organisationnel

Critères économiques
    E1 : apport local ou communautaire au financement de la généralisation
    E2 : apport de l'État

Critères sociopsychologiques
S-p1 : enseignement des langues comme une ascèse, c'est-à-dire comme antidote à la résistance psychologique des populations elles-mêmes, des politiques linguistiques négatives et de l'inertie des institutions particulièrement concernées. L'on doit aller au-delà des supposés devenus rétrogrades et humiliants qui ne reconnaissent pas aux langues africaines leur efficacité et viabilité, leur importance cardinale comme médium d'instruction et d'éducation sur les plans formel, informel et non formel. Cette acceptabilité doit être et demeurer le fondement essentiel de l'action pédagogique.

S-p2 : enseignement des langues comme une nécessité. Cette nécessité doit se matérialiser par l'identification des domaines stables, réservés ou tout simplement potentiels où l'usage oral et /ou écrit des langues africaines s'épanouirait avec beaucoup de bonheur au regard du principe de multiculturalisme et du plurilinguisme qui, plus que jamais fonde l'avenir de la communication sociale.

Critères politiques
    P1 : matérialisation du discours politique
    P2 : appropriation et capitalisation de la politique du bilinguisme identitaire
    (L1-LO1) comme élément du développement national.

La présentation de ces critères nous laisse observer que la généralisation de l'enseignement des langues maternelles repose beaucoup plus sur le scientifique et le technique que l'économique, le sociopsychologique et le politique. Ceci confirme la hiérarchisation proposée des critères, bien que le technique et le scientifique ne puissent se réaliser pleinement sans le concours des autres critères.

Visualisation schématique des critères et sous-critères

La lecture de ce schéma se fait selon le sens indiqué des flèches. Un plus grand espace est couvert par les critères scientifiques et techniques qui sont au nombre de neuf (9) sur les quinze (15) sous-critères inventoriés. Ces sous-critères constituent la gamme des éléments d'évaluation de toute situation d'enseignement des langues dans le contexte global de la généralisation. Quelques-uns des sous-critères, comme nous l'avons indiqué précédemment, se raffineront davantage pour permettre une plus grande aisance de manipulation et d'évaluation.

Visualisation de certains sous-critères

Les sous-critères Sc2 (identification du parler de référence et élaboration du système d'écriture), Sc5 (niveau de développement écrit des langues), T2 (existence des manuels d'enseignement), T3 (formation du personnel) et T4 (mise en place d'un appareil organisationnel) peuvent connaître des développements ultérieurs tels qu'esquissés ci-dessous:

SC2

| Adoption des graphèmes | Harmonisation des systèmes d'écriture et fonctionnement des orthographes | Principes de lecture et d'écriture | Orthographe idéale |

SC5

| de niveau des publications scientifiques | niveau des publications de vulgarisation écrite de la langue | niveau de formation du personnel | niveau de l'utilisation orale et |

T2

| Syllabaire 1 Manuels | Syllabaire 2 | Post syllabaire 1 | Manuel de transition LO1 | Manuel de lecture suivie | calcul 1,2,3 de sciences d'observation |

T3

| Corrélation entre formation et objectifs | formation des encadreurs locaux administratif | Formation du personnel éducationnels |

T4

| Institut de recherches | Institut de formation | Écoles d'application | structures locales de sensibilisation aux innovations |

Les structures locales de base sont absolument nécessaires pour la promotion de l'usage oral et écrit des langues maternelles et pour la mobilisation de l'opinion populaire et du support pour le développement. Si la recherche et la formation peuvent être entreprises aux niveaux national et régional, cela ne saurait être le cas pour la mobilisation et la sensibilisation qui à notre sens, doit prendre racine chez les détenteurs naturels et locuteurs des diverses langues.

Valeur des critères retenus

Les cinq (5) critères répertoriés sont les outils d'application et de mesure d'application de la généralisation de l'enseignement des langues maternelles. En d'autres termes, ils sont la grille de réalisation effective de la généralisation et de l'évaluation de cette généralisation. Chaque critère peut donc se lire et s'interpréter à travers une échelle de valeurs propres, qui détermine le niveau atteint par une situation linguistique ou une situation d'enseignement. Les cinq (5) critères se résument en quinze (15) sous-critères qui, eux aussi, peuvent connaître des divisions internes. Par exemple, le sous-critère sur la disponibilité du matériel didactique pour être rempli doit nécessairement comprendre des éléments tels l'existence des syllabaires 1 et 2, des post-syllabaires, des ouvrages de calcul, des sciences d'observation, de transition de la langue maternelle à la langue officielle. Aussi en est-il du sous-critère relatif au personnel formé qui s'étend non seulement aux maîtres, mais aussi aux superviseurs et aux responsables administratifs (Inspecteurs, Secrétaires à l'éducation).

Hiérarchisation des critères

Les critères répertoriés relèvent tant de la planification de corpus que de la planification de statut. En clair, les activités d'enseignement généralisé des langues maternelles concernent les mécanismes internes de développement de chaque langue et les mécanismes de politique des langues. Les actions à entreprendre impliquent le linguiste et le politique. Un troisième partenaire et pas des moindres se trouve être la masse des locuteurs natifs ou non natifs des langues en présence. Ce partenaire est à la source des usages, des attitudes langagières, des comportements et de l'organisation linguistique qui alimentent à la fois les décisions du linguiste et du politique.

Les activités scientifiques du linguiste en matière de mise par écrit des langues ou leur développement tout court sont des activités programmables. Elles vont de la description même des langues à leur utilisation effective par les locuteurs natifs ou les apprenants dans la forme écrite.

Les interventions de l'homme politique sont de nature à donner un statut légal aux langues. Non pas qu'elles (ces langues) n'existent pas déjà, mais plutôt qu'il convient de manière officielle, c'est-à-dire par lois et décrets, de régler, de fixer les fonctions dévolues à telle ou telle langue. Les interventions de l'homme politique sont – nous sommes parfaitement convaincus – des motifs de réorientation et d'amélioration du travail du linguiste en matière de planification et de programmation des travaux de la recherche elle-même.

La hiérarchisation des critères ira du scientifique au technique, du technique à l'économique, de l'économique au sociopsychologique, et enfin au politique. De plus, au niveau de chaque critère, un ordre ou une certaine priorité quant à l'exécution de certaines opérations cardinales est à établir. On ne peut par exemple imaginer la rédaction d'un post-syllabaire avant un syllabaire, ni la production d'une grammaire pédagogique efficace sans les éléments d'une grammaire descriptive, d'une grammaire théorique, fiable.

De même, il est inconcevable qu'une action de généralisation de l'enseignement des langues maternelles soit faite sans qu'au préalable des expériences sur une échelle réduite soient entreprises, évaluées et les résultats pris en compte. C'est plus cette suite dans l'accomplissement des opérations qui est à prioriser pour chaque critère. Cette hiérarchisation qui obéit à une organisation pratique du travail de standardisation des langues ne trahit pas cependant la complexité des critères et sous-critères. Il faut plutôt et bien mieux, regarder l'ensemble dans une synergie d'actions et d'interventions.

Simultanéité d'intervention des critères

Les critères de généralisation de l'enseignement des langues maternelles pour être fiables, efficaces et puissantes doivent être appliqués simultanément. Les éléments de politique linguistique éducative qui, à certains égards, sont primordiaux, conditionnent les efforts des uns et des autres et orientent les discours politiques. Mais, tout ceci ne saurait porter fruit dans une société qui n'a pas la conscience claire et nette de ce qu'est la langue, son pouvoir, son ascendance sur la vie sociale. Toute politique linguistique éducative réelle ne peut se fonder que sur une analyse des coûts et bénéfices d'une telle entreprise. La valeur économique, mais aussi la valeur culturelle de la langue, qui se mesurent en gains tangibles et intangibles, constituent des paramètres d'une telle évaluation. Toutes ces données si elles ne sont pas étudiées, fixées et appliquées simultanément ou presque, fausseraient la fiabilité et la puissance de tout modèle éducatif dont les langues maternelles constitueraient un élément cardinal. L'absence ou la quasi-absence d'un de ces critères minerait fondamentalement les effets attendus. Cependant, à scruter de près l'interaction des critères scientifiques, organisationnels, sociopsychologiques, politiques et économiques, l'on pourrait penser que le critère politique est de loin le critère dominant ou encore celui qui sert d'effet d'entraînement.

Interaction des critères

La constatation ci-dessus faite participe de la nature même du critère politique. De ce critère dépend la vitesse à imprimer au travail purement scientifique de développement d'une langue plutôt que d'un autre et parfois même la priorité à accorder à certaines opérations nécessaires. Ceci veut dire que le travail scientifique serait à cet égard un travail sur commande, taillé sur les normes du vouloir politique et non un travail en série comme on l'observe souvent. Ceci contribuerait à répondre spécifiquement à la question de savoir quelles études scientifiques pour quel but précis, pour quel objectif de développement ? Historiquement parlant, ceci n'est pas vérifiable car la standarisation des langues s'est faite toujours sans qu'aucune décision de nature politique n'ait été prise. Les linguistes et quelquefois des anthropologues ont procédé à la description de plusieurs langues par curiosité scientifique et non sur une quelconque pression politique.

Ainsi, les chercheurs se mobiliseraient d'abord à hâter les travaux et études scientifiques, les publications de vulgarisation et les activités de formation sur des langues ou des groupes de langues prédéterminées par la planification linguistique issue du vouloir politique. Les ressources humaines impliquées dans la mise des langues par écrit et leur utilisation effective dans l'enseignement ne se libéreraient d'un secteur ou d'un groupe de langues données qu'une fois les activités programmées complètement au point ou une fois que celles-ci auront atteint un seuil d'accomplissement qui permette un auto-développement.

Sur le plan des attitudes linguistiques ou ethnolinguistiques, une politique linguistique globale décrisperait les consciences et laisserait libre cours à des attitudes plutôt ouvertes, plus facilement décelables, identifiables et surtout qui peuvent être orientées dans le sens de cette politique. Le manque de politique de langues noie à la fois les attitudes réelles envers ou contre les langues, même celles que sont supposés posséder les citoyens. Les réticences psychologiques à l'utilisation des langues locales sont moins bien perçues parce que mêlées au statu quo que l'absence d'une politique explicite des langues crée forcément. Ce statu quo dans le domaine de la politique linguistique, au moment même où des applications concrètes et réussies d'enseignement des langues locales voient le jour, complique plus la tâche du décideur qu'il ne la facilite. Car, au moment où des langues prennent le chemin de l'école, s'incrustent dans le cursus scolaire des jeunes Africains, il est plus aisé du dehors de demander qu'on y mette une fin. Mais, on aurait créé ce qu'on voudrait éviter, à savoir la désintégration culturelle et partant la désintégration nationale.

Une autre constatation qui vaut la peine d'être soulignée à grand trait ici n'est que ce qu'il est convenu d'appeler l'engloutissement de tant d'efforts dans le développement écrit des langues « sans avenir national ». En clair, une mise en place d'une politique des langues règlerait les statuts des unes et des autres et permettrait un investissement conséquent des efforts nationaux. Ces efforts qui sont de l'ordre financier, humain, intellectuel, social, structurel, etc., seraient en revanche mieux canalisés, mieux orientés, mieux exploités. L'enseignement formel ou informel des langues exige un certain sacrifice financier inéluctable en formation des hommes, en production de matériel didactique et surtout en orientation psychologique des hommes et des femmes d'une région donnée. Il convient donc de ne pas perdre de vue cet aspect à cause de l'absence d'une politique de langues ou d'une politique toujours à refaire, à examiner ou à réexaminer. Schématiquement, le critère politique se présente ainsi qu'il suit :

Schéma synthétique du critère politique

L'orientation des activités scientifiques et organisationnelles implique la « sélection » des langues à développer dans une période précise ou mieux, la reconnaissance des fonctions spécifiques à des langues précises, les opérations de formation des formateurs avec des contenus fidèles aux objectifs généraux du décideur ou des communautés mises en cause.

Les attitudes des membres des diverses communautés linguistiques sont gérées de manière à cultiver davantage une attitude plus intégrative. Ceci veut dire que la reconnaissance des différences qui existent entre les groupes linguistiques distincts et surtout en capitalisant ces différences comme éléments fondamentaux d'un véritable rapprochement des groupes ethnolinguistiquement différents. C'est ici que l'étude des rapports de complémentarité et non d'exclusion radicale entre les langues officielles et les langues locales aboutit à une claire conscience des fonctions que les unes et les autres remplissent dans la société ainsi que les domaines où leur utilisation n'interfère pas.

La politique des langues définit l'utilisation des langues en présence, en spécifiant les rôles de chacune d'elles. Sont-ce des langues d'utilisation provinciale, régionale, véhiculaire, nationale, officielle ou des langues à utilisation limitée au petit espace géographique de ses locuteurs natifs ? Les statuts éducationnels ainsi fixés influencent le planning d'exécution des études scientifiques en montrant selon le statut de chaque langue, jusqu'où il faut pousser les travaux de recherche et l'articulation de ces recherches avec le statut des langues se côtoyant dans le même planning des fonctions éducatives.

Conclusion

Dans le cadre de cette réflexion sur la généralisation de l'enseignement des langues maternelles dans le système éducatif, cinq (5) critères ont été proposés comme conditions essentielles et grille d'évaluation. Tous ces critères bien que n'ayant pas la même valeur doivent s'appliquer de manière simultanée dans tout contexte pour permettre à la fiabilité, à la puissance du modèle en cours d'expérimentation ou à expérimenter, de s'exprimer de façon optimale. De même, les différents types de généralisation esquissés sont de nature à donner une chance à tout État de s'engager à utiliser les langues maternelles parlées par les populations dans le système éducatif, soit de manière orale, soit de manière orale et écrite. Les critères énoncés serviront – nous en sommes convaincus – d'éléments de contrôle et d'appréciation.

Références

Bearth, T., 1997, « Introduction » in *TRANEL* (Travaux neuchâtelois de linguistique appliquée) n° 26, Institut de linguistique de Neuchâtel, Suisse, Université de Neuchâtel, pp.5-13.

Gfeller, E., 1997, « Pour un modèle africain d'éducation multilingue : le trilinguisme extensif », in *TRANEL*, Institut de linguistique de Neuchâtel, Suisse Université de Neuchâtel, pp.43-47.

Gfeller, E., 2000, *La société et l'école face au multilinguisme*, Paris, Éditions Karthala, France, 242 pages.

Mba, G., 2002, « Pour une application des modèles généralisables d'enseignement des langues nationales au Cameroun» in *African Journal of Applied* Linguistics (AJAL) n° 3, NACALCO Center for Applied Linguistics pp 17-32.

Tadadjeu M. et Mba G., 1997, « L'utilisation des langues nationales dans l'éducation au Cameroun : les leçons d'une expérience » in *TRANEL* n° 26, Institut de linguistique de Neuchâtel, Suisse, Université de Neuchâtel, pp.59-75.

9

Efforts and Challenges Involved in Establishing an Adult Literacy Model for Cameroon

Emmanuel Nforbi

Introduction

When we view the overall system of adult literacy, we can identify the outstanding components that make up a model, as Bhola (1988) observes in his overview of adult education programmes in various parts of the world. After examining Bhola's systems and others, Nforbi (2000) presents a model for Cameroon made up of the following components: finance and equipment, language, material production, training, organization and research. For these components to become functional, several challenges need to be handled with care. The multilingual nature of Cameroon calls for a bottom-up model in which bi-literateness (competent use of mother tongue (L1) and an official language (OL) should be the minimum skills for a literate citizen. The ideal situation will be tri-literateness (mother-tongue, French, and English). Tadadjeu (1997) further argues that a Cameroonian who can only read and write in one language is, therefore, not functionally literate. If only literate in their mother tongue, then they are cut off from the rest of the world. If literate in one or two official languages, they are still cut off from their own roots. This problem will be discussed in this chapter among other things involved in establishing an adult literacy model for Cameroon. We start by examining the language problem since it is central to all literacy programmes.

The Language Problem

Literacy involves ability to read and write in a given language. In a monolingual situation, there is no problem of choice. However, the language in question must be standardized and accepted by the community. In a multilingual context like Cameroon, the challenge is that of choice, standardization, and acceptance. English and French, which serve as official languages, are not mother tongues of Cameroonians. Pedagogically, the literacy process should start from the known to the unknown; that is, from the mother tongue to the official language. For this to be done, the mother tongue must be standardized.

The standardization of African languages, as Nforbi (2001) has analysed, is very expensive, especially as it is done alongside literacy in the official languages. Besides the cost involved, the orthographies need to be accepted. There is a harmonized alphabet for Cameroonian languages, which everybody should adopt. The challenge here is two-fold: accepting this harmonized alphabet, especially by people who had started using other alphabets, and accepting the alphabet of African languages in place of the Roman alphabet used for the official languages.

When people accept the orthographies and even the didactic materials developed, they still need to be convinced that literacy in mother-tongue is not a waste of time but a key to the development of their local communities in particular, and Cameroon in general. Adults will learn to read and write faster through the languages they already speak, since reading and writing are predicated on oral competence.

The consequence of a system that does not have a bridge from the mother tongue to the second language, is a deterred linguistic competence. As earlier indicated, reading and writing are predicated on oral competence. The scientific approach to the study of this oral competence is phonology—the study of human distinctive speech sounds. The fact that these sounds are universal and are produced from the same articulatory organs, which all human beings have, means that phonology can be learned through all languages. These sounds are discovered more naturally from the mother-tongue perspective. The learners are made to discover the language they already speak. This is a means of exploiting and developing their linguistic competence. In other words, they are led to the exciting discovery that what they say has meaning and can be represented in writing.

Knowledge of Adult Literacy Needs

No educational institution can function without well-trained educators. This is true of adult education as well. Teachers trained for formal education with a focus on children in the primary and secondary schools need to pass through a refresher course before they can teach adults. The ideal is to equip trainers purely for the training of adult education animators. This requires having adult education departments in the universities of Cameroon.

Didactic Materials for Adults

One of the challenges of adult literacy in Cameroon at the moment is to develop didactic materials for adult literary (Nforbi 2000). Most of the existing ones in the official languages are intended for the formal school system. There is need for materials that will meet the needs of literacy in French and English. Besides, the focus on literacy in mother tongue equally implies adaptable materials for adults. The existing primers in mother tongue, which follow the Gudschinsky method, are good for children.

These primers pay a lot of attention to the smallest components of language; how sounds form syllables, how syllables form words and how they are written. This could be very useful for analytical learners since it gives careful attention to all the items to be taught and each has a lesson designed for it. Learning through similarities and contrasts is a positive aspect. The concentration on details, such as the position of consonants, functors (grammatical markers), and capitals, however, do not work well for adults whose learning habit is usually global. Language is not always seen in minute units. It also needs to be seen as a whole so as to give its full meaning, which is what adults will immediately look for in whatever they learn.

The Problem of Women in Literacy

According to recent UNESCO sources, there are one billion illiterate adults in the world; two thirds of these are women. In January 1996, at a literacy instructors training course organized by the Summer Institute of Linguistics (SIL) in Maroua, out of the over 30 participants, there was no female participant. After enquiries, it was discovered that the men leave their wives behind because it was not their tradition for their women to leave the homes and stay out for two weeks. One of the participants asked, 'Who will take care of the children, prepare food for them and take care of the house?'

A similar course organized in the North-West Province of Cameroon, registered 35 participants in which there were only three women. The response of the men was not very different from that of the group from the Far North. The women needed to take care of the family in their absence. In the Far North province of Cameroon, about 90 per cent of the girls get married before the age of twenty and most of them do not complete primary education, if at all they start. About 80 per cent of the pupils in the primary schools are boys.

Traditionally, women have come to take marriage and home-making as their vocation. This has not always been the case; rather, it is due to the harsh economic situation. Women have come to shoulder much of the responsibility of the family economically and socially. Hence, they need education that will prepare them for a profession. Providing special educational facilities for adult women is nothing more than paying an old debt that is long overdue; it is certainly not a favour.

As reported in the *State of the World Population* (1990), that the results of studies carried out in 46 countries indicated that a 1 per cent increase in women's literacy rate is three times more effective in reducing infant mortality than a 10 per cent increase in the number of doctors. As women's level of education rises, the number of malnourished children declines. Unfortunately, mature women remain unemployed because of lack of necessary educational qualifications. There is a need for re-schooling to prepare them for a place in the working world. This problem is already faced by women groups in Cameroon like the Women's Department of the Federation of Protestant and Evangelical Missions in Cameroon (FEMEC) and other women non-governmental organizations like the Association of Women Information Coordination Office (AWICO). Through the integration of literacy programmes into their schemes, functional literacy can be attained.

Women's Involvement in Literacy in Cameroon

Through the efforts of non-governmental organizations helping women to improve themselves through self-help activities, most illiterate women are beginning to see the need for literacy and are asking to be educated. A women's group based in Balikumbat expressed the need to learn how to read and write because they realized they could not manage their activities by themselves. They ran a corn mill but could not record the income and expenditure. They could count their money but couldn't keep the accounts in writing. They had to collaborate with AWICO, which guided them on how to achieve literacy. AWICO sent a note to the women, indicating a date for the meeting in their village. The women received the letter and, realizing that the date was a market day, sent another letter asking that the programme be deferred till the next day. AWICO did not receive the letter. The AWICO delegation arrived on the planned date and found that all the twenty members of the group were in the market. They needed to sell their okra, tomatoes and groundnuts, which costitute their only source of income. When a meeting was held, they indicated that it was impossible to stay at home on the market day because it came only once a week. Surprisingly, however, some of them left their articles with their friends to continue selling when they heard that a relative had died.

What is interesting in all this is that their interest in literacy still remained a felt need but was always subordinate to the more immediate needs and to traditional communal events like funerals. It should be noted that the meeting with them did hold in the market near their articles of trade to plan with them how to start off a literacy programme for them. About 90 percent of those present wanted to know how to write their names, how to record their money, write names on their trade items and also write letters. During this meeting, a few men were present, most of them literate. After the meeting, one of the women indicated that they allowed the men to join their group because they themselves could not read and write. So the men had to be there to write their minutes and letters. She regretted this fact and pointed out that immediately they learned how to read and write, the men would only play a passive role in their group as they would have acquired the skills to read and write and consequently would be able to direct their own affairs.

Women need to be trained as adult literacy instructors. They need special attention, especially in the rural areas. When women teach other women how to read and write, they go deep in meeting their needs, and try their best to make their meetings functional literacy classes. For instance, in matters relating to family planning are handled with much more ease than when men are teaching them. They can equally plan their meetings to make room for their numerous domestic activities. The Ghanaian experience is a testimony of the involvement of women in adult literacy.

The Ghanaian Experience

A positive experience of the Ghanaian Institute for Literacy Linguistics and Bible Translation (GILLBT) is the creation of the Women in Literacy and Development (WILD) department. Creating a women's department in a literacy programme empowers them. It has been established that women's needs are different from men's. Women, therefore, need literacy programmes adapted to their realities, as well as primers that handle issues of interest like gender and childcare. They need to organize their classes when they are free, since they have much to do in the home. More important is the fact that most communities are male dominated. Thus, women and men would not work well together in the same class. Women are, therefore, encouraged in the GILLBT programme to take part in writers' workshop where they write on topics that meet their own needs. GILLBT proposes the following for active involvement of women in literacy:

– Involve women as members of the language committee;
– Involve female participants in training courses as well as design some of these courses specifically for them;
– Involve women in leadership and managerial positions within literacy projects; and
– Encourage women to develop income-generating projects that can help them to cater for the needs of their various families.

Income Generating Projects (IGPS)

Even though GILLBT projects depend highly on foreign donors, much is being done to put local projects in place, which, in the long run, can generate income for self-funding. IGPS are, therefore, a very important component of the programme. IGPS are funded as part of the overall literacy and development programme for the following objectives found in GILLBT guidelines for IGPS 1999:

- To give experience in small- and medium-scale income generating activities;
- To afford communities the opportunity to develop managerial and entrepreneurial skills;
- To help communities raise funds to support individual literacy projects;
- To help literacy projects relate literacy to community-based projects;
- To encourage both men and women to work together and develop a sense of self-confidence;
- To serve as a base for communities to work towards financial autonomy for each literacy project.

In order to realize these objectives, training courses are organized on Participatory Rural Appraisal techniques as a means of identifying promising IGPS that will be community based. Training is given on financial management, which includes loans and repayments. The language committee identifies the IGP and proposes it to the IGPS and development coordinators of the literacy and development department. This department, in collaboration with the language committee, studies and assesses the project to see its utility to the community and its cost benefit before granting the funds of which 50 per cent is refundable.

This effort is yielding a lot of fruit as a good number of women groups are able to run micro-projects which enable them to take care of the daily needs of their families as they progress in literacy. Some literacy projects are equally able to raise money from the projects (like the Dagbani project in Northern Ghana) whose sales go a long way to support the project.

There is controversy over the management and remuneration of adult literacy instructors. Usually, those who rush to literacy classes first in the villages are those who can hardly support themselves and who see in literacy a means of coming out of their suffering. After these people have learnt to read and write and find that they have to teach on a voluntary basis in a society that is fast becoming individualistic and capitalistic, there is a problem. The traditional African society was essentially a communal society. But with modernism, which came with colonialism, the African communal lifestyles were destroyed by the various philosophies of the West. It is true that in purely traditional African societies, the chief or the elders reward one for meritorious services. There is community work. The roads, the bridges and the water points are taken care of. There is a day for the Fon's (i.e., traditional ruler's) work. The community will come out on such a day and clear the Fon's farm. Each year, those who have shown their prowess in the defence of the village are rewarded. Today, people are still rewarded in the palaces, even in greater numbers than in the past but for a price. Voluntary literacy animators have virtually no chance of ever being rewarded because they are often so poor that they cannot offer the goats, fowls, money and wine needed today in order to receive a reward. They will probably need to abandon the classes to go for some paid job elsewhere to raise money and the items required for them to be on the list of those to be rewarded. If they succeed in raising these items, they will actually be recognized by the palace as the best literacy workers. Reward in the African traditional society is, therefore, gradually tilting towards those who can pay for it rather than to those who deserve it. If you are wealthy in the village, you have more chances of receiving groups of villagers coming to 'help' you in your farms on 'voluntary' basis because what you will offer to them will be more than what they will receive as wages from another poor villager.

The Challenge of Local Ownership in Cameroon: The Structure and Management of Language Committees

In Cameroon, which has about 256 national languages, the question of which language should be used for teaching of literacy is a complex issue. Trihus (1992) explains the role of language committees in handling this rather complex situation. The National Association of Cameroonian Languages committees (NACALCO) has opted for an approach that enables any one of these languages to be used in teaching literacy. This approach is implemented through a decentralised system of management. The language committees of each language are supposed to take care of the day-to-day running of the literacy enterprise. At the moment, the membership of this Association cover one fifth of the languages spoken in Cameroon. The fifty languages cover about two thirds of the entire population of of the country. It should be noted that a majority of the mother tongues in Cameroon are actually minority languages. Thus, the forming of Language Committees by each language makes that community responsible for the development and preservation of its culture. The language committee is playing as important a role in the development of the indigenous languages as the state. If the language committee is the steering body of the literacy project, then it must be adequately constituted.

The indigenous people are doing the work that foreign missionaries started on some of our national languages. These indigenes learnt to read and write the language through the foreigners and could have been very useful to their communities when the foreigners left. Unfortunately, most of them inherited a western attitude which made them feel superior and unwilling to collaborate with the illiterates.

If the language committee should play more of a technical role than a political one, we should start reflecting on an adaptable structure.

The Konzime Experience

A language committee was formed for the Konzime language (spoken in the Eastern Province of Cameroon), following the traditional association structure. The president was at the same time a political leader. In a multi-party system, this was going to be a problem even though, incidentally, this community was in favour of the party of the language committee member. This notwithstanding, the structure did not reflect the technical needs of mother-tongue literacy. The dense forest which separates hamlets hundreds of kilometres in the same language community, made accessibility to all the community difficult. Gradually, some parts of the community lost contact with the committee. Dialects started claiming their autonomy. The SIL consultant in the language committee, who had spent years developing and translating the language, realized that a way out could be to decentralize the committee. This was done, and a sub-committee was set up in Lomie and another in Somalomo, two different quarters in the language speaking village.

People who were not experienced in the work that had been going on in the language formed the sub-committee in Somalomo. The president, who was chosen because of his age and stability in the society, and not for experience and zeal for the development of the language, could not do much. Structures such as councils of administrators which had been formed never met during its two years of existence. At the end of the two years, the result was a failure. No functioning language committee could be boasted of and no literacy work had been realized. Meanwhile the SIL consultant had been training some interested youths on computer work, literacy and translation. He had also, with the consent of the community, established a literacy office with equipment. The need to revitalize the language committee arose.

The experiences of Lomie and the former committee of Somalomo taught the SIL consultant and the representative of the NACALCO technical team a lesson: they saw the need for a technical functional language committee rather than a political body. As a result, it was necessary to avoid what carried political airs, pride and power. The titles of president, secretary general, and president of the council of administrators, for example, ignited pride rather than responsibility in those who occupied those positions. Hence, the dire need for titles tied to responsibility.

Responsibility Titles and Training of Language Committee Members

The need to have a technical language committee can only be achieved if the posts of the executive are tied to responsibility and experience. It is the responsibility that gives the post, and not the contrary. As such, the specialists were guided by the principal responsibility of the committee, which was to achieve literacy in the language. They were equally guided by the task of animation (since literacy is actually a very important component of socio-cultural animation) to define the titles for posts of responsibility in the executive.

The titles agreed upon were the following:

1. Principal animator, assistant
2. General secretary
3. Literacy animator
4. Training animator
5. Publication animator
6. Treasurer
7. Auditors
8. Advisers

This structure brought the post of responsibility to the hands of those who had been trained and who had the zeal to sacrifice for the success of specific objectives. Those who had been trained by the SIL consultant occupied the main posts and those with no experience in the discipline occupied the minor posts. This kind of structure has the following advantages.

1. It reduces superiority complex.
2. It gives the occasion for those with technical knowledge to be elected, hence giving direct opportunities to use their technical knowledge. (Note that in a traditional structure, such people will end up occupying technical posts but with no power of managing the resources of the committee).
3. A technically inclined structure gives room for those working to actively participate in decision-making and implementation. Decisions are taken on a technical and scientific basis and programmes of activities drawn up in this respect.
4. Projects are drawn up and submitted for funding on priority basis, not just on emotional and subjective basis.
5. Decisions are taken and implemented by those who have trained or, at least, possess some experience in the field. They manage the available resources for the implementation of the project.
6. There is a possibility for such a team to attract funds from the community. When the president of a language committee is rich and influential, he expects the community to support the committee financially. Unfortunately, people expect him to fund the committee from his own funds since he is rich. But when the committee sees the result of work done by technicians and those who know what they are doing and are committed, they tend to support such a team.
7. The chances of a technically inclined team to attract community and external support are higher than the chances of a team that has a socio-political structure.

How can we create a technically functioning language committee that represents all the sectors of the community?

Conclusion

Establishing an adult literacy model for a multilingual nation like Cameroon has many challenges. They include the appropriate handling of the mother tongues in the education system, knowledge of the needs of adults, an understanding of the vulnerability of women and of the role of the community in handling their own issues.

The Ministry of Youth and Sports in Cameroon is already involved in the fight against illiteracy among adults. Unfortunately its efforts are not yet focused on mother tongue education. Non-Governmental Organizations like SIL-Cameroon (SIL), the National Association of Cameroonian Languages Committee (NACALCO), and the Cameroonian Association for Bible Translation and Literacy (CABTAL) have seen the need for using the mother tongue in the fight against illiteracy in Cameroon. In order to adequately coordinate these efforts, there is need for the creation of adult education departments in the universities of Cameroon. This will provide room for further research into the domain of adult education. The overall process of adult education will then be given the attention it deserves and a functional model for adult education in Cameroon will hopefully emerge.

References

Agneta, L. and Anton Y., 1990, 'Adult Literacy', in *A Review of Objectives and Strategies*, Stockholm: Swedish International Development Authority.

Bamgbose, A.,ed., 1976, *Mother Tongue Education: The West African Experience*, Paris: UNESCO.

Bhola, H.S., 1984, *Campaigning for Literacy: Eight National Experience of the Twentieth Century with a Memorandum to Decision-Makers*, Paris: UNESCO.

Bhola, H.S., 1988, *World Trends and Issues in Adult Education*, London: Jessica Kingsley.

Bendor-Samuel, D. and Bendor-Samuel, M., 1983, *Community Literacy Programmes in North Ghana*, Dallas, Texas: SIL.

Nforbi, E., 2000, 'In Search of an Adult Literacy Model for Cameroon', unpublished Ph.D thesis, University of Yaounde I.

Nforbi, E., 2001, 'The Challenges of the Basic Standardization Process of Minority African Languages', *African Journal of Applied Linguistics*.

Tadadjeu, M., 1997, 'Cost Benefit Analysis and Language Education Planning in sub-Saharan Africa', in P.A. Kotey and H. Der-Houssikian, eds, *Language and Linguistic Problems in Africa*, Columbia, Ohio State.

Tadadjeu, M., 1977, 'A Model for Functional Trilingual Education Planning in Africa', unpublished Ph.D thesis, University of Southern California.

Trihus, Margaret S., 1992, 'The Role of Language Committees in the Development of the Indigenous Languages of Cameroon', unpublished master's thesis, University of Southern California.

10

The Rivers Readers Project as an Attempt to Develop Communities

Kay Williamson

The Rivers Readers Project was established to enable children of the Rivers State in Nigeria to learn to read and write their own language. It began following the first creation of states in Nigeria, when it was immediately apparent that the newly created Rivers state (now subdivided into Bayelsa State and Rivers State) was a multilingual area that could not conceivably use a single indigenous language in education. A group of three concerned academics at the University of Ibadan (E.J. Alagoa, a historian, O.A. Nduka, an education specialist, and myself, a linguist) presented a proposal to the first government of the Rivers State, which was accepted in 1967 and put on a more formal footing in 1970 when the area was recovering from the effects of the civil war. It was placed under the Ministry of Education and received a small subsidy from the Ministry until the coming of the civilian government in the Second Republic. Initial take-off grants were also received from UNESCO and the Ford Foundation. The three academics named (with others joining at a later date) were constituted as the Rivers Readers Committee and served as a link between the communities of the State and the Ministry of Education.

The committee agreed to encourage grassroots participation as much as possible, and treat all the languages equally. Because the project operated in an area of great linguistic diversity (the old Rivers State of Nigeria), we had to establish the communities involved. We took them to be those who were self-defined as speaking the same language. This meant that in some cases communities whose speech-forms were mutually intelligible were treated as distinct, because they had always been treated as distinct political entities and had previous separate traditions of writing: an example is the Kalabari-Kirike (or Okirika)- Ibani cluster of lects, which, in linguistic terms, are dialects of one language but require separate readers. On the other hand, the communities which consider they speak Ikwere (Ikwerre) have a great deal of dialectal diversity, but have a common political organization and require a single reader. We adopted the term 'local language' to name the entities for whom a single reader was provided; this cannot be equated with either 'language' or 'dialect' as usually defined by linguists. In the early days, we contacted individuals from the communities involved and asked them to invite others to form a language committee. Later, as a result of experience, we emphasized that the language committee should be as inclusive as possible: different dialect areas, chiefs, teachers, who must include women, different churches, etc., should all be involved. The language committee formed a bridge between the community and the Rivers Readers Committee, and the Rivers Readers Committee formed another bridge between the community and the Rivers State Government.

The language committee selected speakers who were to produce the first draft of all materials. In most local languages, we produced an orthography booklet, then an initial reader, and lastly a set of teachers' notes to help the teachers use the readers effectively. The language committee studied the drafts of the orthography and the readers. The orthography was discussed in detail, and where changes were proposed from what had been in use previously, being able to convince the language committee was the most important step in convincing the community. Once they were convinced, they explained it to the rest of the community, with the seriousness borne of conviction. They also went through the reader, line-by-line, word-by-word. Mistakes were corrected, and many dialectal differences gave rise to long discussions before a text was agreed. The arguments, which convinced the members of the language committee, were also those, which later convinced doubters in the community. If a community, especially with a distinctive dialect, was not represented on the language committee, it was quite likely that that community would refuse to accept the books at all. There were also long discussions whenever English loan words, even those in everyday use in the community, were used in the reader. Concern for the purity of the language led many to argue that children ought to learn the older words for 'mother' and 'father' and not mama and papa, or long compounds meaning book-learning-house instead of sukulu (or similar forms) for 'school'.

When we finally had an agreed text, we printed copies of the books and arranged as grand an occasion as possible to launch them. All traditional rulers, all local government functionaries, Ministry of Education officials, churches, and schools were invited. The books were introduced and explained, and speeches were made extolling the value of the local language and exhorting teachers to teach it properly. As time went on, we used to follow up this grand occasion with practical workshops for the teachers. First we taught them the orthography; then we made them practise writing in the language; then we introduced the readers and the teachers' notes. Workshops were very popular when small allowances were paid to those attending and certificates were awarded at the end. We gave grades on these certificates; there was a private agreement that everyone who attended properly received a certificate, but for more advanced work or job recommendations we chose only those who had obtained the higher grades. From that point, we hoped that the Ministry of Education and the language committee would take over and ensure that the books were properly used in the schools.

Because the original members of the Rivers Readers Committee were academics with full-time university posts, we were unable to spend as much time as we would have liked on checking how things were going. The rest of this chapter will give an informal discussion of how far we succeeded and failed in the enterprise.

We succeeded in devising or revising orthographies for some twenty-five local languages and in producing a first reader in them, usually with teachers' notes. In many language communities, we were able to work with people, especially retired teachers, who were both knowledgeable and enthusiastic about their languages. Quite a number of such people already had, or were inspired to create, books of their own, which they often asked us to help get published. Where these were initial readers, we had to regretfully decline, as we already had our own pattern; but in a number of other cases we were able to publish other manuscripts as supplementary reading materials; vocabularies and a dictionary of proper names. We count it a success to have tapped into local enthusiasm in this way.

Because we were working on a shoestring budget, we used a general common pattern for the readers. Initially we began with a look-and-say method, supplemented by word-building exercises. Variations were, however, allowed where necessary. First, an object, which had a simple name in one language, might have a long name in another. Second, the communities had differences in culture; while the usual occupation in some was fishing, in others it was farming. In all these cases we provided alternative pictures where necessary. Finally, in communities where the SIL, later succeeded by the Nigeria Bible Translation Trust, had already begun work and were producing readers following a different pattern, we arranged to accept their books into the project and publish them with our cover design where requested.

We later discovered problems with the look-and-say method. We had originally understood that this was the method in which teachers had been trained, but we discovered that the older teachers, who were often the ones most interested in teaching the languages properly, invariably taught the letters of the alphabet first, then built them up into two-letter words, three-letter words, etc. This method appears to have been handed down from the first missionary schools in the nineteenth century; it appears in countless old primers and is the model followed by almost all those who spontaneously write new materials, which are often submitted to me in the hope of getting them published. Even teachers trained in more modern methods in the Teacher Training Colleges, once they were faced with an actual class, reverted to what they remembered from their own days in the primary school. For a more recent generation still, many had never even learnt to write their own language in primary school, and were unable to transfer and adapt what they had been taught about English to a first-language situation. Although no proper evaluation of our readers and their effectiveness was ever carried out, informal reports made it clear that what we had initially designed for three terms of the first year of primary school ended up, even with a dedicated teacher, taking two years. As a result, we began devising simpler introductory books in which each vowel and then each consonant was introduced with a picture of an object; this was intended to precede what had originally been intended as Book 1. We can claim partial but not complete success with our method.

To become fluent readers in their language, children need a constant supply of new materials. After the first reader, we tried to go on to a more advanced one. Texts were produced in a number of the languages, but the only ones published were those handled by the Nigerian Bible Translation Trust teams, who were, unlike us, full-time on the job and were only dealing with one or two languages. Apart from the shortage of time to properly check the texts, we lacked money to produce them. The project, which was intended to cover the six years of primary school, was thus limited to the first two.

The financial limitations were not confined to new readers, but also affected the reprinting of the first readers and even the day-to day running of the project. The project was run with the utmost economy; the members of the Rivers Readers Committee worked for years with no honorarium for their contribution and often did not even request a refund of their expenses. One typist was employed for some years, but efforts to attract a senior person with linguistic training failed because he could not perceive it as leading to a reliable career structure. Our funding from the Rivers State Government was placed under a heading in the Ministry of Education, but to claim it became increasingly difficult. Under the Second Republic we found that to meet the Commissioner for Education and his Permanent Secretary (or Director-General), explain the position, and follow up with a formal letter as requested, was no longer enough to secure the release of funds. We were once told that under a civilian government we had to lobby for contracts! As senior academics involved in full-time teaching and research, working on the project on an essentially voluntary basis as a contribution to the State, we did not see it as our place to lobby for the miniscule funds budgeted for the project like contractors aiming for contracts in the million (or multi-million) range. Consequently, we ceased to receive any annual subsidy, and the project therefore ceased to operate formally except where a local community was willing to sponsor the production of their own reader and asked for our technical assistance. The lack of a proper funding relationship with the government must be counted one of our failures.

This failure is connected with the biggest problem of all; the lack of a whole-hearted commitment at both state and local government levels by the Ministry of Education and its officials. We came to perceive statements of support for the project as mere lip-service. The Ministry of Education proved unable to ensure the distribution of the books to the schools as arranged or to ensure that they were used in the classrooms. They did sponsor a few workshops for teachers, which generated some degree of interest, but they consistently failed to adopt the constant recommendation which emanated from these workshops: that the local languages should not only feature prominently in the timetable but should be examined at the end of the school year. The absence of this requirement reinforced the existing perception of the local language as unimportant compared with English. The school authorities, the teachers, the parents and the children themselves perceived the acquisition of English as all-important, the chief reason for attending school and the means to acquiring a good job afterwards. This perception, a deep-seated prejudice stemming from attitudes instilled in the colonial era, can only be modified by an active campaign, by increasing numbers of committed people, leading to a new vision of the place of local languages in relation to English; we were unable to achieve it.

I present this largely negative picture with reluctance. I would like to point to signs of hope, but there seems to be few of these. Rather, English appears to be becoming a first language for increasing numbers of children, not only those in multilingual urban areas but even for those in rural areas who aspire to imitate the 'sophisticated' township children. I believe that, in this period increasingly dominated by global concerns expressed through the global language, English, speakers of West African languages, especially the small ones, should decide whether they really want their languages to die out. This will be the result of allowing children to grow up with fluency only in English. What will be the effect on communities? Traditionally, they have been defined by language; but if the languages die, will the local communities die, or will they re-define themselves in English? What will happen to traditional values of courtesy, sensitivity and cooperation? Will they be replaced by ideas of competition, market values, and commercial viability? Is it possible to find ways of combining the good traditional values with the good of modern ideas, while rejecting the parochialism of the former and the selfish extremes of the latter? Surely these matters deserve serious debate; and surely the debate should be carried out in African languages as well as English and French. The linguists assembled here who represent different areas of Africa should consider these matters. What should be done, and how do we play our full part in bringing about constructive change.

11

Barriers to Effective Implementation of Multilingual Education in Cameroon

Blasius Agha-ah Chiatoh

Introduction

The promotion of social programmes is a challenging process because these programmes involve reshaping the cultural and linguistic attitudes of the communities concerned. But if one were to wait until the right conditions were in place before such programmes were implemented, then probably no programme would ever get started. Prior to, during and after the establishment, programmes encounter numerous and usually enormous problems. Problems emanate from weaknesses in conception, planning and implementation or from the socio-cultural, economic and political environment. In this chapter, we examine some major practical problems that affect the promotion of multilingual education in Cameroon. From local communities through private institutions of promotion to the government, multilingual education in this country remains an issue of public debate and reflection. For over two decades attention has been paid to basic and applied research in a bid to establish common grounds for developing multilingual education. Significant progress has been made both within the perspective of research and that of application of operational models. But this notwithstanding, policy implementation is extremely slow and public appreciation and support still leaves a lot to be desired.

The government has adopted a 'laissez-faire' policy where it neither encourages nor prohibits the process. This has resulted in the emergence of enormous and commendable private initiative. Local communities are increasingly recognizing the need for multilingual education and the reality of promoting national languages in the educational system. Together with local communities and international organizations, they have sought to transform the educational landscape by proposing the teaching of national languages as an indispensable component of a more efficient and more authentic educational system for Cameroon. In the course of our discourse, we examine the present state of multilingual education in Cameroon and the motivation for such an approach. We also present the application of extensive trilingualism as the framework for promoting the multilingual education model in Cameroon. More importantly, some of the key barriers to effective implementation are highlighted and some major remedial orientations presented in a bid to proposing lasting solutions to the multilingual education promotion process.

Multilingual Education in Cameroon

The history of multilingual education in Cameroon dates back to 1978 when the Operational Research Project for Language Education in Cameroon (PROPELCA) was created. Its goal was to experiment with the complementary teaching of mother tongues and official languages. In 1981, the first experimental schools became operational. Since then, the process has witnessed significant progress both in its legislation and in the application of the model in schools. In its first congress in Bamenda in 1985 the Cameroon Peoples Democratic Movement (CPDM), the ruling party, adopted the promotion of national languages as an indispensable component of the promotion of national cultural heritage. This vision was later developed in *Communal Liberalism* (Biya 1987). In 1995, the General Forum on Education recognized the importance of national languages in education and, in 1996, the Revised Constitution recognized and recommended the teaching of national languages. In 1998 parliament passed a bill, which was later promulgated into law (No 98/004 of 14 April 1998), laying down guidelines for education in Cameroon. It recognized the teaching of national languages alongside the official languages (English and French). A partial text of application of the 1998 law was signed in 2002. It formalized the teaching of mother tongues by creating Provincial Pedagogic Inspectors of mother tongues. Apart from progress made in legislation, there has also been tremendous progress in the implementation of the programme, especially in the private school system.

However, the application of L1/OL education in the official programme has remained an unaccomplished dream. The participation of public schools has remained relatively low. In 2000, and thanks to a convention signed between the government of Cameroon and UNICEF, experimental public schools became operational in the North, Adamawa and East provinces. Meanwhile, the promotion of the programme in other public schools has benefited more from the motivation of individual decentralized authorities and local communities. Globally, however, the experience has expanded significantly with private schools continuously involved in its implementation and generalization. Today, over 280 schools (private and public) are practising either the formal or the informal models of PROPELCA. The government, private institutions as well as local communities are more than ever conscious of the need for multilingual education. Unlike the early years, motivation for participating in the programme comes essentially from the communities themselves.

The Approach

Multilingual education is based on the use of two or more languages in the transmission of knowledge and know-how. Each society designs its linguistic policy in line with the numerical and functional status of its languages within a national perspective. Cameroon has over 250 languages used daily either orally or in the written form. Given this multilingual situation and faced with the challenge of promoting education that responds to the needs of the citizens, decisions have to be taken concerning the languages of education. But most of Cameroon's national languages are not yet developed and thus cannot serve as written media for transmitting modern knowledge. At the same time, English and French, as official (majority) languages, are overshadowing local languages, hence the need for immediate solutions to the problem of education and language use in Cameroon.

The approach consists in the use of all national languages alongside official languages, in formal education and in literacy. It recognizes English and French as majority languages in their own right, and also that these languages are indispensable for wider communication. National languages are recognized not only as minority languages but also as the languages of everyday use of local communities and, therefore, most efficient instruments of learning. The approach proposes that every community undergoes basic education in its language and systematically transit into the first official language. Accordingly, therefore, if all the languages were developed, then one would have over 250 languages taught simultaneously in schools and in literacy centres. For both formal and non-formal learning, the approach is bilingual. At the level of the primary, it involves the use of mother tongue as the medium of instruction within the first three grades with a transition into the official language from the second grade. At the secondary level, the approach is extensive trilingualism with the teaching of an additional national language known as the language of cultural opening (L2) together with the second official language (OL2). The adult component too is bilingual and involves first the learning of L1 and then the learning of OL2.

Relevance of a Specific Cameroonian Approach

Every country adopts its educational policies in accordance with its specific national development needs. Normally, the approach takes into account the learning and communicational needs of the citizens and the opportunities available for the use of each language. Consequently, the choice of an appropriate linguistic policy cannot be made without taking into consideration the opinions of decision-makers, specialists and the communities of native speakers. In proposing the multilingual model, this factor has been duly considered. But concerted action and national consensus have not, however, guided its application. On the contrary, individual actors have used their motivation and commitment to contribute variously to the process. As a result natural and sometimes inappropriate roles and responsibilities have emerged. The government has provided legislation while specialized institutions and local communities have ensured research and application. Yet the overall guarantor of education in the country, the government, has not yet committed itself to participating actively in the implementation process. This is why Cameroonians look down on the programme.

The model has been influenced by a wide-range of factors, including:
i) Multiplicity of minority languages;
ii) The desire to encourage culture learning and preservation;
iii) The need to encourage cultural and linguistic integration as a vital step towards national integration; and
iv) The need to ensure quality and accessible education.

These factors can be grouped conveniently into five categories: political, cultural, linguistic, pedagogic and social. The linguistic category takes into account not only the linguistic diversity of the country but also the fact that the languages are basically minority ones. This means that it would be inappropriate to encourage minority language teaching in some languages and not in others. For any model in this context to be appropriate, it should not undermine the existence and value of other languages. The approach thus seeks to provide every community the opportunity to carry out basic education in its language. According to the model, there is no need for a single national language for Cameroon. Although the languages have minority status and cannot assume national functions, some of them could easily assume provincial or regional status and be taught as such. But for the moment, Cameroon has not yet come to this stage.

The cultural factor concerns the desire of communities to preserve their cultural and linguistic identities. It is based on the premise that our cultural and linguistic heritage is ideally preserved through the written use of the languages that express it. This is the underlying motivation for most Cameroonians wishing to see their languages written. Whether or not the languages are used in education, literacy and religion is, in fact, only secondary. Some Cameroonians do not fully recognize the need for teaching these languages in schools. Those who have already acquired reading and writing skills in the first official language (OL1) learn their mother tongues purely for cultural identity reasons. They want to strengthen attachment with their cultural and linguistic groups. This has been referred to as identity bilingualism (Tadadjeu 1998).

The political factor is motivated by the desire to achieve national integration through maximal exploitation of Cameroon's rich linguistic and cultural diversity, which is an enormous resource that should be used to enhance national unity. Politicians (to a lesser extent) and linguists (to a larger extent) see this as an ideal framework for building a common nationalistic spirit through which Cameroonians integrate freely into the national community. To enhance this process, first, there is the harmonization of the alphabet of Cameroonian languages (Tadadjeu and Sadembouo 1979), which enables every citizen already literate in his/her language to read and write any other Cameroonian language. Second, there is the extensive trilingual education model, which proposes a language of cultural opening that allows the child, on leaving secondary school, to acquire cultural and linguistic knowledge in a national language other than his/her own.

The last factor is pedagogic. It is based on the premise that the acquisition of basic literacy skills in the mother tongue (L1) facilitates the learning of the official language (L2). It acknowledges initial learning in the L1 as reinforcing the quality of, and accessibility to, education. By encouraging cultural identification and edification, multilingual education is seen to strengthen self-confidence and to lay the foundation for building creative and critical competencies.

Extensive Trilingualism as the Basis for Multilingual Education

The L1/OL education programme is based on the theory of extensive trilingualism (Tadadjeu 1984). This theory proposes that the Cameroonian child who leaves school should be able to communicate in at least three languages one of which should be a Cameroonian national language and, by preference, a mother tongue.

The second language should be the first official language (OL1), that is, English for Anglophones and French for Francophones while the third should be a vehicular Cameroonian language and for other children a second official language (OL2), French for Anglophones and English for Francophones.

According to the theory, at least four languages will be used in the Cameroonian educational system, the mother tongue (L1), the first and second official languages (OL1 and OL2) and a second Cameroonian national language (L2). If the Cameroonian child, on leaving school, is capable of communicating effectively in two languages (L1 and OL1) and then minimally in two others (OL2 and L2), then that child will be appropriately prepared to operate in his/her community and then in the national community. This theory thus constitutes the ideal foundation for building the linguistic competence of the Cameroonian child. Its relevance lies in the fact that it is based on the linguistic and cultural realities of multilingual societies par excellence. The use of the four different languages implies careful planning in which both languages and sentiments (cultural impact) of the people are given careful and equal consideration.

Barriers to Effective Implementation

Although the model presented above is practically operational and pedagogically enriching, it has not been implemented without numerous difficulties. The present climate of application reveals that Cameroonians recognize mother tongues more as instruments of preserving cultural heritage than as efficient instruments of basic education. This is a position commonly held by the literate people, particularly the intelligentsia. Such an argument is not sufficient to justify the development and promotion of programmes. The challenges encountered thus far revolve around the use of national languages as media of instruction and involve economic pressure, lack of political commitment, absence of written languages, teaching materials, and implementation personnel.

Lack of Political Commitment

The successful implementation of a language policy demands strong support from policy makers because this involves changing the function of a language, and, consequently, the rights of those who use it. The choice of languages affects various aspects of the life of a society so that government intervention is inevitable. Language choice and language education depends on the political, cultural and technical factors that must be made by government. But there is need for collaboration from specialized institutions and the target communities. The government should appreciate educational needs in line with national development priorities, set the stage for application and oversee the entire process. The Cameroonian situation has been rather peculiar. Government favours multilingual education, as seen through present legislation. But this is not backed up by official support. There is no functional implementation and follow up mechanism. Institutions in charge of policy implementation are lukewarm either because they lack the necessary resources or simply the will and enthusiasm to enforce application. The resulting effect is that government support has remained essentially one of lip service.

Judging from the prevailing situation, implementation has continued to depend entirely on the support of private institutions and on the local communities. They have accepted and encouraged its experimentation and application. The problem here is that while the former are not well equipped to assume this enormous responsibility; the latter are, in fact, under no obligation to promote the programme.

Unwritten Languages

Effective implementation of programmes requires that every language be developed into writing. But of the over 250 languages in the country, less than 100 of them have writing systems and, of this number, only about 38 have actually attained some satisfactory levels of development. As such, the programme cannot implemented in all the communities. Private institutions have been instrumental in the development of national languages. Working together with university researchers, they have succeeded in carrying out groundwork research leading to standardization and development of writing systems for national languages. These institutions have also provided basic training in order to build competencies in writing systems, materials development and programme management. But these actions alone are not yet sufficient to establish the basis for sustainable promotion of programmes.

So far, the primary criterion for language development has been the enthusiasm of the communities to participate in and support the process.

The basic indicator for enthusiasm has been the establishment of language committees responsible for conception, co-ordination and management of literacy at the level of individual communities. Private institutions thus depend on the prior acceptance, enthusiasm and commitment of communities to engage in the development of their languages. Almost everyday, new committees are emerging, an indication that the communities are really enthusiastic. But considering the number of languages that are still unwritten and given the economic difficulties involved, a majority of the communities are unable to go into the educational system. This is noteworthy, given that the programme is built essentially on private initiatives which, alone, cannot provide the impetus and resources needed to realize such a goal.

Teaching Materials

In a context where mother tongue education does not yet enjoy concrete public support and where different domains of implementation are not developed into professional fields, implementation is bound to encounter difficulties. The area of materials production is particularly preoccupying. Very little expertise has been developed in the domain at the national and local levels. There is, therefore, a crucial problem of materials elaboration, follow up and distribution. Local communities do not possess the necessary capacities. Local personnel trained in the process soon drop out because the enterprise is unprofitable, leaving behind vacuums that take time to fill. Initially, institutions such as NACALCO assumed the responsibility of materials production but now the local communities should take over the task. This means, providing the personnel and engaging in minimal, if not maximal, local financial support. But the prohibitive costs of production make it impossible for this responsibility to be fully assumed locally. Moreover, there is almost no ready market for the books produced since readership is not yet well developed. Sales are low and the committees are unable to establish a strong financial basis for sustainable production. Funds come mainly from private institutions and communities provide the content and services of elaboration. But still, authorship motivation is low and this is another crucial aspect of the whole issue. Therefore, materials production becomes an activity that is neither paid nor compensated for since the entire literacy process is essentially based on volunteerism. When one considers that the teaching-learning process requires a regular and permanent flow of materials production, then the overall effect of the present situation becomes quite obvious.

Human Resources

The problem of human resources is crucial in programme implementation. This area is marked by cruel insufficiency; and so smooth development becomes really challenging. Since the programme relies on institutions whose personnel have not been trained in its promotion, training programmes are designed for personnel. This implies taking decisions relating to who assumes the costs of training and other major aspects of the programme. The local community lacks the required expertise. Given the absence of government input, personnel remuneration is poor, and, consequently, general motivation is low. The result has been the misappropriation of expertise, whereby specialized institutions become programme managers and funding agencies rather than promoters of the scientific and technical aspects of the programme. At the level of individual schools, poor remuneration and indiscriminate transfers of personnel are rife. Acute personnel shortages further compound the situation. These factors have had serious repercussions on programme implementation. Teacher and child attrition has become a permanent worry. Most classroom situations are complicated with teachers handling two to three classes, thus rendering application ineffective if not impossible. Yet, successful application demands that teachers be permanently assigned, at least, in the first three classes of the primary. In many cases, this is impossible because of personnel shortages and because those trained drop out sooner or later; so programmes start off and discontinue in many schools and restarting them is even more challenging than initial introduction. Authorities interpret this as the inability of promoters to ensure continuity. The whole issue, however, is that private institutions cannot efficiently handle the activities of research and application alongside administrative responsibilities such as personnel management. Above all, they do not own schools and so cannot engage in such a process.

Community Resistance

In some communities, implementation suffers from resistance from some parents who underestimate the value of learning in national languages because they consider them inferior. Some withdraw their children from school while others harass teachers applying the programme. These communities do not recognize the value of national languages as a key component of everyday value systems. Most of them perceive education as a means of obtaining white-collar jobs and since official languages are the only languages used by the institutions providing these jobs, there is a general reluctance to promote the written use of local languages. The stiffest opposition comes from parents who are not native speakers of the languages taught in schools. They see education in these languages as a systematic imposition of different ethnic cultures on their children, thereby threatening their individual native cultures. Nevertheless, a good number of them are beginning to understand the use of these languages in initial education. The few who have recognized the benefits of the system fully support it. They acknowledge that the programme facilitates official language (OL1) acquisition.

Social Mobility

Social mobility is a common characteristic of all emerging communities. People keep moving from one part of the country or community to another, and they move with their language and culture. But they encounter new languages, which they must acquire in order to interact freely in the receiving community. So, each time that the child moves, he encounters a new linguistic and social reality. For most parents, this is traumatizing for the children.

The problem is compounded when the new school does not apply the programme. The child has to adapt to a new system that makes exclusive use of the official language. In this case, the switch into the official language is abrupt and unsystematic and could have negative effects on the child's academic performance. A majority of those who oppose the programme use this argument. According to them, the programme should wait until its application is officially generalized.

Insufficient Financial Resources

For multilingual education to succeed, it requires huge financial resources. Personnel have to be trained and remunerated, teaching materials have to be produced and followed up and evaluation ensured first at the level of each community and then at the national level. The costs and charges are so enormous that neither the local community nor private institutions nor even the government working alone can easily afford them. The task has been rendered even more challenging by the government's lukewarm attitude. With the legal dispositions already taken (the laws of 1998 and 2002), the pace may be set for concrete government commitment. But as to when this will happen, it still remains uncertain because policy implementation in the country is extremely slow. Private institutions are themselves very insecure financially and so cannot ensure long-term support. Moreover, there is no formal partnership between them and government institutions so that participation depends exclusively on the motivation of respective institutions. Until such partnerships are established not much success can be expected.

How do we Overcome these Challenges?

The Cameroonian multilingual education process is unique in Africa. The context of application is extremely complex (about 250 languages), and the process is managed exclusively through private initiative. In the light of this, we shall propose some remedial orientations and guidelines for lasting solutions to the present situation. These are local ownership, private institutional input and partnership and national level management.

Local Ownership

Local ownership refers to the ability of communities to assume the responsibility for the multilingual education process, at least the mother tongue component of it, in the long term. Experience in Cameroon reveals this could serve as the most reliable and sustainable framework for building the process. Communities recognize themselves as direct beneficiaries of programmes and also as potential guarantors of long-term promotion. Through language committees and with the support of local and national institutions, they conceive, plan and manage activities especially in the areas of personnel training, materials elaboration, follow up and short-term funding. Local councils and elite development associations have made significant input into the process.

In addition, teams of local specialists are systematically established at the level of each community to ensure management. Private institutions provide scientific, technical and financial support. Thanks to their support, multilingual education has become a living reality in the country. NACALCO, SIL, CABTAL and the Catholic and Protestant churches have played an outstanding role in the process. Today, it is clear that local communities can assume minimal self-reliance development. The vision currently developed by NACALCO is for all local institutions to become permanent stakeholders in the multilingual education process. This is the potential framework for building local ownership. Participation has come to represent a key parameter for determining local motivation and commitment. If this is achieved, then it will significantly reduce the promotion burden and set in motion a more coordinated and accelerated process given that each stakeholder will contribute permanently in its own area of competence.

Private Institutional Input and Partnership

In a context where government input is almost completely non-existent, the role of private institutions is indisputably indispensable. This is precisely the framework within which the Cameroonian experience has evolved. Private institutions have constituted the basis for experimentation bfore the nationwide generalization of the programme. Even with the concept of local ownership, it is not certain that local communities will be able to operate successfully without outside assistance. They will continue to depend on private institutions for assistance for many years to come. Through them, communities have been able to design and manage their programmes. They provide orientation on planning, management and building of capacities for local generation of financial resources. But the daily running of the programme has remained in the hands of the communities themselves. This is an essential step towards building self-reliance and continuity. But their presence on the field is not officially recognized and encouraged by government so that the programme itself tends to be regarded as purely a private issue. The role of private institutions definitely needs to be acknowledged and supported. These institutions should be brought into the mainstream of education planning and management if the multilingual model has to be successfully implemented. Recognition also implies formal joint participation whereby both government and private institutions become permanent actors.

National-Level Management

For smooth functioning of programmes at the national level, there has to be a national mechanism for overall coordination and follow up of activities. Such a mechanism will not only harness the various efforts of development by different actors but will also provide impetus for local and national commitment to programme application. The Ministry of National Education (MINEDUC), through the services of a specialized and fully empowered department, should play this role.

At the private institutional level, NACALCO, in its capacity as the federation of language committees, serves as the platform for the coordination and implementation of the activities of language committees. However, NACALCO's influence is not quite felt among government circles. It is now evident within both circles that such a mechanism is indispensable. In some circles, the absence of government involvement has affected support. Absence of support continues to be interpreted as indicative of the lack of importance of the programme. A multi-sectoral mechanism, involving education non-governmental institutions, would probably reverse the present trend. Such a mechanism should operate within MINEDUC. In this way, common problems such as improvizations, unnecessary bottlenecks and other forms of weaknesses in the application policies will be checked. These have proven to be the greatest pitfalls of most government actions in the domain of policy implementation in general and multilingual education policy application in particular.

Conclusion

Our examination of the barriers to effective implementation of multilingual education in Cameroon has revealed that the Cameroonian model is based on the development and use of all Cameroonian languages in education. We have presented the extensive trilingual model as the general framework for the promotion of the model. Some of the most prominent barriers we discussed fall into five categories: political, linguistic, pedagogic, human and financial resources. Some key lessons to be drawn from the experience, and which should serve as the basis for breaking existing barriers, have been highlighted. On the whole, we have sought to demonstrate that although great progress has been recorded in the implementation of the model, enormous problems still persist particularly with respect to full government involvement. This is an indispensable factor in the development of nationwide impact and meaningful commitment.

References

Biya, P., 1987, *Communal Liberalism*, London and Reading: The Eastern Press Ltd.

MINEDUC, 1998, Law No 98/004 of 14 April 1998 to lay down guidelines for education in Cameroon. Yaoundé.

MINEDUC, 1995, *Rapport des Etats généraux de l'Education nationale*, MINEDUC.

Tadadjeu, M., 1984, 'Pour une politique d'intégration linguistique camerounaise: le trilinguisme extensif'. Quelle identité culturelle pour le Cameroun et l'Afrique de demain? APEC (Assemblée Nationale des poètes et écrivains camerounais), Yaoundé.

Tadadjeu, M., 1998, 'Bilinguisme identitaire et apprentissage d'une troisième lang-age: Le cas du Cameroun', unpublished paper, University of Yaounde 1 and NACALCO Centre for Applied Linguistics (CLA).

Tadadjeu, M. & Sadembouo, E. ed., 1979, *General Alphabet of Cameroon Languages*, PROPELCA Series No. 1, University of Yaounde.

12

Rescuing Endangered Cameroonian Languages for National Development

Emmanuel N. Chia

Introduction

A language is said to be endangered or under threat of extinction when it is spoken or used actively by less than 100,000 people (Gina Cantoni 1995:viii). It is said to be moribund or at an acute state of endangerment when less than 1,000 people speak it. Generally, in this situation, children no longer learn the language and only a handful of elders of over sixty years still speak it. For example, it is reported that somewhere near Garouain in 1974, Dieu Michel (ALCAM:115) stumbled upon the last surviving speaker of Ngo, the most northerly of the Bantu languages, and elicited from him a list of 200 words. In time, these few surviving elders die and the language dies with them. A language is declared dead when no speaker of it is still alive. It is from this point of view that ALCAM declares Nagumi, Nimbari, Gey and Oblo to be dead Cameroonian languages. Considering the global situation of language endangerment and death, as reported by Crawford (1995:17), as many as half of the estimated 6,000 languages of the earth are moribund. According to this same report, an additional 40 per cent of these languages would be declining. This means that 90 per cent of existing languages today are likely to die or become seriously embattled during this millennium. As can be deduced, this leaves only about 600 languages, that is, about 10 per cent of the world's total. Researchers from different parts of the world, including Africa, confirm this assessment. This global situation makes the estimate of four dead languages for Cameroon extremely conservative. It would be safer to say that the situation is not known since dead languages leave no traces behind.

Interest in Language Endangerment

The question that obviously arises is why would anybody be interested in this area of language study. This question is pertinent particularly within the context of the debate on whether multilingualism is an asset or liability in nation building.

Language Plurality as a Liability

Most scholars of the Third World argued around the 1960s that multilingualism was a burden and a definite impediment to national unity, integration and development. In discussing the language issue in Nigeria before the civil war broke out, Schwarz (1965:38-9), describes the linguistic differences as 'the seed from which secession can grow'. According to him:

> ... differences between indigenous languages keep the people apart, perpetuate ethnic hostilities, weaken national loyalties and increase the danger of separatist sentiment. For this author and others of the same school of thought for whom monolingualism is a definite asset for nation building, the extinction of any of the myriad of languages in developing countries would be a welcome reduction of the burden (cited in Bamgbose 1991:14).

What these scholars fail to see, however, is that language, like the national flag, is only symbolic of a pre-existing common feeling of togetherness and belonging. People of different ethnic and linguistic groups can be moulded into one solid political unit with common aspirations and destiny. Switzerland is an eloquent example. On the other hand, the cases of Burundi (with one national language, Kirundi), Rwanda (with a single national language, Kinyarwanda) and Somalia (with only Somali) are but few examples of many monolingual polities that have met with disasters of scandalous proportions in nation building. The argument according to which a single common language is a necessary requirement for nation building is, therefore, a myth (Bamgbose:ibid). The problems of nation building lie elsewhere and they cannot be blamed on the multiplicity of languages. We shall come back to this problem later when discussing literacy.

Language Plurality as an Asset

This is the view to which we subscribe and many strong arguments can and have been adduced in support of this position.

i) In the context of developing nations, their many languages constitute a precious source of enrichment. Besides the fact that these languages are both an embodiment and expression of a rich and variegated national culture and philosophy, they are the most effective vectors of vital information on development issues pertaining to agriculture, health, commerce, etc., in rural areas.

ii) According to Crawford (1995:32-5), language constitutes for the linguistic science the basis for the study of general human grammatical competence, and the disappearance of any human language represents an incalculable loss for the science. In this respect, the destruction of data by the disappearance of a language would be regrettable. Each language is a window on the human mind, which should be maintained and exploited, not pushed into extinction.

iii) It has also been argued that the loss of linguistic diversity means the loss of intellectual diversity which loss can only make man the poorer for it. The less variety in language, the less variety in ideas.

iv) Language loss is part of the more general loss that the world suffers in all things, for example, the loss in biodiversity. But whereas scientists are continually documenting the ripple effects of such loss on our global ecosystem, no evidence is left for study in the case of loss of linguistic species.

v) In view of the foregoing, perhaps the most salient of the arguments is that, since the extinction of languages implies human costs for those directly affected, everything should be done to prevent language loss. Loss of a language is tantamount to the destruction of a rooted identity for both language communities and individual members. Along with the concomitant loss of culture, language loss can destroy a sense of self-worth, limiting human potential and complicating efforts to solve other problems such as poverty, family breakdown, school failure and substance abuse. After all, language loss does not happen in privileged communities. It happens to the dispossessed and disempowered peoples who most need their cultural resources to survive.

Considering, therefore, the obvious interest attached to the problem of endangered languages, it is important to first identify and discuss the threats to the survival of Cameroonian languages, examine the ravages already done and are still likely to be done to them, look at the processes involved in language death, and, finally, consider possible lines of action to stem the tide of language erosion. The discussion henceforth will follow in that order.

The Threat to Cameroonian Languages

In the same way in which environmental factors threaten biodiversity, rendering some species endangered, as hinted above, there are easily identifiable factors that have killed and have continued to threaten the existence of many indigenous languages in the country. Some of these factors or causes of endangerment are internal to the language, some are external; but both act occasionally and synergistically.

Internal Threats

The threats envisioned here arise from within the language community and not from the language corpus itself. These threats range from the numerical strength of the native speaker population through internecine wars to lack of prestige.

Population of Speakers

The native speaker population of the indigenous languages in Cameroon ranges between 1 and 700,000. A sizeable number of the languages boasts 2,000 and 50,000 speakers; very few count over 500,000 speakers, and, at the moment, none of them has a population of over 1 million speakers. It has been noticed that within minority language communities, the feeling of numerical inferiority complex pushes the members (especially the young) to identify with the more popular neighbouring language communities. This frequently happens if members of the minority group depend on the larger community for access to school and other facilities. The risk of absorption of minority groups in such a situation by larger ones is rather high. Since their group is little known outside their immediate local habitat, their point of reference, once they are out of the region, is the better-known larger language community. Thus, people from Bueni, Mmen and Bum, once out of the Province, will identify themselves with Kom in the Boyo division in the North West Province of Cameroon. In the same way, once out of the village where their language is spoken, many speakers of Yasa, Basaa, Bagyeli and Bakoko, identify themselves with Duala in the Littoral Province. This phenomenon of the minority identifying with larger linguistic groups is one of the causes of linguistic erosion that eventually leads to language death.

Internecine Wars

Villages or dialect groups of the same language community are known to have wrangled, fought and parted ways over questions of land ownership or the exercise of authority or power over the group. The Balis, one of the big Chamba groups, in their southward drive, probably fleeing from the horse-riding Fulani warriors from the north are said to have disagreed, fought, separated into many splinter groups, and, finally, settled in different areas in the grasslands. As evidence, four of such groupings are found today in the North West and Western Provinces far flung from each other: Bali-Nyonga (the largest), Bali-Gashu, Bali-Galim, Bali-Kumbat, speaking different languages but claiming the same origin. It is not clear which of these languages is their original language. It is likely that they fused into other language communities that they encountered on their way occasioning substantial modifications to the languages in contact, such that the original language of the Balis would be completely dead today.

Settlement in High Risk Zones

For purposes of security, and protection from attacks by stronger and belligerent groups seeking territorial expansion, many minority language groups have elected to take refuge in rocky, infertile, inhospitable and often risky areas; the only advantage being that these locations are difficult to access and, thus, provide security. But the same rocky desert areas of the northern part of Cameroon and the Kirdi country, for example, are known to record high death tolls when famine strikes as a result of long periods of drought or the onslaught of locusts. In the volcanic mountainous regions, eruptions in the past have reduced language groups, dispersed some and completely swallowed up others. Only legends about these dramatic catastrophic events of the past remain to tell us how many nations were buried in the entrails of our volcanic lakes. The Nso, Noni, Oku, Kom and Aghem legends and songs attest to this. The most recent cases of such devastation are the eruptions of lakes Menoun and Nyos. In the case of the latter, 1,700 souls perished at once and this does not tell the story of the myriads of living species in the area.

The Incidence of Disease

Although the danger of disease is truer of the past than of the present, pandemic diseases such as the smallpox, the pest and typhoid, have swept away large populations of Africa. It is not impossible to imagine that such plagues could have decimated entire language communities. Malaria, to a smaller extent, and sleeping sickness (especially in swampy areas such as the Mbam area in the Central Province) are still responsible for many deaths in Cameroon. But because the high mortality rate in many village communities in the tropics is attributed to witchcraft, many youths are scared away from their native areas. The result is that only the elderly can stay there. This drastically reduces the vitality of the language, and when the vitality of a language is affected, it is headed for extinction since the younger populations that are forced to stay in metropolitan areas no longer need their MT where they live, work and educate their offspring. Again, while the war against malaria has not been won in that no vaccine has been developed against it, another pandemic, AIDS, which is more ravaging than malaria has come, targeting the youths in particular. There is a real fear that large populations (and, therefore, large linguistic groups) will disappear, as there is no cure in sight for AIDS and preventive measures are not succeeding.

Change of Attitudes and Values

In the face of richer, more advanced and attractive cultures, some less fortunate language communities have changed their lifestyle. Nomadic peoples have become sedentary in some parts of the country, modifying or rejecting their original cultures. Also in the face of official languages (English and French), many native communities have come to the conclusion that their indigenous languages have no worth and, therefore, no place in modern society. Those educated in the official languages think that local languages do not deserve to exist. Language teachers and educators in general forbid school children from speaking these languages. When others speak near them, they react with derogatory remarks such as 'you are causing rain to fall' or insults them that they are 'uncouth', etc. Not only do teachers with these attitudes prohibit the use of these languages in the school premises, they sanction defaulters. Some educators claim that speaking these languages constitutes an obstacle to the proper acquisition of the official language. Such attitudes are a very real threat to our languages.

Lack of Prestige

Cameroonians who are bilingual in their MT and Pidgin English (or other languages of inter-group contact, such as Fulfude), even though they are illiterate, automatically rank the three languages commonly used in society in a descending order of prestige as follows:
i)   The official language (English or French)
ii) Pidgin English (or Fulfude)
iii) Mother Tongue (Duala, Kom, Mankon, etc)

This ranking comes from their understanding of government policy requiring that they send their children to school to learn the official language which is the language of government, administration and justice. Their hope is that their children will gain employment after school and become divisional officers, teachers, doctors, nurses, etc. These are the people who matter in society. The language they use (the OL), is the most coveted, the most desirable and the most prestigious. Pidgin English, in the village context, comes next to the OL because it is used in trade exchanges, in the markets around and to make contact or communicate with people who do not speak the language of the locality. An MT monolingual illiterate would automatically rank a bilingual in MT and PE, or even a monolingual in PE is regarded as superior to him/her. It seems people covet what they do not have. Consequently, the MT or the indigenous language is placed at the lower end of the prestige scale. This, in itself, is a serious threat to the native languages.

External Causes of Endangerment

The threats to the indigenous languages to be discussed here are those that originate from outside the language community such as invasion, conquest and occupation by a warring group, wars of territorial expansion, economic exploitation and competition between strong and weak languages.

Occupation by a Foreign Power

During the internecine wars that characterized the grasslands, beginning from the 14th century up to the 18th century, it was common for warlike tribes to invade an otherwise peace-loving community and simply occupy it, reducing the original occupants to subservience. This is how the Kom people are said to have moved into their present site (Kiawi 2001). The original inhabitants, the 'Ndonalu' people were simply silenced in their own land and, today, they only count as one of the 20 Kom clans. The question of interest is, what happened to their language? It stands to reason that, they gave up their land, their culture and language to the belligerent Kom people. Such invasions, though rare today, still exist.

Wars of Territorial Expansion

Once settled, the Kom people engaged in expansionist wars during which they defeated neighbouring tribes such as Bueni, Ake, Achain and Ajung. Bueni still speaks an impoverished variant of Obang in Befang but all adult Bueni natives are bilingual in Bueni and Kom and shifting to Kom and English. However, the languages of the other tribes that had become vassal states to the Kom fondom are no longer spoken. This phenomenon of territorial expansion that put small or weak languages at a terrible risk are common to all major grassfield chiefdoms. The same thing can be said of Bali-Nyonga and its neighbours in Mezam and Nso and its neighbours in Bui.

Sandwiched Minority Languages

These are cases of minority groups that find themselves between feuding tribal groups. Their very insecure location between warring groups makes them suspects of either neighbour. In these circumstances, the members of the sandwiched community become trilingual or bilingual ,at least, as a necessary imperative. When they are with one of the neighbours, they speak the language of the neighbour and so on. For as long as they find themselves in this uncomfortable situation, their language and culture are at great risk. The Mbesa people in Boyo division caught up between the Oku and Kom people, who for long have been contesting the ownership of the Ijim Forest, are a case in point. This would also be the fate of language groups situated along and across national borders, what Chumbow (2000) refers to as ' Transborder languages' in the condition of the 'trojan horse syndrome' (cf. his study of transborder languages of Africa and transnational co-operation).

Commercial Invasion by a Foreign Language

As a result of colonial subjugation or trade relations between a powerful industrial country and an underdeveloped one, the poor country, which is situated on the receiving end, consumes the goods and must borrow the names of these numerous commodities into its lexicon. In a sense, they sell their goods along with their language to the consumers. What is dangerous in the exercise is the replacement of vocabulary and expressions of the local languages with equivalent expressions from the colonizer's idiom for aesthetic purposes, i.e., just so that the speaker sounds 'civilized' or sophisticated even in speaking his/her MT. In this way, instead of the local languages getting enriched, they are constantly becoming impoverished. This, again, comes as a result of the unconscious rejection of self or the willing acceptance of the foreign element at the expense of self. This is another form of linguistic erosion.

The Western School System

The Western school system, which was imposed on us by the colonial masters, was essentially aimed at replacing our 'barbarous' languages with the languages of our colonizers referred to as 'civilizing' languages. We accepted our situation willy-nilly, since these are the languages without which you cannot gain employment either in the private or public sector. Since the future of our children depends on the acquisition of these foreign languages, parents make every effort for them to acquire these official languages but at the expense of their indigenous languages. This has been further strengthened by misconceptions or myths such as 'you must give up your language if you want to learn another'. Also, for most parents, the children gain apparently nothing by knowing the indigenous languages. Some parents prohibit and sanction severely, the use of MTs within the family setting especially in urban areas.

There is another facet to this form of western education. By introducing bilingual education in the official language and the child's MT as a solution to our problem, the MT is only used as a pedagogic strategy to teach the official language better. Thus the child's MT is used to teach the OL and once the OL is acquired, the MT is abandoned. There is no further interest in continuing education in the MT. There is no programme that provides for deepening of knowledge in the indigenous language neither is there room for the use of the MT for the rest of the child's career. This is transition or subtractive bilingualism and it is, indeed, a threat to our indigenous languages since it provides a bridge out of the MT for the child but no return to it again.

The Growth of Towns in Minority Language Areas

The growth of most towns begins with the creation of a divisional headquarters in a native area. The presence of a divisional office where all official business is transacted, the presence of government services such as the health centre (hospital), agricultural posts, finance services, police and justice, etc., that accompany the new creation, attract in their wake an influx of population hitherto unknown in that area. Since this population is drawn from different linguistic backgrounds, the common language of interaction will not be the language of the native area but the official language used in schools and offices and pidgin in social and commercial interactions. As the population grows, and the demand for land rises, the natives sell their holdings and retreat to the backwoods. However, their young ones hardly follow them. The elders soon disappear and the languages disappear with them. The closest example here is the Bafaw language listed in Ethnologue as having only 8000 speakers. Kumba used to be its native area but now a big town has grown up there, putting the natives and their language in danger.

The Actual Situation

In an attempt to determine the actual status of the Cameroon indigenous languages found in Atlas Linguistique du Cameroun (CERDOTOLA-ACCT-DGRST:1983) and taking only demographic information (as found in Ethnologue 2000) into consideration, the classification in Table 1 emerged.

Classification of Endangered Languages

The classification in Table 1 is solely based on the population of speakers. Other criteria, such as the degree of development, number of publications and rate of literacy in the language (etc.), were not available at the time of research. As can be seen from the table, only two of the myriad of languages in Cameroon has a population of above 500,000 speakers and, as earlier indicated, none of them attains 1 million. Nevertheless, the languages in categories A and B are considered 'fairly safe' because, by our definition, a language is said to be endangered or under threat of extinction when it is spoken by less than 100,000 people. The rest of the languages are, therefore, in the danger zone. Ninety are 'not safe' and 94 are at 'high risk of death' with 20 dying because these have less than 1000 speakers.

Table 1: Degree of language endangerment

Category	Population of Speakers	No. of Languages	Remarks
A	500,000+	2	
B	100,000+ − 500,000	14	Fairly safe
C	50,000 + − 100,000	20	Not safe
D	10,000+ − 50,000	70	
E	1,000+ − 10,000	74	High risk of death
F	0001 − 1,000	20	

Since Table 1 takes into account only 200 languages, it means that more than 40 languages are left out of our analysis here. This is because there were no population figures indicated against these languages in our source document (Ethnologue) cited above.

It should also be noted that the area of unparalleled linguistic fragmentation marked by concentrations of minority languages is situated in the difficult high savannah grassland region of the West and North West Provinces and the borders of the Northern Akwaya region of Manyu division. Again this concentration continues towards the north of the country, covering the hilly region to the west of the Adamawa Province and extending northwards along the border with Nigeria to the jagged almost desert area of the North and Far-North Provinces. On the other hand, the low lying plains of the country, East, Centre and South, experience higher degrees of linguistic homogeneity marked by fewer languages, sometimes far flung from each other. The concentration of languages in difficult terrain thought to provide security constitutes in itself, as indicated earlier, a serious risk to the survival of minority languages. Because of the high competition for arable land, which is rare, inter-tribal wars are frequent and famine is perennial especially as one approaches the advancing desert north. These are serious threats to the language communities in place.

Process of Endangerment and Loss

Considering the causes of endangerment that lead to the total extinction of a language as discussed above and what obtains on the field for most languages destined for death, a five-step process can tentatively be sketched:

Marginalization → Contraction → Devalorization → Zero transmission → Extinction.

1) Marginalization of language occasioned by reduction of the numerical strength of its speakers, their financial potency and status.
2) Contraction or reduction of the domains and functions of the language, for example, restriction to use only in traditional ceremonies.
3) Devalorization of the language and culture in terms of loss of prestige and self-worth. Negative attitudes about the language generate disloyalty and shift or abandonment by its speakers, especially the youths, a situation that some scholars refer to as being 'tongue-tied' (Okwudishu in this volume) .
4) Arrest of language transmission: Children no longer learn the language. The use of language is limited to the elderly who soon pass away with their knowledge of it.
5) Extinction: All speakers of the language are dead, and, of course, the language vanishes.

This would be the process by which languages die but is there no way out?

Possible Remedies

In the light of the foregoing discussion, the following suggestions are submitted as possible remedies to the endangerment of African languages. Whereas it is understood that some of these measures will precede others in time, for example, those that have to do with fact finding on some of the little known languages, etc., many of the measures are urgent and can be tackled immediately and simultaneously:

1. It is urgent to carry out a head count of the population of speakers, both natives and non-natives of each of these languages, or, at least, include it in the next demographic survey of the country. This will help to make the status of each language clearer: dead, dying, endangered or secure. (We are aware that different people especially politicians, give different meanings to census exercises and are quick to falsify or misinterpret them.)

2. Priority should be accorded to the linguistic study of these languages: Tape recording them, producing orthographies, grammars and dictionaries, beginning with category F languages as a matter of priority down in descending order to category A languages. If the languages in category F and E must be rescued, there is little time for delay.

3. There will be need to procure funds for the activities of language planning, language engineering, language standardization, the production of didactic materials, training of teachers, and the production of bilingual education programmes in the languages in question.

4. Language resuscitation can be envisioned for those declared dead or dying, but the principal problem here would be that of getting the required resources. It must be emphasized, however, that resuscitation is perfectly possible from the example of Hebrew, which was once dead but is now the national language of Israel.

5. Educate the native speakers to see the value and need of saving, developing and using their language and to be committed to this cause. The elite should be encouraged to take up the challenge of developing their language. They should be the ones to initiate and control the endeavour; otherwise it stands no chance of succeeding.

6. In order to protect these languages from the onslaught of predator languages, such as English and French, subtractive bilingualism, must be avoided. Instead, stable bilingualism must be adopted, ensuring careful specification of domains and functions of each language. The development and expansion of lexicons, insofar as borrowing is concerned, should not be done at the expense of the local idiom.

7. Sandwiched minority languages like transborder languages (Chumbow 2002 manuscript) should be studied, developed and used as bridges for peace and

cooperation, instead of being looked at with suspicion or as 'l'enemi dans la maison'.

Use of the Indigenous Languages in National Development

The idea of national development, which the use of indigenous languages aims at achieving, should be understood to refer to an authentic African renaissance whose sole objective is to close the gap between developed countries and ours in the health, agricultural, communications, technological fields, etc. This renaissance should begin with education in the local language first before instruction in any other medium.

In the foregoing discussion, under different lines of argumentation, we pointed to a number of crucial areas in which our indigenous languages can be used, for instance, to convey vital information for the well being of the native speakers. We stressed the imperious necessity for campaigns against ravaging pandemics like the AIDS to be carried out in the language of the potential victim or the target population. These languages have been and can also be used to great effect by the politician seeking votes at elections. We equally indicated the gainful use of these languages to convey information to farmers on insecticides, fertilizers, new farming methods and tools, etc., information that will lead to increase in their yield and, therefore, contribute to their socio-economic growth. We also briefly mentioned the possibility of using our indigenous languages in local newspapers, community radio and in satellite communication, which in particular is pregnant with felicitous ramifications for economic development of the entire African continent (Tadadjeu & Chiatoh 2002:1-14). Basically we are saying that these languages will better serve the traditional function of communication than a foreign medium in these contexts.

One other use of indigenous languages that has been touched on obliquely above is their use in literacy. Ever since the UNESCO meeting of experts on the use of vernacular languages in education in Paris (1951) and their report in 1953, it has become axiomatic that the mother tongue is the best medium for imparting literacy skills to children and adults alike. The explanation is simple: psychologically, the MT is the system of meaningful signs that, in the mind of the learner, works automatically for expression and understanding. Sociologically, it is a means of identification among members of the community to which the learner belongs. Educationally, a learner learns more quickly through it than through an unfamiliar linguistic medium (UNESCO 1953:11). Thenceforth, it is an inalienable right for all children to learn in their mother tongues.

These authoritative statements have been very instrumental in influencing support for MT education in Cameroon and throughout the world. When children begin their education in the mother tongue they do it more easily, more quickly and so much better than through a foreign medium that they can even learn other national languages, a fact that works in the interest of national unity and integration. But what is even more important is the fact that MT education is the best way to fight illiteracy. Illiteracy has a direct link with socio-economic development. The 1976 UNESCO reviews of literacy in the world since the 1965 Teheran Conference stipulates clearly that 'illiteracy has a close correlation with poverty'. It has also been shown that highly industrialized and economically advanced countries of Europe and North America have the lowest illiteracy rates while the developing countries have the highest illiteracy rates.

In the third place, publishing, a profession in which many people have grown fabulously rich elsewhere, can provide a living for indigenous language authors. An interesting novel, a collection of poems, a history book, children's bedtime folktales in an indigenous language, properly done and well distributed can pay good royalties to the author (Chia 1996).

Russ Bernard (1997) who argues forcefully for publishing in non-literate languages provides an eloquent example from Oaxaca in Mexico. The beginning may be riddled with problems, but patient application and commitment brings, as in the case cited, huge successes. Some of Ngugi wa Thiongo's novels, published in English, now recast in the author's native language (Kikuyu), have found a new audience and a huge market (personal information from Professor Chumbow). Besides, this is the type of endeavour that, more than anything else, helps to rescue and preserve endangered languages.

It is thus clear, that the uses to which the indigenous language can be put are numerous, gainful, and challenging. Besides the fact that the native speakerneeds to use it just to be himself or herself, effective use of these languages will engender national unity and integration, social and economic development.

Conclusion

This chapter has defined and delimited the endangered languages of Cameroon. It has shown that there is a definite interest in the study of the phenomenon of language endangerment. Our languages are dying at an alarming rate. The chapter has traced the causes and process of death. But this calamity can be avoided. Suggestions to this effect, beginning from an urgent count of the speakers of each language, to the effective planning, development and use of these languages, have been presented. What is left now is the political will to provide resources for timely intervention. There is no time to waste if these languages must be rescued. Finally, it is shown that these languages need to be rescued because they serve as the most effective tools of national development.

References

Bamgbose, A., 1991, *Language and the Nation: The Language Question in Sub-Saharan Africa*. Edinburgh: Edinburgh University Press.

Chia, E., 1983, 'Cameroon Home Languages' in E. L. Koenig, E. Chia, and J. Povey, eds, *A Sociolinguistic Profile of Urban Centres in Cameroon*, Waltham, Mass.: Crossroads Press.

Chia, E., 1976, Linguistic Democratization (unpublished manuscript).

Chumbow, B. S., 2000, 'Transborder Languages of Africa', *The Journal of Social Issues*, PRAESA, South Africa.

Crawford, J., 1995, 'Endangered Native American Languages. What Is to be Done and Why?' *Bilingual Research Journal*, Vol. 19 No. 1.

Crawford, J., 1996, 'Seven Hypotheses on Language Loss Causes and Cures' in G. Cantoni, ed., *Stabilising Indigenous Languages*, Flagstaff: Northern Arizona University.

Dieu, M. and Renaud, P., 1983, *Atlas Linguistique du Cameroun : Inventaire Préliminaire*, Y'de, Paris: ACCT.

Fasold, R., 1984, *The Sociolinguistics of Society*, Vol. 1, Oxford: Basil Blackwell.

Grimes, Barbara and Grimes, Joseph E., eds, 2000, *Ethnologue*, Vol. 1: Languages of the World, Dallas Texas: SIL.

Kiawi, P., 2001, 'The Kom-German War 1904-5: The Kom War Tactics', University of Buea: Dissertation.

Krauss, M., 1992, 'The World's Languages in Crisis', *Language*, 68, pp. 6-10.

Krauss, M., 1996, 'Status of Native American Language Endangerment' in G. Cantoni, ed., *Stabilizing Indigenous Languages*, Flagstaff, A.Z.: Northern Arizona University.

Okwudishu, A., 2002, 'Of the Tongue-Tied and the Vanishing Voices: Implications for African Development' (Published in this volume).

Ruis, R., 1995, 'Language Planning Considerations', in *Indigenous Communities in Bilingual Research Journal*, Vol. 19, No. 1.

Tadadjeu, M. and Chiatoh B., 2002, 'The Challenge of Satellite Communication in African Languages', in *AJAL* No. 3.

13

Of the Tongue-Tied and the Vanishing Voices: Implications for African Development

Okwudishu Appolonia Uzoaku

Introduction

> If you look in detail why languages are dying out, it is because there are real pressures on people that are not democratic and not very progressive. Perhaps their land is being taken away from them. Perhaps their environment is being destroyed, so language can be marker of something more profound or more troubling that's going on.
>
> ----Daniel Nettle, *Vanishing Voices*.

Among the social processes that have ushered in the global village phenomenon is one, which has been described as cultural and linguistic meltdown in progress all over the world. This process involves an extraordinary language shift (Fishman 1991), which has, within the last hundred years, seen the demise of several languages. Literature on endangered languages reveals that the problem has become pandemic. Research in this area has become so crucial to linguistic organizations that there is a clarion call on linguists to form committees on endangered languages. Data on the endangered languages of various areas of the globe have been compiled and made available on websites for interested scholars to access easily. There is ample data on the endangered languages in the Americas, Asia, the Pacific and Europe with information on when the last speakers of some of these languages died.

A careful look at the data on languages of Africa, generally, and those of Nigeria, in particular, reveals that there is still a dearth of information on this phenomenon from Africa. Our objective in this chapter is to make a contribution to the ongoing research on endangered languages. The area covered by our study is the Federal Capital Territory in Nigeria where there has been a displacement of indigenous populations for the purpose of building a new national capital.

Conceptual Framework

In this chapter, the two concepts, being 'tongue-tied' and 'vanishing voices' are used to depict the factors that contribute to language shift. The term 'tongue-tied' has been used in previous studies to describe apathy toward a language use by its native speakers or second language learners (Simon 1980; O'Connor 1983; and Patir 1993). Fishman (1991) locates the key to indigenous language preservation in the transmission of the tongue in the home by families. Where there is no commitment to such transmission, resulting in the non-use of the language by the youths, we say that they (the youths) are tongue-tied. With the passing away of the older generation of speakers, the voices that formerly spoke the language also vanish. This is aptly captured in Nettle and Romaine's (2000) landmark book, *Vanishing Voices,* in which language endangerment is shown as resulting from powerful forces that combine to shape people's lives and interactions with each other. Voices begin to vanish when tongues (languages) are threatened and such voices are completely obliterated when the languages are vanquished. Terms such as 'death' (Brenzinger 1992b) murder, genocide (Crystal 2000) suicide and silence (Nettle and Romaine 2000) are metaphors that have been applied to vanished languages. Languages are also described in metaphoric terms as fading (Uko 2002), endangered, decayed, diseased, moribund, obsolete or extinct. Krauss (1992) defines moribund languages as those that are no longer being learned as mother tongue by children. He distinguishes them from endangered languages which may still be learned by children during the next century. He contrasts these two types with safe languages, which are languages with official state support and very large numbers of speakers.

Theoretical Framework

According to Sanburg, 'languages die like rivers' (see Hortz 2002). Thus, the phenomenon of language death is as old as history. What is disturbing is the fact that more languages are dying today than at any other time in the world's history. It is predicted that by the end of the twenty-first century, about half of the world's 6,000 remaining languages are expected to disappear (Klaus 1992; Hale 1992). Some extremist versions suggest that by the year 3000, only 600 languages will be left. Data released by the Summer Institute of linguistics (SIL) in its database known as the Ethnologue show that there are 51 languages with only one speaker left with 28 of them located in Australia alone; fewer than 100 speakers, and another 1,500 speak 500 languages by fewer than 1,000 speakers.

SIL's Ethnologue report of nearly extinct languages indicates that 417 of the languages in the list are classified as nearly extinct. Out of these, 157 are in the Pacific, 161 in the Americas; 55 in Asia; 7 in Europe and 37 in Africa. Among the African countries that feature in the Ethnologue, Nigeria records the highest figure, with 12 out of the 37 nearly extinct languages. Cameroon comes second with 8 nearly extinct languages while 4 languages (Gey, Nagumi, Duli, and Yeni) are described as already extinct.

Adopting the definition of endangered language, based on the numerical strength of its speakers, Brenzinger, Heine and Sommer (1991); and Ugwoke (1999) list 152 Nigerian languages with less than 5000 native speakers as endangered. Using parameters other than numerical strength, Woff (2000) defines languages as endangered when they lose communicative functions because, quite characteristically, the next generation no longer acquires the mother tongue language as first language. In other words, languages die out for lack of active speakers. Brezinger (1992, 1998) lists over 100 African languages as seriously endangered in this sense of language death.

Reporting the situation in Adamawa State of Nigeria, Fakuade (1999) lists Yungur, Mboi, Bata, Chamba, Vere, Tambo, Bura, Ga'anda and Lala as ethnic groups that have completely abandoned their language in favour of Fulfude. To this list, Ahmed Gella of the House of Representatives (personal communication) adds the Gude ethnic group, also in Adamawa. He laments that the indigenes of Gude aged 60 and below can no longer communicate in their language since they have adopted both Fulfude and Hausa. The oldest speaker of the language, according to him, is about 92 years old, implying that when the older speakers die off, the language dies with them. Similar situations are reported for languages of ethnic groups in Bauchi, Gombe and Taraba States (Fakuade 1999), and for Plateau, Kaduna, Niger, Benue, Kebbi, Nassarawa, Sokoto and Borno States, (Ugwuoke 1999; Kuju 1999), which have completely given up or are gradually bowing out under the influence of Hausa, Fulfude and Pidgin English. Barely three days to the take off of the 23rd West African Linguistics Congress, language endangerment made the headlines in a famous Nigerian newspaper. A special report was made on extinct and fading tongues, listing 23 languages all previously listed in Crozier and Blench (1992) and Ugwuoke (1999) as victims.

Focusing on Brazilian languages, Rodrigues(1993) states that two forces account for the extinction of over 75 per cent of Brazilian indigenous languages within the past 500 years: the assimilation of an indigenous group into the expanding national culture with consequent language shift; and the decimation of indigenous populations by disease or through violence.

Fishman (1991) isolates symptoms of language endangerment by using an eight-stage international disruption scale to show that the most threatened languages are those used only by socially isolated folks, by a socially integrated population beyond child-bearing age, and orally with no literacy.

Some critics, especially those who do not appreciate the value of indigenous languages, argue that languages have the right to die (Bamgbose 1991) and that if so many minority languages lack vitality, they should be allowed to die in peace (Malik 2000). For these critics, SIL has a contrary view, which is that 'no language is too small'. Language and human dignity are inherently linked since a people's identity and culture are intimately tied to their language (Cahill 2002).

Crystall (2000) presents five-arguments to show why we should care about language death. His arguments highlight the value of languages as:

- diversity
- expressions of identity
- repositories of history
- part of the sum of human knowledge.
- interesting subjects in their own right.

Nettle and Romaine (2000) seem to sum up this debate by arguing that the loss of so many languages should be seen as an environmental disaster threatening the fundamental well being of humanity. Humankind itself, they suggest, is an ecological system that depends for its survival on cultural and linguistic diversity, just as the health of a rain forest or an ocean depends on the diversity of its flora and fauna. For these authors, the loss of linguistic and cultural diversity should be seen as an integral part of larger processes threatening bio-diversity on earth.

Method

The fieldwork focused on the languages of the Federal Capital Territory in Nigeria. This territory, now the seat of the government, occupies a sizeable portion of the landmass that was formerly known as the Abuja Emirate (Heath 1962). Data was gathered through the use of a questionnaire and personal interviews with the natives of this area, in the new locations they have been moved to in the process of building the national capital. Before presenting a summary of the findings, below is a brief discussion of the people and their languages.

Original Inhabitants of Abuja and their Languages

Abuja was previously populated by several ethnic groups, namely the Gwarin Genge; the Gwari Yemma, (also known as the Gwari of the West); the Koro; the Gade; the Ganagana; the Gwandara and the Bassa. The languages spoken by these tribes are: Gbagyi, Ebira, Bassa, Ganagana, Gade and Gwandara.

The list of those groups, as in Heath (1962) and Hussaini (2000), includes the Arago and the Ebira. With the transfer of the seat of government from

Lagos to Abuja, the indigenous communities occupying this landmass were moved to new locations and resettled there. These new locations now bear the tags 'new' to differentiate between them and the former places of abode. Thus, one hears of New Karu, New Lugbe, New Bussa, Sabon Wuse, to mention a few. The consequences of resettlement have been enormous. It has depleted former homogenous communities. Some sold the new structures erected by the government and fled into the thick forests and behind the mountains where they formed new settlements. Others migrated to other areas of the territory and remain swallowed up by the dominant population in these areas. For those who preferred to remain in the new settlements constructed by the government, their fate is not different. Hussaini (2000) reports that the housing policies in the new locations are modern and completely different from the traditional architecture of the people. Secondly, there is an influx of immigrants into these locations creating a new class of businessmen and women who are in control of the economic activities of the areas. Thus, the indigenous people who lack both the financial base and skill to compete with this new class is gradually being marginalized, implying that they may eventually have to move again out of this environment to a new one where they could fit in. The question one needs to ask is: with these movements, what happens to the cultures and languages of these indigenous people?

Focusing on the situation in New Karu, Hussaini (2000) speaks of:

> ...their inability to unite against a strange force or development. [Rather] they prefer to migrate and in the process, deplete their strength. What one gathered is that in the next century or so, Gbagyi culture would disappear in both the old and new Karu because it is undergoing transformation due largely to the influx of immigrants from other areas of the country.

Of course, the erosion of the culture, the language that is the repository of this culture, will be drastically affected.

Okwudishu (1997) warns that the scattering of these indigenous populations would have adverse effects on their cultures, languages and their collective identity.

Findings

In this section, we shall briefly discuss some observations based on an analysis of the data gathered from the fieldwork.

i) *Gbagyi*

A survey of six area councils (Local Government Areas (LGAs)) of the Federal Capital Territory (Abuja; Kwali; Gwagwalada; Kuje; Bwari and Municipal) shows that Gbagyi speakers are found in all the LGAs with a strong presence recorded at Gwagwalada, Bwari and some settlements that form part of the municipal area, such as New Lugbe and New Karu. However, unlike Bwari and Gwaagwalada where there are autonomous communities with a strong collective identity, the Lugbe and Karu settlements have been heavily encroached upon by civil servants and a new class of business people and their culture. Gbagyi is used as a medium of instruction in the local schools in Gwagwalada for the first three years of primary school, following the provision of the National Policy on Education. In the Municipal, Kuje and Bwari, only Hausa and English are used for instruction at this level. The Gbagyi speakers generally feel that their language is under threat as it is heavily influenced by Hausa whose speakers are considered to belong to a more civilized class. Thus, anyone who cannot communicate in Hausa is looked upon as uncivilized. Efforts to maintain the language at home are dampened by the situation in the schools where Hausa and English are the main languages used for instruction, taught as subjects and used for communication with peers.

ii) *Ebira*

Speakers of Ebira were located mainly in Abaji and Kuje. However, it is only in Abaji that it is reportedly used for instruction in the first three years of primary school. In Kuje, only English and Hausa are used for instruction. Apart from Hausa, the Gbagyi speakers of Kuje see Ebira as a strong influence.

iii) *Bassa*

Speakers of Bassa, like those of Gbagyi, were reported in all but one LGA, that is, Bwari. They are mainly in Kwali and Kuje, but the language is not used for instruction in any of the locations. Though spoken in Kuje, it is not popular. Bassa speakers, especially in Kuje, claim that their language is strongly influenced by Gbagyi which most of them speak.

iv) *Ganagana*

Speakers of Ganagana were reported only in Abaji where it is listed among the languages used for instruction. In Kuje, Ganagana is reported as a language under seriously threat.

v) *Gade*

Few speakers of Gade were reported in Kwali and Kuje. The original home of the Gade people was Kuje, but with the recent developments, they were forced to move to Niger State where they were resettled at Sabon Wuse. After they moved, Gbagyi speakers migrated and took over Kuje. The few Gade speakers left behind consider their language as endangered as it is practically being displaced by Gbagyi and dominated by Hausa. It is not used as a medium of instruction; only English and Hausa are used for such in this area.

vi) Gwandara

Few Gwandara speakers were also reported in Kwali Local Government Area. It does not feature as a language of instruction and it is strongly influenced by the other languages, especially Gbagyi and Hausa.

In addition to Gade, which appears in Crozier and Blench (1992) as a full language, it was reported that Mwanwa, Koro and Bwawaa were no longer thriving in the Federal Capital Territory. However, as they are not listed in Crozier and Blench (1992), we consider them as dialects of some of the major languages discussed above. For example, Mwanwa was said to have formerly thrived in the Gwako area of Gwagwalada, but those who speak it now number only about 100. The drastic reduction in the number of speakers of Gade, Mwanwa, Koro and Bawaa is as a result of the implementation of the resettlement policy in the territory, which has forced some of the indigenes to constantly be on the move.

Implication for Development in Africa

The case studies presented in this chapter have implications for development in Nigeria and Africa generally. Languages express identity. They are repositories of history that contribute to the sum of human knowledge. Crystal (2000) considers language extinction as a great tragedy for human culture, as a kiln to the burning of a library of historical documents, or the extinction of the last species of a phylum.

In Nigeria, the situation in the Federal Capital Territory, Abuja, calls for special attention. Gbagyi, the dominant indigenous language, from the account given here, appears to be resisting the pressures from Hausa and the other languages. But with the steady influx of people into the new settlements and the irregular implementation of the language policy in schools, one wonders how long this resistance will last; more so, as the new generation of Gbagyi speakers cannot be a reliable force to reckon with. There is also the problem of those dialects of Gbagyi that are fading away probably due to constant movement of the indigenes who eventually get swallowed up in an alien community where they may be forced to adopt a new language for survival.

It has been rightly observed that a national development plan that has not given a pride of place to indigenous languages as vehicles for national development is likely to be a wasted effort. Africa should, therefore, strive for development beyond in the narrow sense of economic development only. Development in Africa should focus on the cultivation of a literate citizenry that can participate effectively in the socio-economic, political and cultural life of the nation.

Development, in this sense, is human-based and languages chosen for that purpose must be those that will facilitate access to information for the masses at the grassroots (Babalola 2000).

Recognizing the role of languages in the development of the Africa, the Asmara Declaration spells out the following guiding principles for safeguarding the indigenous languages of the various African nations:

1. African languages must take on the duty, the responsibility, and the challenge of speaking for the continent.
2. The vitality and equality of African languages must be recognized as a basis for the future empowerment of African peoples.
3. The diversity of African languages reflects the rich cultural heritage of African unity.
4. Dialogue among African languages is essential: African languages must use the instrument of translation to advance communication among all people, including the disabled. All African children have the inalienable right to attend school and learn in their mother tongues. Every effort should be made to develop African languages at all levels of education.[4]
5. Promoting research on African languages is vital for their development, while the advancement of African research and documentation will be best served by the use of African languages.
6. The effective and rapid development of science and technology in Africa depends on the use of African languages; and modern technology must be used for the development of African languages.
7. Democracy is essential for the equal development of African languages and African languages are vital for the development of democracy based on equality and social justice.
8. African languages, like all languages, contain gender bias. The role of African languages in development must overcome this gender bias and achieve gender equality.
9. African languages are essential for the decolonization of the African mind and the achievement of African Renaissance.

Suffice it to say that if we allow the depletion of indigenous populations to continue and their languages to continue to be eroded and vanquished, African Renaissance will remain forever a dream.

Conclusion

In line with the Asmara declaration, we end this chapter by making some suggestions and recommendations for the government, linguists and parents. Given the seriousness of the problems discussed, our objective is to sensitize all stakeholders in national development to the need to evolve strategies for dealing with the problems of indigenous languages, especially those 'teetering on the brink of extinction' (Cook 2000).

Government should:
- be careful not to sacrifice indigenous culture and languages in the guise of development; where movements of populations are inevitable, as was the case in Abuja, resettlement projects should take into consideration the need to protect the indigenous people from forces that marginalize them and threaten their collective identity;
- promulgate laws for the protection of the rights of indigenous peoples to preserve their languages and cultures;
- collaborate with affected communities to set up and fund projects for language maintenance; such projects should be consistent with the values, priorities, and language needs of indigenous communities and focus on language development; this should include strategies such as literacy education, materials production, writing of literatures, translation, etc. Such strategies have been successfully applied in an experiment involving the small Rivers State languages (Williamson 1976);
- give indigenous languages a strong presence in the educational system and access to electronic technology; the media should play an active role in the promotion of local languages.

Linguists, especially those residing in affected areas should:
- embark on purposeful documentation of languages and dialects of unstable communities, recording as much data as possible. Such documentation, according to Crystal (2000), safeguards linguistic diversity and contributes to a knowledge base for linguistic universals; and
- create awareness in local communities and foster positive community attitudes toward their languages and cultures.

Parents should:
- expose their children as early as possible to a stimulating local language, cultural and learning environment that is consistent with the best local and early childhood practice; and
- insist that, in their local schools, children should have early access to proficient local language speakers as teachers.

References

Asmara Declaration, 2000, 'Conference Declaration: Against all Odds: African Languages and Literatures into the 21st Century, Asmara, Eritrea, 11-17 Jan'.

Babalola, V.O., 2000, 'Nigerian Languages as Agents of National Development: Strategies for the Year 2000 and Beyond', in *New Frontiers*, Vol. 1, No. 1, pp. 1-9.

Bamgbose, Ayo, 1991, *Languages and the Nation; The Language Question in Sub-Saharan Africa*, Edinburgh: Edinburgh University Press for IAI.

Brenzinger, Mathias, ed., 1992, *Language Death [...] Factual and Theoretical Explorations with Special Reference to East Africa*, Berlin and New York: Moton de Grayter.

Brenzinger, Mathias, 1998, *Endangered Languages in Africa*, Cologne: Koppe.

Brenzinger, Mathias, Bernd Hind and Gabriale Sommer, 1991, 'Language Death in Africa', in Robert H. Robins and Engenias M. Uhlenbeck, eds, *Endangered Languages*, 19-44, Oxford and New York: Berg.

Cahill, Michael, 2002, *Endangered Languages in Endangered Language Groups*, Dallas: SIL International.

Crystal, David, 2000, *Language Death*, Cambridge: Cambridge University Press.

Fakuade, Gbenga, 1999, 'Language Endangerment in North Eastern Part of Nigeria: Instances and Strategies for Averting it', in E. Nolue Emenanjo and P.K. Bleambo, eds, *Language Endangerment and Language Empowerment in Nigeria*, Aba: National Institute for Nigerian Languages, pp 58-67.

Federal Government of Nigeria, 1979, Revised 1981 and 1998, *National Policy on Education*, Lagos: Federal Government Printer.

Fishman, Joshua. A., 1991, *Reversing Language Shift*, Clevedon, England: Multilingual Matters.

Grimes, Barbara F., ed., 1996, *Ethnologue: Languages of the World*, 13th Edition, Dallas: Summer Institute of Linguistics, Inc.

Crozier, D. H., Blench, R. M., 1992, *An Index of Nigerian Languages*, Dallas: Summer Institute of Linguistics, Inc.

Hale, Ken, 1992, *On Endangered Languages and Safe Guarding of Diversity, Language*, Vol., 68, No. 1: 1-3.

Hansford, K., Bendor-Samuel, J. and Stanford, R., 1976, *An Index of Nigerian Languages*, Ghana: Summer Institute of Linguistics.

Heath, Frank, 1962, *A Chronicle of Abuja*, Lagos: African University Press Limited.

Hotz, Robert Lee, 2002, *Speak Memory, Los Angeles Times*, December 10, 2002.

Hussaini, Aliyu, 2000, 'The Implications of Moving the Federal Capital Territory to Abuja [on] the Inhabitants of the Federal Capital Territory: The Case of KARU Community', *New Frontiers in the Humanities*, Vol. 1, No. 1 pp. 62-5.

Krauss, Michael, 1992, 'The World's Languages in Crisis' in *Language*, Vol. 68, No. 1:4-10.

Krauss, Michael, 2001, 'Mass Language Extinction, and Documentation: the Race Against Time', in Osama Sukiyama, ed., *Lectures on Endangered Languages: 2. From Kyoto Conference 2000- ELPR publication Series C002* 19-39.

Kuju, Mathew, 1999, 'Language Endangerment: An Appraisal of Non-Major Nigerian Languages in Northern Nigeria', in E. Nolue Emenanjo and P.K. Bleambo, eds, *Language Endangerment and Language Empowerment in Nigeria*, Aba: National Institute for Nigerian Languages, pp 37-59.

Malik, Kenan, 2000, 'Let them die: Essay on Death of Languages', in *Prospect*, November.

Nettle, Daniel and Suzanne Romaine, 2000, *Vanishing Voices[:] The Extinction of the World's Languages,* Oxford: Oxford University Press.

O'Connor, Maureen, 1983, 'How to Loosen Tongues', *Guardian,* Nov. 8.

Okwudishu, A.U., 1997, 'Endangered Languages and Endangered Communities: A Call to Action', paper presented at the 15th Conference of the Linguistic Association of Nigeria (CLAN), Sokoto, 3-7 Nov.

Pakir, Anne, 1993, 'Two Tongue Tied: Bilingualism in Singapore', *Journal of Multilingual and Multicultural Development,* Vol. 14, Issue 1, pp. 73-90.

Pinker, Steven, 2001, *Vanishing Voices: Book Review.* U.S.A.: O.U.P.

Rodrigues, Aryon Dall'Igna, 1993, 'Línguas indígenas: 500 anos de descobertas e perdas', in DELTA., Vol. 9 (1): 83-103.

Simon Paul, 1980, *The Tongue-Tied American: Confronting the Foreign Language Crisis,* New York: Continuum.

Summer Institute of Linguistics, 1996, *Ethnologue: Languages of the World,* Dallas Texas: SIL.

Ugwuoke, I., 1999, 'Nigerian Languages in Danger of Disappearing', in E. Nolue Emenanjo and P.K. Bleambo, eds., *Language Endangerment and Language Empowerment in Nigeria,* Aba: National Institute for Nigerian Languages, pp. 14-31.

Uko, Utibe, 2002, 'Extinct and Fading Tongues', *This Day,* Sunday, 4 August, p.14.

Williamson, Kay, 1976, 'The Rivers Readers Projects in Nigeria', in A. Bamgbose, ed., *Mother Tongue Education: The West African Experience,* London: Hodder and Stoughton; Paris: UNESCO press, pp. 135-53.

Williamson, Kay, 1999, 'Use Your Language—or Lose Your Language', in E. Nolue Emenanjo and P.K. Bleambo, eds., *Language Endangerment and Language Empowerment in Nigeria,* Aba: National Institute for Nigerian Languages, pp 162-67.

Wolff, H. Ekkehard, 2000, 'Language and Society' in Bernd Heine and Derek Nurse, eds., *African Languages: An Introduction,* Cambridge: Cambridge University Press, pp. 298-374.

Section II

Applied Linguistics

14

Initial Assessment of the Performance of Lamnso PROPELCA Children at the First School Leaving Certificate Examination

Emmanuel N. Chia & Laura Berinyuy Jumbam

Introduction

The children whose performance at the First School Leaving Certificate examination (FSLC) will be assessed in this chapter speak Lamnso as their mother tongue. Lamnso is one of the Ring Languages of the Western Grassfields Bantu spoken in Bui Division of the North West Province of Cameroon. In September 1981, the first batch of children instructed in this language were introduced on experimental basis, into a bilingual education system using the mother tongue (Lamnso) and English, the first official language (OL1) of Anglophone Cameroon.

This experiment was the brainchild of a research team referred to as PROPELCA, meaning operational research team for language education in Cameroon (Tadadjeu 1990:138). Taking a cue from the 1953 UNESCO report on fundamental education, PROPELCA had in 1977–78 proposed a major curriculum reform consisting of the experimentation and eventual introduction of a bilingual education system to supplant the hitherto, colonial monolingual education in English or French (both foreign to Cameroonian children). The early years of elementary education would be taught in the child's mother tongue with a provision for a smooth transition into the OL1 as the child approaches the final lap of primary education. The time table was patterned in such a way that as the child progressed from the first year to higher classes, the heavy doses of indigenous language instruction gradually reduced as corresponding instruction in OL1 increased. This was motivated, among other things, by the requirement that the First School Leaving Certificate (FSLC) examination had to be done only in the OL1. The objective was that by the time the child completed elementary school, he/she should be able to speak, read and write both languages equally well. Since government at the time was not disposed to entertaining any such venture, the PROPELCA team went for private (mission) schools. The first such school in the Anglophone part of the country was the Catholic School (CS) Melim in Nso, Bui Division. In 1986 another Catholic School in Nkar joined the experiment in the Lamnso zone. But, unfortunately, by the beginning of the 1990s, the bilingual programme in the two experimental schools had run out of steam and come to an abrupt halt. A number of reasons have been advanced for this failure. Teachers trained for the programme found themselves transferred away from the experimental classes by school hierarchy for no good reason. Secondly, teachers on the programme asked for incentives, which were never forthcoming. The economic crises that rocked the country and reached its peak in the early 1990s must have had as negative an impact on the management of these schools as on many other areas. Finally, government reticence in the area of mother tongue education only made matters worse.

This notwithstanding, the PROPELCA team never gave up and the evidence to that effect is that the situation was soon redressed. By 1995, many other schools had joined the experiment in the Lamnso area. At the time we went to the field, that is, in the second semester of the 2001–02 academic years, 34 schools had picked up the experiment and were doing pretty well. Government attitude towards mother tongue education had changed remarkably. The 1996 Constitution recognized the importance of preserving and developing national languages and a law passed in 1998, provided the general orientation for education in the country, laying particular emphasis on the promotion of native cultures and languages. This explains why a sizeable number of the 34 schools mentioned above are government schools.

Objectives of the Study

Our main objective was to compare the performance of children in this bilingual programme in the Lamnso area with that of children in the monolingual (English) schools at the First School Leaving Certificate (FSLC) examination for the same period. This assessment will be carried out at regular intervals (of six years) as many more schools attain the FSLC level. This exercise would eventually highlight the importance or not of beginning the educational career in the mother tongue. Additionally, we would identify the barriers that hamper the smooth functioning of the bilingual programme and propose possible solutions.

To achieve the above objectives, we drew up the following hypotheses:
i) PROPELCA (or bilingual) and monolingual (English education) children will not differ significantly in their performance at the FSLC.

ii) PROPELCA and monolingual children will not differ significantly in their performance in the English language at the FSLC.

iii) PROPELCA and monolingual children will not differ significantly in Arithmetic at the FSLC.

Data Collection

The principal type of data we needed for our study was the FSLC examination results for the experimental and non-experimental schools in the area and we got them beginning from 1995. But despite the many schools involved in the bilingual programme, only two schools; Government School (GS), Kikaikelake, and Catholic School (CS) Ndzeru had graduated 406 children at the FSLC. For purposes of comparison we randomly selected the following two monolingual education schools: St Theresa's School (STS) Kumbo and Catholic School (CS), To-oy. Both schools together had graduated 412 children during the period under study. We were able to obtain the data on past FLSC examination from the Divisional Delegation of National Education in Bui. In addition, we visited the schools and talked to the managers, headmasters and teachers involved in the two programmes about their experiences and motivation on the job.

We also collected information about the provenance, training and qualification of the teachers in the two sets of schools and were satisfied that they were all native speakers of Lamnso and almost all invariably Grade II trained. We also discovered, to our satisfaction, that all the teachers in the bilingual classes had received PROPELCA training in the use of Lamnso as a medium of instruction. PROPELCA regularly organizes training seminars for teachers on its programme during the long vacation. We also noted that the bilingual schools used the same Lamnso didactic materials prepared for the purpose and the same method and instructional materials prescribed by government for the mainstream English monolingual schools. The cultural and linguistic background of the children, this being generally a rural area, was virtually homogeneous. From the above findings, we were pretty certain that variables such as background, personality, IQ, and setting of both the teachers and the children (among other things) did not interfere significantly with the results. There were no known cases of mentally retarded children in the schools.

Since primary schools aim at teaching the three Rs, we were not only satisfied with pass percentages in the overall performance but also with their performance in Arithmetic and the English language skills.

Method of Data Analysis

The first step in analysing data began with preparing frequency distribution tables representing the different performance rates of pupils in the different schools. Measures of relative frequencies, such as percentages, were used to allow for comparison of results across studies with different sample sizes. Measures of central tendency, such as mean and measures of dispersion like the standard deviation, were also used to summarize the performance of pupils at the FSLC examination.

Since our main goal was to describe the relationship between the variables, MT education and performance, so as to provide a basis for prediction, analysing correlation between these variables entails using statistical tests. The t-test was used to determine whether the sample means was sufficiently different to be unlikely to have been drawn from the same population and to determine the statistical significance of a mean difference in the schools. The analysis of variance was also used in this study to determine the variation between and within the schools concerned.

The inferential statistical procedures provide a means of testing whether the differences in the dependent variable (performance) should be attributed to an effect of the independent variable—MT education.

The following are some of the data on the FSLC results from 1995 to 2000 collected (from the Bui Divisional Inspectorate of Education). Tables 1 and 2 provide data on the bilingual schools

Table 1a: G.S Kikaikelaki Lamnso / English

Year	Number Sat	Number Passed	% Passed
1995	44	43	97.7
1996	32	31	97.12
1997	46	46	100
1998	40	40	100
1999	34	32	94.11
2000	33	33	100
Total	229	225	Mean=98.15%

Mean = 588.93/6 = 98.15

Table 1b: C.S Ndzeru Lamnso / English

Year	Number Sat	Number Passed	% Passed
1995	19	17	89.5
1996	40	40	100
1997	26	26	100
1998	34	34	100
1999	31	29	93.54
2000	27	27	100
Total	177	173	
Mean=97.17%			

Mean = 583.04/6 = 97.17

Table 2a: S. T. S. Kumbo / English

Year	Number Sat	Number Passed	% Passed
1995	56	55	96.42
1996	61	60	98.36
1997	58	57	98.28
1998	70	66	94.28
1999	46	46	100
2000	40	34	85
Total	331	318	Mean=95.39%

Mean = 572.34/6 = 95.39

Table 2b: C. S. To-oy / English

Year	Number Sat	Number Passed	% Passed
1995	19	16	84.4
1996	18	18	100
1997	11	11	100
1998	12	9	75
1999	12	8	66.6
2000	9	9	100
Total	81	71	Mean=87.6%

Mean = 526/6 = 87.6

Table 2c

Lamnso / English			English		
Total	Total passed	Total mean performance	Total	Total passed	Total mean performance
406	398	97.66	412	389	91.49

Table 3: Summary of Means

Lamnso / English		English	
G. S. Kikaikelaki	98.15	S. T. S. Kumbo	95.39
G. S. Ndzeru	97.17	C. S. To-oy	87.6

The major preoccupation of this study was to find out if there is a statistical difference between the performances of pupils who go through a bilingual education vis-à-vis those who pursue the monolingual programme. The results show that generally, the performance in the two sets of schools is good. There are good years when they score 100 per cent and bad years when they score below 90 per cent. Neither of them is consistently good and the other consistently poor. However, looking closely at the statistics above, one realizes that PROPELCA children have an edge as far as the results of the FSLC are concerned. The two PROPELCA schools have mean performances of 98.18 per cent and 97.17 per cent respectively while the monolingual schools have 95.39 and 87.6 per cent respectively.

In order to properly ascertain the impact made on the pupils' performance by MT education, this study also set out to compare the performance of these schools in the individual subjects of English and Arithmetic. The following statistics are the performance of PROPELCA children and monolinguals in the English language.

Lamnso / English

Table 4a: English Language Results - G.S Kikaikelaki

Year	Number Sat	0-49	50-70	80-100	% Passed
1995	44	-	15	29	100
1996	32	-	9	23	100
1997	46	-	20	26	100
1998	40	-	6	34	100
1999	34	1	18	15	98.05
2000	33	-	10	23	100
Total	229	1	78	150	598.05
Percentages		0.43	34.06	65.50	Mean = 598.05%= 99.50

Lamnso / English

Table 4b: English Language Results - C.S. Ndzeru

Year	Number Sat	0-49	50-70	80-100	% Passed
1995	19	2	5	12	89.5
1996	40	-	4	36	100
1997	26	-	2	24	100
1998	34	-	5	29	100
1999	31	-	2	29	100
2000	27	-	4	23	100
Total	177	2	22	153	598.05
Percentages		1.12	12.42	86.44	Mean = 589.5/6= 98.25

English

Table 5a: English Language Results - S.T.S. Kumbo

Year	Number Sat	0-49	50-70	80-100	% Passed
1995	56	1	40	15	96.42
1996	61	2	52	7	96.72
1997	58	2	46	10	96.55
1998	70	5	44	21	96.85
1999	46	-	40	6	100
2000	40	6	15	19	85
Total	331	16	237	78	Mean =
Percentages		**4.83**	**71.60**	**23.56**	567/6= 94.59

English Only

Table 5b: English Language Results - C.S. To-oy

Year	Number Sat	0-49	50-70	80-100	% Passed
1995	19	3	14	2	84.4
1996	18	1	13	4	94.4
1997	11	-	11	-	100
1998	12	3	6	3	75
1999	12	4	6	2	66.6
2000	9	1	5	3	88.8
Total	81	12	55	14	Mean =
Percentages		**14.80**	**67.9**	**17.28**	509.2/6= 84.8

Table 6: Summary of Means

Lamnso / English		English	
G. S. Kikaikelaki	99.50	S. T. S. Kumbo	98.15
G. S. Ndzeru	98.25	C. S. To-oy	98.04

Even though there is no great difference in the mean performance of the two school programmes, the bilingual PROPELCA children are seen to have an edge over their monolingual counterparts with 99.50 per cent and 98.25 per cent as against 98.15 per cent and 98.04 per cent respectively. The difference in performance is however, more evident in Tables 4 (a) and (b) and Table 5 (a) and (b) when one looks at the percentage in relation to the score range. While a majority of PROPELCA children fall withinthe range of 80-100 per cent in English Language, monolinguals do the reverse with very few pupils obtaining such a range. The Table reveals that 65.50 percent of pupils in G.S Kikaikelaki, representing 150 out of 229 of them, perform excellently in English language with scores ranging from 80–100 per cent. The trend is the same for G.S Ndzeru with 86.44 per cent representing 153 out of 177 pupils falling in this range. The reverse is true for monolingual schools where statistics indicate that only 23.56 percent and 17.28 percent of the pupils in STS Kumbo and C.S To-oy respectively, obtain as high as 80–100 per cent scores in English language. This clearly reveals that despite the apparently slight difference in the mean performance of pupils in the two programmes, there exists a marked disparity between these schools as far as grading is concerned.

It is observed that statistics for results in Arithmetic follow the same trend as for those in English language whereby PROPELCA schools generally perform better and obtain higher scores than the monolingual schools.

Statistics on Arithmetic Results

Lamnso / English

Table 7a: Arithmetic Results -- G.S Kikaikelaki

Year	Number Sat	0-49	50-70	80-100	% Passed
1995	44	1	30	13	97.7
1996	32	2	10	19	97.12
1997	46	-	15	31	100
1998	40	-	21	19	100
1999	34	2	18	14	94.11
2000	33	-	20	13	100
Total	229	5	114	109	
Percentages		**2.18**	**49.78**	**47.59**	Mean = 588.93/6= 98.15

Lamnso / English

Table 7b: Arithmetic Results -- C. S. Ndzeru

Year	Number Sat	0-49	50-70	80-100	% Passed
1995	19	1	6	12	94.7
1996	40	-	20	20	100
1997	26	-	10	16	100
1998	34	-	12	22	100
1999	31	2	20	9	93.54
2000	27	-	8	19	100
Total	177	-	76	98	
Percentages		**1.69**	**49.78**	**55.36**	Mean = 588.24/6= 98.04

English Only

Table 8a: Arithmetic Results - S. T. S. Kumbo

Year	Number Sat	0-49	50-70	80-100	% Passed
1995	56	3	45	5	94.64
1996	61	1	40	20	9836
1997	58	1	42	15	98.28
1998	70	10	48	12	85.71
1999	46	-	30	16	100
2000	40	6	20	18	85
Total	331	21	228	86	Mean =
Percentages		6.34	68.88	25.95	561.99/6= 93.66

English Only

Table 8b: Arithmetic Results -- C. S. To-oy

Year	Number Sat	0-49	50-70	80-100	% Passed
1995	19	4	10	5	78.94
1996	18	2	8	8	88.88
1997	11	-	8	3	100
1998	12	4	5	3	66.66
1999	12	4	4	4	66.66
2000	9	1	6	2	88.888
Total	81	15	41	25	Mean =
Percentages		18.5	50.6	30.86	490.02/6= 81.67

Table 9: Summary of Means

Lamnso / English		English	
G. S. Kikaikelaki	98.15	S. T. S. Kumbo	93.66
G. S. Ndzeru	98.04	C. S. To-oy	81.67

Verification of Hypotheses

This section tests the hypotheses postulated earlier. Two statistical tests are used: the t-test and the analysis of variance (ANOVA). Hypotheses are negatively stated (the null hypotheses). The null hypothesis is rejected if the independent variable has an effect on the dependent variable. The hypotheses postulated earlier on and repeated here for easy recall will be tested in this section:

H_o^1: PROPELCA and monolingual children will not differ significantly in their overall performance at the FSLC.

H_o^2 : PROPELCA and monolingual children will not differ significantly in their performance in English language at the FSLC.

H_o^3 : PROPELCA and monolingual children will not differ significantly in their performance in Arithmetic at the FSLC.

H_o^1: **Table 10**: T- test values showing the effect of mother tongue education or not on pupils' performance at the FSLC results.

Sample	Freq	Df	Mean diff	Standard deviation	t-value	Critical value	Result
Lamso/Eng.	406						Significant
English	412	3	6.17	2.02	3.05	3.18	

$P > 3.05$, $t_o = 3.05$, $t_{0.0.5.3} = 3.18$

$P > 3.05$ is significant at the 0.05 level of significance. The results of hypothesis one, tested at 5 per cent level of significance, show that there is a significant difference between the performance of PROPELCA children and the monolinguals, which, otherwise, means that the teaching of Lamnso in schools positively influences performance in FSLC. This is because the critical value, 3.18 is greater that the t-value, 3.05. The hypothesis that the performance of PROPELCA and monolingual children will not differ significantly is, therefore, rejected.

H_0^2 PROPELCA and monolingual children will not differ significantly in English language at the FSLC.

Table 11: Analysis of Variance on the Performance of PROPELCA and Monolingual Children in English at the FSLC

Source	Df	Sum of Squares	Mean Squares	F-ratio	Critical value	Level signifi-cance	Result
Between Schools	3	2590.72	18.76				
Within Schools	180	611.81	3.382	5.547	2.60	0.05	Significant
Total	183	3202.53	22.142				

F-ration=5.547, $F_{0.05.3.180}$= 2.60, $P< 0.05$

The results are significant at the 5 per cent level of significance because the F-ration, 5.547 is greater than the critical value of 2.60 where level of significance = 0.05. Using the measure of mother tongue education, the null hypothesis is rejected. This reveals a tendency for Lamnso PROPELCA children to perform better even in English language than English monolinguals. As surprising as it appears, this tendency can be explained by the fact that once the psychological trauma of beginning education in a foreign medium is removed and the child is fully integrated into his socio-cultural and spiritual milieu, his natural scientific and technological urge is awakened and he can perform better than one who is still wrestling with the trauma. This might be the case here, which means that the trend has to be watched closely in future assessment exercises.

Summary of Findings

From the above analysis of the data collected from the inspectorate of education in Kumbo, the following tentative findings have been synthesized.

1) It was found that Lamnso PROPELCA children perform well at the FSLS with a mean percentage of 97.66 from 1995 to 2000. This contrasts with 91.49 per cent for monolingual schools. This would suggest that the teaching of mother tongue in primary schools might have had a positive influence on the performance of pupils at the FSLC.

2) The results also show that PROPELCA children and monolinguals are not equally proficient in English language. PROPELCA children surprisingly perform better than their monolingual counterparts with a majority of them (75.97 per cent) scoring between 80 and 100 per cent in English language. This contrasts with 20.42 per cent for the monolingual children who tend to cluster around the average score of between 50 and 70 per cent. We suggest that this could have resulted from the possibility that the 'monolinguals' here are still wrestling with the trauma of learning in a language other than their mother tongue.

3) The same thing holds for performance in arithmetic where PROPELCA children again excel with a mean percentage of 98.09 as against 87.66 for monolinguals. The difference is clearly evident when one looks at the score ranges where PROPELCA children who fall between the range of 80-100 per cent constitute 51.47 per cent while monolingual children falling under this range make up for only 28.42 per cent of the total number of pupils. All these tend to confirm the general hypothesis that PROPELCA children perform better in school. This will have to be confirmed by future assessments.

4) The results also show that even though the PROPELCA programme is an additional charge on the children since they learn to read and write in their mother tongue, which the monolinguals do not do, this has no adverse effect on their learning. On the contrary, it is an added advantage to their learning

and understanding. If future assessments hold up this tendency it would be a big boost to the bilingual programme.

Problems and Challenges for Mother Tongue Education in Cameroon

There have been many objections to the use of African languages in education. Many people question whether these languages are able to perform their functions in the modern context, especially in science and technology.

In an interview with Mr William Banboye who doubles as the national president for the National Languages Organization (NLO) and co-ordinator for the Lamnso Language Committee, he intimated that there is a real technical difficulty involved in the teaching of these languages. Most of them are purely instruments of oral communication, not easy to put into writing in order to prepare appropriate textbooks for use in schools. However, this is precisely what the National Association of Cameroon Language Committee (NACALCO) is doing.

He talked of the political fear that teaching these languages would strengthen tribalism rather than promote national unity. Another fundamental hindrance that he points out is socio-psychological in nature. The colonial school, according to him, succeeded in teaching us to look down on our own cultural values, including our national languages. We still have to rise above these obstacles.

He finally concluded 'it is now understood that national languages are indispensable if a country based on consumption and importation is to be enriched and transformed into a society oriented towards production and development'.

With regard to these obstacles on the use of African languages in education, Chumbow (1982a) simply dismisses them as mere rationalizations devoid of any substance and designed to check the development of African countries. The opinion of experts is that, when the pros and cons are put in the balance, the advantages of using the mother tongue in education outweigh the disadvantages.

Suggestions

Efforts should be made to motivate national language teachers if the bilingual education programme involving national languages has to be sustained. This could take the form of an additional pay package.

In addition to financial incentives, the government should make the programme compulsory for all schools in language communities where the programme has proved to be successful. Greater efforts should be made to standardize all the other languages that are still unwritten. This will ensure that the academic gains that accrue from the use of these languages in school (such as better FSLC results) are enjoyed by all Cameroonians.

The public needs to be constantly sensitized on these advantages of instituting mother tongue in schools so that parents can sufficiently encourage their children and ease the teachers' task.

It is high time government passed from simple recognition of MT/OL bilingual education to concretely instituting the FSLC examination in the language that the child commands. This would be excellent motivation for the bilingual education programme.

Conclusion

The initial results of the PROPELCA bilingual education programme in Lamnso and English in Bui division are very promising. The assessment of the performance of children at the FSLC must continue as many schools attain this level. Only then can these findings be valid. The stakes are high for the successful implementation of this programme nationwide. However, only with the concerted efforts of the National Association of Cameroon Language Committees (NACALCO), the Government and civil society, can the PROPELCA programme be sustained.

References

Chia, E.N.,1985, 'Second Language Teaching and Learning in Cameroon Today and Tomorrow', in K.R. Jankowsky, ed., *Scientific and Humanistic Dimensions of Language*, Amsterdam/ Philadelphia, John Benjamins Publishing Co.

Chumbow, B.S., 1985, 'Linguistics and National Development' University of Ilorin inaugural lecture, Ilorin, University of Ilorin press.

Legere, K., ed., 1995, 'African Languages in Basic Education: *Proceedings of the First Workshop on African Languages in Basic Education*, National Institute for Educational Development (NIED), 18-23 Sept., Windhoek, Namibia.

Mba, G. and Chiatoh, B., 2000, 'Current Trends and Perspectives in Mother Tongue Education in Cameroon', *African Journal of Applied Linguistics*, Yaounde, Cameroon, pp. 1-22.

Tadadjeu, M., 1990, *Le défi de Babel au Cameroun*, Collection PROPELCA, no.53, 1990.

Tadadjeu, M. et Chia, E., 1981, 'Projet de recherche opérationelle pour l'enseignement des langues au Cameroun'.

Tadadjeu, M., Mba G., and Chiatoh, B. 'The Process of Local Ownership of Multilingual Education in Cameroon', *African journal of Applied Linguistics*, Yaounde, Cameroon.

UNESCO, 1953, *The Use of Vernacular Languages in Education*, Monograph on Fundamental Education, 8, Paris, UNESCO.

15

A Linguistic-Based Language Teaching Model for Deaf Communities

John Ogwana and Pius Tamanji

Introduction

All over Africa, governments recognize the role of language as a powerful instrument for mass training to achieve a skilled manpower base capable of functioning as viable agents of change in national development. As such, national language policies seek to target as many sectors of the community as possible. Unfortunately, however, from one African country to the other, the tendency is to give very little consideration to the deaf and dumb since, to the policy makers, nature has refused this group of people the ability to use language (speech). The few attempts to help deaf people communicate are made by human interest groups whose methods are so diversified that two deaf people from two different institutions specialized in the education of the deaf can hardly communicate with each other, let alone communicate with people whose hearing is not impaired.

This article first demonstrates that, contrary to the views of policy makers, a significant percentage of children termed deaf (and consequently dumb) can actually be brought to use certain aspects of language to a level that almost equals that of children with unimpaired hearing. Focusing on the methods of language teaching employed in two different institutions for the deaf (ESEDA and EPHATA), this chapter proposes a method of language teaching to the deaf which is based on firm linguistic considerations and which, technically speaking, is a synthesis of the two methods employed in these institutions. This model, if stringently employed and with due consideration to time of exposure to the communication system, will help all categories of deaf people to communicate (although to different degrees) with both deaf and hearing-unimpaired people. Considering that the two institutions examined are widely representative of the general tendency in Cameroon, the upshot of the article is that the method proposed herein can be exploited to good effect by other institutions for the deaf in Cameroon.

In the first part of the chapter, we present the two institutions for deaf education that we have chosen for this study alongside the methods they employ in teaching language to the deaf. The next section presents methods of classifying deafness, pointing out that combining the methods yields a language acquisition negative index which presents a clearer picture of the degree of deafness that each deaf person is suffering from. With this clearer picture, the task of assigning the learners to appropriate classes and adapting the language teaching method to suit the needs of each class becomes easier and more objective. Next, we examine the weaknesses of the institutions with regard to the enterprise of language teaching. The following three sections present a method of teaching language (communication) to the different categories of the deaf which benefits from the two methods employed in the institutions under study. The chapter concludes by pointing out that different institutions in Cameroon specialized in the education of the deaf stand to benefit a lot from the proposed hybrid method.

Institutes of Specialized Education in Cameroon

Cameroon has a fairly good number of institutions that specialized in the education of the deaf These institutions largely pattern into two main groups, based on the system of communication used in the institution as medium of instruction. In the first group we find institutions that use sign language (American sign language) as medium of instruction and, in the second group, we find institutions that use lip-reading[1] and oral speech as the principal medium of instruction. For the purpose of this study, we have chosen two institutions that are representative of these two tendencies. These are ESEDA (École spécilaisée pour enfants déficients auditifs), Yaounde, Cameroon, and EPHATA Institute for the Deaf, Kumba, Cameroon. EPHATA represents the first tendency which employs sign language while ESEDA represents the second tendency where communication is achieved via lip-reading and, occasionally, oral speech.

Categorizing Deafness

Deafness has been discussed at length in the literature but the focus differs from one discussion to the other. Thus one comes across such terms as 'hard of hearing', 'hearing deficiency', 'dysaudia', 'half deafness', 'complete deafness', etc., used in relation to the phenomenon of deafness. One of the relatively satisfactory definitions of deafness, which we have come across, was proposed by Gribenski André (1964) who defines deafness as 'the diminishing or absence of the sensitiveness of the ear to sound'. This definition is incomplete for, as we will see later, the auditory mechanism extends beyond the ear and includes organs such as the auditory nerve and the auditory centre of the brain. All the same, we stick to this definition as a starting point because it has the advantage of being a broad definition, which takes into account varying degrees and types of deafness.

Deafness can be characterized based on three parameters: physiological, acoustic and developmental (or chronological) parameters. Each parameter is discussed in turn below.

Physiological Parameter of Deafness

According to Ross and Wilson (1987), there are two major types of deafness: perception deafness and conductive deafness. *Perception deafness* is caused by the dysfunction of the nervous system which extends from the organ of corti to the auditory centre of the brain. *Conductive deafness* is caused by some physiological damage within the external or middle ear without affecting the internal ear or the auditory centre of the brain.

Our preliminary investigation shows that perception deafness is more damaging than conductive deafness. Several cases of conductive deafness can be overcome by either surgical intervention or by the introduction of hearing aids. Surgical intervention and the introduction of hearing aids seems to be less effective in cases of perception deafness. Another interesting observation is that, in the case of perception, deafness is mild; it affects only selected frequency ranges. Hence a victim may be deaf either in the high frequency or low frequency range. But in most cases, perception deafness leads to very serious hearing deficiencies, so serious that surgical operation and hearing aids are of no use.

Acoustic Parameter of Deafness

Deafness may also be characterized in terms of the degree of sensitivity of the ear to sound. The less sensitive the ear is to sound, the louder the sound has to be in order for it to be perceived. The minimum hearing range (expressed in decibels – dB) is very low for people who are slightly deaf and very high for people with a deeper hearing defect. When we talk of degrees of deafness, we are dealing with a continuum on which various researchers in this field have established a series of reference points and then given them labels. In this chapter, we shall use the deafness evaluation model proposed by Borel-Maissony (1970).

Using French as the language of experiment and using dual face-to-face communication at a distance of two meters between the speaker and the listener, Borel-Maisonny arrived at six degrees of deafness based on increasing minimum hearing range in decibels (dB), as presented in Table 1.

Table 1: Ranges of Acoustic Deafness

Degree	Nomenclature	Minimum Hearing Range
1st	Very Light Deafness	30-35 dB
2nd	Light Deafness	40-45 dB
3rd	Serious Deafness	50-55 dB
4th	Severe Deafness	65-70 dB
5th	Deep Deafness	75-85 dB
6th	Total Deafness	90-100 dB

1st degree: Very Light Deafness (30-35 dB)

Deaf people within this category can perceive sounds if they are spoken at above 30 dB. It should be noted that normal dual conversation is at 30 dB. Hence, special extra loudness is required when speaking to these people. Whispering, which ranges between 20 dB and 25 dB, will not help them.

This type of deafness is often not easy to detect in children who at first are often mistaken for being either distracted or stubborn when they fail to respond to vocally directives.

2nd Degree: Light Deafness (40-45 dB)

Deaf people in this category can perceive isolated speech sounds produced above the 40-45 dB range. However, when such sounds are fused in syllable and word structures they are difficult to identify.

3rd Degree: Serious Deafness (50-55 dB)

Deaf people in this category need a minimum intensity of 55 dB to perceive speech sounds. Even then, the identification of most sounds is very limited, especially as regards vowels. These people often fail to identify entire words to such an extent that comprehension of language is only partial even in the best of circumstances.

4th Degree: Severe Deafness (65-70 dB)

Victims in this category cannot perceive normal speech sounds even in isolation since normal conversation intensity does not exceed 60 dB. When speech sounds are amplified beyond 60 dB, they cannot be used to form understandable words.

5th Degree: Deep Deafness (75-85 dB)

Deaf people in this category can perceive only amplified speech sounds incompatible with ordinary human speech. Such people can hardly rely on acoustics to identify any speech sound even if they may hear some sort of noise.

6th Degree: Total Deafness (90-100 dB)
Deaf people in this category cannot perceive any speech sound below 90 dB.

Developmental Parameter of Deafness
Another interesting factor in characterizing deafness is based on the stages that normal hearing children go through in the process of acquiring language. Using this factor, Ogwana (1998) conceived a five-stage developmental model indicating the various age ranges at which a child may become deaf. These are presented in Table 2.

Table 2: Ranges of Developmental Deafness

Stage	Age Range in Months	Deafness Label
1	0-12	Prelabic Age Deafness
2	12-18	Holophrastic Age Deafness
3	18-33	Telegraphic Age Deafness
4	33-48	Recursive Age Deafness
5	48-60	Adult Grammar Age Deafness

Prelabic Age Deafness (0-12 months)
In this category are found children who are born deaf and those who become deaf before the age of 12 months, i.e., before they utter any word. In the rest of the chapter, we will refer to this group as suffering from congenital deafness.

Holophrastic Age Deafness (12-18 months)
This category includes children who become deaf after they have produced their one-word utterances but before they can produce two-word utterances.

Telegraphic Age Deafness (18-33 months)
Here are included children who become deaf after attaining the ability of expressing their ideas by putting together two or more words but before they are able to produce recursive structures.

Recursive Age Deafness (33-48 months)
Children who become deaf after attaining the ability of embedding several ideas in simple sentence structures but before they are able to produce adult-like sentences are found in this category.

Adult Grammar Age Deafness (48-60 months)

In this category, we include children who become deaf after mastering the basic elements of simple sentence structure and who have started learning the production of complex sentences.

The Language Acquisition Negative Index

Knowledge of the acoustic and developmental parameters of deafness constitutes an essential instrument to the teacher of language to deaf children. Each parameter, by itself, establishes the degree of offering to work with CDEO are received with lukewarm interest and eventually discouraged in various forms from working with them. To the deaf people, their world is theirs only and no one should come from outside and tell them how to live their lives.

Another negative social effect of the EPHATA system is that some of the children are denied the possibility of using oral speech. Our discussion of categories of deafness above highlights the fact that a good number of children become deaf at an age when they have developed rudimentary skills in speech production. Such children, as mentioned earlier, can be brought to communicate orally if a stringent methodology is applied. In EPHATA, the rudimentary skills that these children brought into the school system are simply allowed to gradually die away since they are taught only sign language with virtually no exposure to oral speech.

Academically, the system of communication (American sign language) is not adapted to reflect the cultural realities of the learners. In the initial years of primary education, the child is expected to be exposed to objects, practices and beliefs in his immediate environment. Most of the signs referring to these objects, practices and beliefs are absent in the communication system, understandably because American sign language was developed for American deaf children and so was based on the American culture. The learning process for deaf Cameroonian children using American sign language is, therefore, slowed down on two counts. First, the child is deaf and so cannot learn as fast as the children with unimpaired hearing, and, second, a number of objects, beliefs and practices cannot be learnt early enough since they are not easily expressed in American sign language.

Overall, from these weaknesses noticed in the communication programmes of two institutions that are widely representative of the situation in Cameroon, it is evident that the whole system as a whole needs a new communication model that will cater for the needs of all categories of deaf children. Understandably, proposing a communication model that caters for all brands of deaf children is easy to propose on paper but very difficult to implement, given the financial implications. However, if the political will to involve all groups of citizens in the development process is there, the means to do so can always be met. Against this background, we propose, in the sections that follow, a model of communication that is generalizable to all institutions specialized in the education of deaf children; a model that will take care of children who are totally deaf, those who are only partially deaf and, above all, that will take the deaf children out of their exclusive world and place them in a broader world where they can communicate with children with unimpaired hearing.

Towards a Common Communication Model

The communication model that we propose here combines the methods employed in ESEDA and EPHATA and adds to this linguistic and extra-linguistic factors that, in our opinion, have not been given due consideration in the course of elaborating a language teaching model for deaf communities. The novelty in the model we propose is that it allows all categories of deaf children to be exposed to both oral and sign language. This has the advantage that, out of school, deaf children will be able to communicate, to a reasonable degree, with non-deaf people. The model begins with the process of admitting deaf children into the school and placing them in different levels of learning based on the degree of deafness of each child. A teaching method adapted to suite each level of learning is then proposed using the teaching of sounds as illustration.

Admission and Placement Procedure

Upon receiving a deaf child into the institution for the first time, the authorities will, as in ESEDA, proceed to test the child for the degree of deafness. This evaluation should obligatorily combine the acoustic and developmental parameters of deafness. This combination will establish the Language Acquisition Negative Index (LANI) for each child and placement in the different levels of learning will then be based on the LANI. Considering the LANI table that we repeat here (as Table 3) for convenience, the placement levels that follow are recommended.

Level Ia

This level contains children who became deaf after attaining at least the holophrastic stage of language acquisition and who can only perceive sounds amplified to at least 65dB. Although the children in this level became deaf after they had acquired the basic skills in speech (sound) production, the process of demutizing them (i.e., bringing them to use oral speech) is difficult because the children can only hear sounds that are amplified to a considerable level. Once speech sounds are amplified beyond 60dB, they cannot be used to produce understandable words. Worse of all, beyond 75dB, sounds produced are no longer compatible with human speech. Children in this category can, however, be made to recognize a good number of speech sounds by watching the shape and movement of the lips and other visible organs of speech; a practice generally referred to in deaf literature as lip-reading (Ogwana 1998). What matters in this level is to employ a careful methodology in teaching lip-reading which takes into account the kinds of sounds to be taught first and the order in which they are introduced to the children. We return to this point later.

Table 3: Language Acquisition Negative Index

Acoustic parameter	Develop. Parameter	Audit age 1	Recursive age 2	Telegraphic age 3	Holophrastic age 4	Prelabic age 5
1st degree deafness Very light deafness -	1	01	02	03	04	5*
2nd degree deafness light deafness -	2	02	04	06*	08*	10*
3rd degree deafness serious deafness -	3	03	06*	09*	12*	15*
4th degree deafness severe deafness -	4	04	08*	12*	16*	20*
5th degree deafness deep deafness -	5	05*	10*	15*	20*	25*
6th degree deafness Total deafness -	6	06*	12*	18*	24*	30*

Key: * = negative index that renders natural language acquisition very difficult and, at times impossible.

Level Ib

This level groups children who are born deaf irrespective of the acoustic level of deafness (light deafness or total deafness does not matter here). The articulatory organs of these children have not been activated and so the children have no latent skills in speech production. Demutizing them is impossible since they have never really used their organs of speech to produce speech sounds. Whether they are exposed to sounds produced at 30dB or 100dB, it makes no difference. The sounds they hear represent simple noise for the sounds cannot be equated to anything already stored in memory. It is rather hard to bring these children to use oral speech unless a very careful and committed teacher teaches them. The children could benefit from a carefully handled lip-reading approach. The success of this will depend so much on the kinds of sounds taught, the order of presenting them and, in particular, the intensity of exposure to the sound in terms of number of times in a day/week.

Level II

In this level we place children who became deaf after attaining at least the holophrastic stage of language acquisition and who can only perceive sounds amplified to at least 40dB. The children who fall into this category have the advantage that they became deaf after they had developed skills of speech production. In principle, therefore, demutizing them should be possible. A problem however arises, because, although they have latent skills in speech production, these skills cannot easily be awakened since they can only perceive sounds that are amplified; and we know the problems that accompany amplification. However, reasonably good equipment for amplification will help and introducing lip-reading early enough will be an added advantage.

Level III

This level contains children who became deaf after reaching the holophrastic stage of language acquisition and who can only perceive sounds produced at an acoustic level slightly higher than that for normal conversation. All the children in this category became deaf after they had mastered the skills of speech (sound) production. Since we are concerned here with the teaching of sounds, it does not matter whether the child learnt to produce only one-word utterances or full adult-like sentences. The process involved in producing sounds in one-word utterances or in full sentences is, generally speaking, the same.[2] Demutizing the children in this level is relatively easy as the teacher only needs to awaken their latent skills by speaking to them at an acoustic level slightly higher than that for normal conversation. Teaching lip-reading to these children is not really important for by speaking aloud, the children can hear the teacher and so readily recollect what they had acquired and add new material to the existing stock of knowledge.

The general picture which emerges from this discussion on admission and placement levels shows that most, if not all, of the deaf children will benefit from a communication system that stresses lip-reading. Lip-reading, in teaching sounds, is a method that needs to be handled with great care, taking into consideration phonetic and non-phonetic, as well as linguistic and non-linguistic factors. We now turn our attention to the various factors to be taken into consideration when using the lip-reading approach in teaching sounds to deaf children.

Steps in Teaching Sounds Via Lip-Reading

Many scholars involved in the principles of course design for language teaching differ with respect to the various procedures in teaching a particular aspect of language but they are all unanimous on the point that while the content of what is taught is important, the order in which the material is presented to the learners is primordial (Yalden 1987, Munby 1978, Krashen 1982, etc.). Designing a language-teaching model for children suffering from different degrees of deafness is even more difficult. We propose to both the designer and the language teacher that in designing a programme for deaf children, phonetic and non-phonetic criteria be taken into consideration alongside the generally recognized factors, such as content of course and order of presentation of material. The phonetic and non-phonetic criteria are briefly discussed below.

Phonetic Criteria

We use the expression 'phonetic criteria' to refer to properties of speech sounds, such as manner of articulation, place of articulation, etc., that need to be taken into consideration when designing a course on the sounds of a language. Our principal concern here is to highlight the properties of sounds that facilitate learning to the deaf child. The first factor that should be taken into consideration when selecting the type of sounds and the progression in the introduction of the sounds is the place of articulation. The rapid chain of events involved in the production of certain speech sounds is visible to an attentive 'listener' who carefully watches the mouth of the speaker. In this respect, it is generally easier for the listener to identify consonant sounds than vowel. Since the model we are proposing here involves lip-reading, we propose that in teaching sounds to deaf children, consonants should be introduced first since the production of a good number of them can be read from the movement of the lips and tongue.

In teaching consonants, which are considered easier than vowels, a certain order must still be followed since not all the consonants are produced with articulatory gestures that can be read from watching the lips and tongue. As such we propose a guide to the order of introducing consonants in Table 4:

Table 4: Order of Consonants based on Ease of Identification

	Easy to Identify	Less Easy	Difficult	Very Difficult
French	p, b, m f, v	t, d, n s, z, ʃ, ʒ, l, r	k, g, ɲ ʁ	ɥ, ɥ, j, w
English	p, b, m, f, v	t, d, n s, z, ʃ, ʒ, l, tʃ, dʒ, r	k, g, ɲ	j, w
Bantu	p, b, m, gb, kp, ɓ, ŋ͡m f, v, ʋ	t, d, n s, z, ʃ, ʒ, l, r ɬ, ɮ, ṣ, ẓ	k, g, ɲ, ŋ, ɣ, ʔ	j, w, ʎ

This general introduction of the sounds, which progresses from the easiest (to identify/produce) to the most difficult, exposes the child to the sound system of the language. Sounds are important in language because they are distinctive in opposition. That is, a change from one sound to another in a particular context corresponds to a change in the meaning of the words in which the sound is used. A necessary step to follow, after teaching the learners to identify sounds from the articulatory gestures, is to gradually lead the deaf child to become conscious of this opposition which plays a distinctive role in language. To help the child develop this ability to distinguish words, we propose the following order in oppositions based on Fourgon's (1979:51) proposal for French.

[p, b, m] ~ [t, d, n]
[p, b, m] ~ [f, v]
[t, d, n] ~ [f, v]
[p, b, m] ~ [s, z, ʃ, ʒ, l]
[p, b, m] ~ [k, g, ɲ]
[p, t, k] ~ [b, d, g]
[b, d, g] ~ [m, n, ɲ]
[f, s, ʃ] ~ [v, z,]
[r] ~ [l]
[w, j, ɥ]

Teaching vowel sounds is usually a difficult exercise even for children without hearing defects since it is not often easy to see the different movements of the speech organs during the production of vowels. Phonetically, vowel sounds are described in terms of position of highest part of the tongue in the mouth, shape of the lips and degree of mouth opening. The French sound system contains 16 vowel sounds. Combining Peytard and Gouvrier's statistics with the phonetic properties of vowel sounds, we realize that front vowels produced with the lips spread as well as central vowels are the most frequent sounds in French.

[a],	[e],	[i],	[ɛ],	[ə]
8.1%	6.5%	5.6%	5.3%	4.9%

In addition to this, front vowels in general (9/16) and round vowels (10/16) dominate the French sound system. On the basis of these facts, we can establish a system for teaching vowel sounds to deaf children that takes into account the relative ease in identifying/producing a vowel sound. We consider spread lips (unrounded), open mouth (low) and front part of mouth as positive factors since they facilitate the identification of vowel sounds more than rounded lips, closed mouth (high) and back part of mouth, which are negative factors that render the identification of vowel sounds difficult. From this, we hypothesize that the more positive features a vowel sound contains, the easier it will be for a deaf child to identify this vowel sound and vice versa. Following is a table classifying French vowels according to ease of identification.

Table 5: French Vowels and Easy Identification

1	Unrounded +	Low +	Front +	a, ɛ (3+)
2	Unrounded +	High -	Front +	e, i (2+)
3	Front +	Rounded -	Low +	œ (2+)
4	Front +	Rounded -	High -	y, ø (1 +)
5	Back -	Rounded -	Low +	ɔ, ɑ (1 +)
6	Back -	Rounded -	High -	o, u (0 +)
7				ə and nasalized vowels

In introducing the vowel sounds of any language to deaf children, the factors contained in the preceding paragraph and table should be taken into consideration. As we pointed out in the case of consonants, it is the opposition between one type of sound and another that is important in distinguishing words. It is, therefore, not so much the manipulation of this or that vowel in isolation but rather the opposition of one type of vowel to another that is important. As such, we propose the following criteria for classifying vowels according to type of opposition (still using French as an illustration).

Table 6: French Vowels and Types of Opposition

	+	−
1	Unrounded i, e, ɛ, a,	Rounded y, ø, œ, o, u, ɔ
2	Low a, ɛ, œ, ɔ, ɑ,	High i, e, u, o, y, ø
3	Front i, ɛ, e, a, y, ø, œ	Back u, o, ɔ, ɑ
4	Oral vowels	Nasal vowels

Considering the distinctive features of each vowel, therefore, we notice that the unrounded/rounded low/high oppositions are easier to manipulate than the front/back and oral/nasal oppositions.

Non-Phonetic Criteria

Another very important factor to consider in introducing speech sounds to deaf children is the frequency of occurrence of the sound in daily speech. We have decided to refer to this criterion as non-phonetic basically because the number of times a sound is used in daily speech does not depend so much on any of its phonetic properties (manner and place of articulation). Let us draw the attention of the reader here to the fact that frequency of occurrence of a sound in daily speech does not depend on ease of articulation, for, if this were to be the case, it would be hard to explain why the frequency of occurrence of a rather difficult (to articulate) sound such as [ɲ] has a percentage of occurrence in Arabic which is as high as 6.8 per cent. Frequency of occurrence of a sound, in a sense, correlates with the usefulness of the sound in speech. A statistical study of French (P.-R. Leon and Peytard) reveals that French consonants have the following percentages of occurrence in daily speech:

Table 7a: Frequency of French Consonants

r	6.9 %	n	2.8 %	z	0.6 %		
l	6.8 %	v	2.4 %	ʃ	0.5 %		
s	5.8 %	ʒ	2.3 %	g	0.3 %		
t	4.5 %	f	1.3 %	ɲ	0.1 %		
k	4.5 %	b	1.2 %				
p	4.3 %	j	1.0 %				
d	3.5 %	w	0.9 %				
m	3.4 %	ɥ	0.7 %				

In a related study, Fourgon (1979) prefers that this frequency factor be linked crucially to child language, that is, the statistical study should be done on child language since the aim is to determine the order in presenting sounds to a category of children. On the basis of this, Fourgon first identifies the consonants attested in child French and classifies them in order of frequency of occurrence. The following table shows Fourgon's classification in which the consonant with the highest frequency of occurrence is at the top of the list.

Table 7b: Fourgon's (1979) Frequency of French Consonants in Child Speech

p, b, m, l, t, d, f,v, s, k, r

Peytard and Genouvrier (1970) established the following frequency chart for French vowels:

Table 8: Frequency of French Vowels

a	8.1%	ə	4.9%	y	2.0%	ɛ̃	1.4%
e	6.5%	â	3.3%	ʒ	2.0%	œ̃	0.5%
i	5.6%	u	2.7%	ø	1.7%	œ	0.3%
ɛ	5.3%	o	2.21%	ɔ	1.5%	ɑ	0.2%

In teaching the identification/production of sounds to deaf children, therefore, it is recommended that the sounds with a high frequency of occurrence (thus more useful) in child speech be introduced first, or, at least, as early as possible, in the learning process.

Certainly, the frequency factor will often conflict with the earlier factor (ease of identification/production) since it is not in all cases that a sound with the highest frequency of occurrence will necessarily be the sound that is easiest to identify/produce. We recommend that in such cases of conflict, the former factor (ease of identification/production) take precedence over frequency of occurrence.

To summarize the discussion in this section, we have proposed that in designing a programme for teaching speech sounds to deaf children, phonetic and non-phonetic criteria, such as frequency of occurrence, opposition between sounds, and ease in identifying/producing sounds, should be taken into consideration. The introduction of the sounds to the learners should be gradual and ordered such that sounds that are more frequent in child speech should be taught before those that are less frequent and sounds that can easily be read from the movements of the lips, tongue and other organs of speech should precede those that cannot easily be read from these movements. If this method is applied stringently with due consideration to exposure time, even children who are "totally deaf" will be able to use oral speech even if their efforts are limited to 'silent speech' (speech which is not accompanied by oral sounds but which can be identified from the movements of the speech organs). If this model is generalized, then institutions like ESEDA will cater for all categories of deaf children and not only those that are 'totally deaf' and institutions like EPHATA will be able to train deaf children to communicate (even if only partially) with normal hearing people.

The Place of Sign Language

The discussion in the preceding section focused on a model that has the potential of bringing all categories of deaf children to use oral speech, even if the speech in some cases is 'silent'. It is evident from the discussion and from our proposals for categorizing deafness that all the categories of deaf children cannot benefit from lip-reading to the same degree. While children who suffer from neonatal deafness will benefit directly from the method and learn fast enough, those with congenital deafness cannot benefit directly, as learning will be slow and painful. This notwithstanding, it is evident that the model, if carefully employed, will benefit all categories of deaf children although to different degrees. In order to complete the language learning exercise so as to reinforce lip-reading and provide children suffering from congenital deafness with an additional means of communication, we propose that the language component of the programme in every institution for the deaf include sign language. From our preliminary study on using the combined method (lip-reading and sign language), we observed that children to whom only lip-reading is taught will learn faster if lip-reading is complemented with sign language and children to whom only sign language is taught will communicate more effectively if sign language is taught alongside lip-reading. In order to allow deaf children to derive maximum benefit from the combined method, it will be appropriate if sign language is introduced after the children are sufficiently advanced in lip-reading. This way we solve one major problem: In sign language, learners are taught to sign letters of the alphabet and not, understandably, the sounds that correspond to the letters. Were we to teach sign language alongside lip-reading in the early stages of the learning process some of the learners will certainly get confused since, to most of them, sound does not represent anything. Since our objective is to develop a model that brings the learner to communicate with both deaf and normal hearing people, we think it appropriate to first allow the learner time to acquire sufficient skills in lip-reading necessary to communicate with normal hearing people before moving to sign language, which, in our model, simply reinforces communication.

There are, however, a number of issues that still need to be resolved before we can seriously consider including sign language in the teaching programme in Cameroon and other African countries. The first of these problems is how to introduce sign language to a child who has acquired skills in lip-reading. Should it be taught as a separate course on the programme or should it be combined with lip-reading in a course titled 'communication'? Teaching sign language as a separate course on the school programme will not, in our opinion, immediately create the impression in the mind of learners that it is a system which serves as a useful complement to lip-reading. And this is exactly what our model wants to stress; that is that communication in deaf communities will be more effective if lip-reading is accompanied/complemented by sign language. We want a system of communication in which a word, or sentence uttered (albeit silently) is accompanied by the appropriate sign so that in the end, the speaker can reach out to interlocutors who are literate either in lip-reading or sign language. Against this background, therefore, we propose that sign language be taught alongside lip-reading as continuation of the same course in communication. When the teacher starts teaching syllables and words after completing the component on lip-reading, the learners should be taught to say the word orally (aloud or silently as the case might be) and, at the same time, they should be taught to sign the word. The same procedure is employed when learning sentences and whole texts.

The second issue, which needs to be addressed, is that sign language, as we know it today in Cameroon, is built on the American culture. To the best of our knowledge, little effort has been made to adapt American sign language to the Cameroonian context. This, in our opinion, constitutes a major drawback in the overall learning process. Education experts recognize the need to begin the learning process by introducing a child to its immediate environment. Evidently, this cannot be achieved if the language of instruction does not have words (signs), which characterize that immediate environment. In order for deaf children to derive maximum benefit from the use of sign language, therefore, it is necessary to first adapt American sign language so that it reflects African realities.

Conclusion

This chapter set out to propose a language-teaching model that benefits from two systems that characterize the general tendency in Cameroon and which has the potential of bringing deaf children to communicate simultaneously via lip-reading and sign language.

The study was motivated by the observation that while some institutions for the education of the deaf in Cameroon are too selective in their admission policies, others seek to establish a 'separate world' unique to deaf people alone. In the first category belong institutions like ESEDA whose admission policies target only children who are 'totally deaf'. The result of this is that children who are considered 'only partially deaf' are abandoned to themselves and their families. In the end, they either enrol in 'normal schools' where they are subjected to the rigours of mainstream education competing (unfairly) with children whose hearing is unimpaired or they stay at home where the latent language skills they acquired prior to deafness gradually deteriorate and vanish, leaving the children totally deaf and, consequently, dumb. In the second category, we find institutions such as EPHATA, which admits all categories of deaf children but trains them to communicate solely in sign language. In the end, the children are obliged to live a life of isolation in a secluded world since the society outside the deaf school is not literate in sign language.

In order to have a world in which the deaf child is given the opportunity to live a life that equals that of the normal hearing child, the chapter made a number of recommendations prominent among which are:

1. Institutions for the deaf should admit all categories of deaf children. Upon admission, each child should be subjected to a physiological, acoustic and developmental evaluation in order to determine the degree of deafness. Based on the results of the evaluation, the child is placed in one of three levels where time and intensity of exposure to knowledge as well as the use or not of technical teaching aids varies from level to level.

2. Institutions for the deaf should employ a common system of communication that benefits all categories of deaf children and permits them to communicate not only with each other but also with people whose hearing is normal.

3. The common system of communication that involves lip-reading and a contextualized form of sign language should be taught.

4. Using a step-by-step approach. In the first step, the deaf children are taught to read speech sounds from the movements of the lips, tongue and other

organs of speech. After lip-reading has been sufficiently acquired, sign language should be taught alongside word and sentence recognition/construction.

5. In teaching sounds via lip-reading, we propose that sounds that are easy to identify from the movements of the organs of speech be taught before those that are difficult to identify and sounds that are more frequent in daily child speech should precede those that are less frequent.

We are convinced that if the evaluation and placement procedure is respected and the teaching methods stringently applied with due consideration to time and intensity of exposure, we would create a 'just' world in which deaf children have fairly equal chances of succeeding in school as other unimpaired children. Also, deaf children will feel free, self-confident and have self-esteem since they would be able to communicate with childrenwithout hearing impairment.

Notes

1. In lip-reading, two people involved in a communication rely on the movement of lips and other visible organs of speech to interpret messages.
2. We ignore here such minor variations that might arise as a result of the fact that sounds are adjacent to one another in words and sentences.

References

Borel-Maisonny, S., 1967, 'Essai de nomenclature pédagogique des déficiences auditives de l'enfant' in *F.I.C.E* n°. 13, pp 63-84

Fourgon, F., 1979, *Précis de Démutation et d'orthophonie,* Rennes: E.N.S.P.

Gribenski, A., 1964, *L'Audition,* Paris, P.U.F.

Krashen, S., 1982, *Principles and Practice in Second Language Acquisition,* Oxford: Pergamon Press.

Munby, J., 1978, *Communicative Syllabus Design,* Cambridge: Cambridge University Press.

Ogwana, J. C., 1998, 'Categorising Deafness: Case Study of ESEDA, Yaounde', MS, University of Yaounde I.

Peytard, J. and Genouvrier, E., 1970, *Linguistique et Enseignement du Français,* Paris: Larousse.

Ross, Janet S. and Wilson, J.W., 1987, *Anatomy and Physiology in Health and Illness,* Edinburgh: Churchill Livingstone.

Yalden, J.,1987, *Principles of Course Design for Language Teaching,* Cambridge: CUP.

16

The 'S' in ESP: Will Teachers' Knowledge of the Learners' Speciality Make a Difference?

Ludwig N. Metuge

Introduction: Background

The acronym ESP stands for English for Special or Specific Purposes. In the context of Cameroon, ESP is usually viewed at the tertiary level as that new EFL fashion which, in the mid 1980s supplanted 'Formation Bilingue'—Bilingual Training (BT) Programmes (Dongmo 1985). However, whilst the university administrators and BT instructors quickly fell sway to promises of the new EFL approach, there didn't seem to be a corresponding change in the teaching aims, materials and methods used. The yester-year BT instructors accepted the new appellation of their profession but weren't quite divorced from the 'General English' approach which, hitherto, had characterized Bilingual Training.

The trouble is, many of the BT teachers, now ESP instructors, could not afford to prepare two or more additional English lessons a week, to meet the special needs of the various groups of students in the different faculties of the University, as ESP teaching would require. Under the auspices of the British Council, and in collaboration with the University of Yaounde 1, ESP seminars were organized (1985 and 1987) with an intent to smoothen the transition from BT to ESP.

Unfortunately, despite the apparent enthusiasm of these tertiary level seminar participants, it is doubtful whether many managed to understand the implications of the letter 'S' in English for Specific Purposes. An excerpt from the 1987 ESP

Seminar Report by Ingram Hill—a British Council ESP advisor at that time—shows his frustration at the apparent inability of the seminar participants (ESP instructors from the university centres and other tertiary institutions in Yaounde) to cope with texts meant for science students:

Micro-teaching:

Each member of the group 'taught' a stage of the lesson to the students [the rest of the participants]. Results were rather wayward...

Another problem was that the science material was designed for use with scientists, not Arts teachers with insufficient background knowledge to make intelligent comments (1987:8).

The above citation is the locus of this chapter. The fear is that ignorance of the learners' subject-speciality would mean inadequate teacher input, with all its attendant evils in the teaching-learning process, one of them being poor learner output.

To put things in perspective, the rest of this chapter will deal with three main areas: theoretical views on ESP; a report of an experimental and control study; and, finally, proposals and conclusions.

Some Theoretical Views on ESP

How Is ESP Construed in the USA and the UK?

Given that most of the EFL materials in our libraries and on our shelves come from either the UK or the USA, it would be helpful to understand the theoretical assumptions that might have motivated researchers in these two places, and how this could impact on our setting in Cameroon.

As Bhatia (1986:67) points out, there is an anomaly between British and American research studies on the conception of ESP. While the British studies (notably those of Allen and Widdowson (1974) assume that the setting for ESP is a second language situation, the American studies have drawn data largely from native and/or first-language settings as evident in the work of Selinker, Lackstrom, Trimble (1976) and others.

The implications of these apparently conflicting assumptions for the EFL setting at the tertiary level in Cameroon cannot be overemphasized, given that English is neither a first nor a second language to Francophone Cameroonians. As Ellis (1984:2) would put it, ours is a 'pure classroom situation', as opposed to a naturalistic context enjoyed by the ESP student studying in Britain or the USA. An awareness of these differences in setting is important for the teacher, as this would affect the learning aims, teaching methods, and achievement levels (Crystal 1988:368).

Other assumptions in the above two countries that might not be quite congruent with the Cameroonian setting include the learner's age, status, level of literacy in English and the mother tongue, motivation, homogeneity and size of the class, etc. (Metuge 1998).

The Specific in ESP

'Tell me what you need English for and I will tell you the English that you need' has been and still remains the ESP motto. As Hutchinson and Waters (1987:21) have observed, ESP is an approach to language teaching that aims to meet the needs of particular learners. This means, in practice, that much of the work done by the ESP teachers is concerned with designing appropriate courses for various groups of learners, which is not a major preoccupation for the General English teacher.

The letter 'S' in ESP thus refers to the special or specific need of the learner. It is this special need or purpose that motivates the learner and forms the basis for the ESP course content to which the ESP teacher must abide. Thus, fundamentally, the ESP course is learner-motivated or learner-centred. The ultimate hope of the sponsors, the school, or the teacher is usually to see the learners function/perform adequately in English, especially in relation to their speciality. If the learner is a chemistry student, for example, s/he is expected, at the end of the English for Science and Technology (EST) course to be able to do basic oral or writing tasks in chemistry. He/she should be able to 'talk chemistry' with some Anglophone students of the same level. Hence, as Robinson (1984:8) succinctly puts it, 'It is the purpose for which the learner is studying that is special or specific and not the language'. Consequently, different purposes expressed by the students, their sponsors or the school, might affect the choice of ESP instructors. This, however, is far from being the case in many developing countries, including Cameroon, where, for want of qualified staff, one EFL instructor is assigned three or more different groups of learners, having different specializations and varying levels of EFL proficiency. In slightly different terms, but with the same focus on the activity or subject matter the class might be engaged in, Corder (1986:187-88) had this to say:

> The acquisition of vocabulary (lexis) seems to be largely context-dependent, that is, we learn precisely that vocabulary which at any particular moment we need to know. It doesn't seem to be profitable to have a lesson dealing with words related to gardens, for example, unless you are actually engaged in gardening - related activities where the words are necessary in order to perform the activity. The priority is the activity, and the words a by-product of the activity, rather than the central focus.

The specific question here, which is the underlying theme of this chapter is: How would the non-specialist 'ESP teacher' manage to animate students' subject-related class activities, exploit the discoursal or rhetorical elements of the specialized text, if he/she is intellectually unequipped with respect to his/her students' speciality? Wouldn't the situation be analogous with a hypothetical Chemistry teacher who, despite her beautiful English, does not succeed in handling the Literature class assigned to him? Collaboration with the subject masters as well as the students themselves would no doubt be called for in this case. However, it would be more reassuring and profitable for both the learners and the teacher, if the latter herself learnt to 'fish' . This is because, given the busy schedule of University teachers, the subject master, despite his or her goodwill to collaborate, might not always be at the disposal of the needy ESP instructors. This rather difficult position the ESP teacher may find herself in, has equally been the concern of many researchers in the field (Howatt 1985:226; Swales 1985:212-23; Strevens 1980:467; Pinto da Silva 1993:40; McDonough, 1981:13; Waters 1979:42; Bhatia 1986:69; Rivers 1981:475). Even though these authors do not expect the ESP teacher to be an expert in the student's field of study, their general attitude seems to suggest that his or her basic knowledge of it would be most desirable.

Some Researchers' Views on the ESP Teacher in Relation to the Students' Subject-Speciality

Perhaps in order not to terrify those involved in the teaching of English for Specific Purposes, some authors writing on the subject have always modestly maintained that the ESP instructor needn't be an expert (Laird 1979; Strevens 1980; Pinto da Silva 1993). This is the first impression one gets. It would be noticed, however, that the same authors always add a 'but' or a 'however' in what would have been an otherwise comfortable position for the non-specialist ESP instructor. This suggests, implicitly, that it would be professionally desirable for the ESP instructor to be familiar with his/her students' subject-speciality. Examples of such rather misleading statements abound in the literature. A few examples would be illuminating in order to preclude any doubts that a basic knowledge of the student's speciality is a prerequisite for relevant teacher-input.

We may start with Strevens (1980:467) who writes:

> The ESP teacher is not, and should not be expected to be a teacher of the speciality (though collaboration between subject specialists and EFL specialists is a valuable approach, **and the teacher who combines in his own personal training the speciality and EFL specialism is in the very best position to succeed).** But the ESP instructor must come to terms with the existence of an unfamiliar universe of discourse within which he or she **must** now perform his teaching duties (emphasis mine).

In her article in *FORUM* Volume 31, No 2, (April 1993), this is what Da Silva (1993:40) recalls with regards to 'teacher's subject knowledge': 'It is now widely accepted that the ESP teacher should not be expected to be an expert in the students' speciality. However, it has also been said that it falls within our professional requirements to be at least interested in the subject, either for purely intellectual or more practical reasons'.

McDonough (1984: 49) reiterates a view that describes the classical ESP practice in the UK where, in most cases, the ESP course and the subject of the student's speciality could be delivered by the same teacher: 'Where the teachers are not subject teachers as well, reference is often made to the cooperation between subject and language teacher'. The same line of thinking can be discerned from Waters (1979: 49) who solicits the presence, among the ESP staff, of a 'teacher whose background is predominantly in the sciences, rather than language teaching'. (The pertinence of Waters' remark will be appreciated in the last part of this chapter—Proposals.)

Commenting on John Swales' Article (1985:212-223), 'ESP-The Heart of the Matter or the End of the Affair', Anthony Howatt (1985:226), supports of Swales' proposal for the apparent elevation of the status of ESP to Research English (RE), but equally expresses his fear as to the consequent weight of responsibility this would place on the shoulders of the RE/ESP teacher, 'since the latter would now be expected to know more about the subject matter rather than less'.

Even more direct and explicit are these last two statements from Strevens (1980) and Rivers (1981) which put to rest any further doubts as to the pivotal role of the ESP instructor in the success of the ESP class: 'The success of the ESP class [Strevens (1980:458) writes], requires more and more sophisticated preparation on the part of the teachers, not less; when that requirement is accepted, rates of achievement and satisfaction tend to be high; when that requirement is not realised, achievement is low and frustration creeps in'. Finally, this excerpt from Rivers (1981:475), elucidates what appears to be a general consensus on the foregoing discussion:

> The conventionally prepared language teacher is usually inappropriate for the task, without re-orientation and supplementary training. Language for Specific Purposes (LSP) requires not only skill in language teaching, and especially in preparing language-learning materials, but also some knowledge of the demands of the specialised field or occupation....

The pertinence of what Strevens and Rivers emphasize above has been tested, as demonstrated in the experimental and control study below:

An Experimental and Control Study

Summary

The study focused on two groups of science students (an experimental and control group) who had followed an ESP course at the undergraduate level, and were about to start a post-graduate course in Applied Biology. The aim of the study was to measure the impact of 'teacher variable' on their performance at the 'End of Semester English Examination'. Hence, a teacher handled one of the groups—the experimental group—with some background knowledge in the sciences, whilst a non-specialist teacher followed the control group. Whereas the differences in performance of the two groups in an earlier pre-test were negligible, some marked difference in performance was recorded in a test administered to these students at the end of the experiment (Table 1).

Students in the experimental group tended to perform better than those in the control group.

Preliminary Assumptions:

a) All those tested Francophone students

b) English has status of a foreign language (FL) on curriculum.

c) P.K: All those tested have a good Chemistry and Biology background.

d) They followed ESP courses at undergraduate level.

Main Variable in the Experiment—Teacher

a. Teacher in Control Group: minus background knowledge of science (Chemistry/Biology)

b. Teacher in Experimental Group: plus some background knowledge of science (Chemistry/Biology).

Hypothesis

Will 'teacher variable' with respect to knowledge of the learners' subject speciality affect the proficiency levels of different groups of learners?

Methodology

Rationale

The rationale in this study derives from Selinker and Tomlin's (1986:227) argument that:

> an increased concern for empirical methodology will necessarily bring ELT theory into closer conjunction with teaching practice. These researchers contend that the

best pedagogical decisions for students can be made only by taking into serious account systematic observations of students performance in specific learning situations...

Experimental Design

- Parallelism

The experimental design in the present study parallels the one reported by Ellis (1984:11). Such experimental studies (e.g., Scherer and Wertheimer 1964) have typically attempted to compare the effects of different 'treatments' on proficiency levels achieved by different groups of pupils.

Design: A pre-test (Appendix 1) based on undergraduate work was administered to both groups. This was followed by separate methodological treatments, as stated above. Results of the pre-test (Table 1 below) are intended to help us determine the approximate proficiency levels of the testees in the two groups prior to the different experimental treatments.

Pre-test: Performance of the Experimental and Control Groups

Content: Undergraduate ESP programme.

Results

Table 1

Experimental Group		Control group	
code	score/20	code	score/20
E.1	08	C1	08
E.2	11	C2	06
E.3	06	C3	07
E.4	05	C4	09.5
E.5	05.5	C5	03
E.6	10	C6	06.5
E.7	08.5	C7	05
E.8	04	C8	11
E.9	02	C9	07
E.10	08	C10	09
E.11	07.5	C11	05.5
E.12	10	C12	05
E.13	11.5	C13	09
E.14	12	C14	10
E.15	07.5	C15	11
E.16	08.5	C16	08
E.17	05.5	C17	11
E.18	11	C18	07
E.19	02.5	C19	11
E.20	01	C20	04
Total =	145	Total =	153.5
Average =	7.25	Average =	7.67

Course Content

Questions in the pre-test and the End of Semester English examination (Appendix 1) contain and reflect the basic contents of the course the two groups were supposed to follow:

> Reading figures involving decimals, fractions, large figures; translation; comparing and contrasting; describing experiments; giving directions; knowledge of community-related issues; names of elements and compounds; describing chemical equations etc.

Summary of Findings

Compared with their performance at the pre-test administered prior to the 'different treatments', students in the experimental group have made marked progress. It would also be noticed that the lowest number of passes for the control group was recorded in Questions 5 and 6 (see Table 2), which were subject-specific. This is understandable, given that the teacher for this group has no knowledge of Chemistry.

The differences in performance between the experimental and control groups are mainly due to 'teacher variable'. Even though both groups tested had the same course contents, the teacher in the control group, it would appear, could not manage to teach the science material (see Table 2 below, and especially items 5 and 6), which involved 'problem-solving'. However, the performance of the experimental group was better because their teacher had some background knowledge of the sciences.

The performance of the experimental group would have been even better if the teacher had an advanced scientific background.

Table 2: Experimental and Control Studies (Continued)
Performance of those Tested on the Individual Questions

Audience: Postgraduate Students of Applied Biology

Task	Experimental Group N(Passed	Control Group N(Passed
1	17	08
2	12	11
3	14	08
4	11	10
5	15*	01*
6	7*	01*

Proposals

a. An immediate and familiar step to take to improve the quality of ESP instruction at the tertiary level is to reactivate in-service training courses where EFL/ESP instructors can be invited to watch subject specialists at work, and thereby get some basic insight into the different subjects.

b. The organization of workshops and seminars at the national level, where ESP experts (foreign or national) can be invited to share their experiences with less experienced teachers, would also be an idea worth putting into practice.

c. Given the large number of unemployed graduates from the science, law, economics and arts faculties roaming our streets, it would be ingenious to launch a new government educational 'crusade' which would encourage the direct recruitment of these graduates into the advanced Teachers Training College (Ecole normale supérieure), where they would undergo specialized training as EFL teachers in general, and ESP instructors in particular. This would be a little bit like 'converting a passenger liner into a war ship' in order to save higher state interests.

On the completion of their courses (whose duration would be at least six to ten months), this new 'breed' of ESP instructors could then be posted to the various tertiary institutions, where they would be put at the disposal of their respective faculties. It is hoped that under such circumstances, optimal output with respect to the learners' communicative skills would be attained.

Conclusion

Insights into the theoretical conception of ESP would contribute to efficient practice and success of the subject. Ignorance of these insights would induce wrong strategies that would adversely affect the teaching-learning process.

Improved proficiency rates would be recorded if the 'specific' in ESP is understood and applied, that is, if students in our tertiary institutions are assigned ESP teachers who have good background knowledge of the students' various areas of specialization.

References

Allen, J.P.B. and Widdowson, H.G., eds., 1974, 'Teaching the Communicative Use of English'. *International Review of Applied Linguistics* 12, 1, pp.1-21.

Bhatia, A.T., 1986, 'ESP for Students of Science', in Forum Anthology: Selected Articles from the *English Teaching Forum* (1979-1983), Washington D.C.: USIA.

Corder, P., 1986, 'Talking Shop: Language Teaching and Applied Linguistics', in *ELT Journal*, Vol. 40, No 3, pp. 185-90.

Crystal, D., 1988, *The Cambridge Encyclopedia of Language*, chapter 62. Cambridge: Cambridge University Press.
Da Silva, P., 1993, 'ESP: Back to Methodology', in *Forum* Vol. 31, No 2.
Dongmo, J. L., 1985, *EAP Seminar invitation letter, addressed to the Director General of the University Centre*, Ngaoundere.
Ellis, R., 1984, *Classroom Second Language Development* (Language Teaching Methodology series), Oxford: Pergamon Press.
Heaton, J.B., 1975, *Studying In English*, London: Longman.
Hill, S.I., 1987, EAP Seminar Report on Dr. Ellis' Visit: 30 March-11 April, Yaounde: British Council.
Howatt, A., 1985, 'ESP-The Heart of the Matter or the End of the Affair? (Commentator 2)', in R. Quirk and H.G. Widdowson (eds.) *English in the World*, Cambridge: Cambridge University Press.
Hutchinson, T. and Waters, A., 1987, *English For Specific Purposes: A Learning Centered Approach*, Cambridge: Cambridge University Press.
Laird, E., 1979, *English in Education* (Teachers edition), London: Oxford University Press.
McDonough, J., 1984, *ESP in Perspective* (A Practical Guide), London: Collins ELT.
Metuge, L.N., 1998, 'European ESP Assumptions, and the Ideal EFL Student at the Tertiary Level in Cameroon', *Annals of the FALSS*, University of Ngaoundere Vol. 3.
Rivers, W., 1981, *Teaching Foreign Language Skills* (Second Edition), Chicago and London: University of Chicago Press.
Robinson, P., 1984, ESP (English for Specific Purposes),Oxford: Pergamon Press.
Scherer, A. and Wertheimer, M., 1964, *A Psycholinguistic Experiment in Foreign Language Teaching*, New York: McGraw-Hill.
Selinker, L., and Trimble, L.,1976, 'Scientific and Technical Writing: The Choice of Tense', English Teaching Forum, 14,4 (October).
Selinker, L, and Tomlin, R.,1986, 'An Empirical Look at the Integration and Separation of Skills in ELT', in *ELT Journal*, Vol. 40, No 3, (July).
Strevens, P., 1980, 'English for Special Purposes: An Analysis and Survey', in K. Croft, ed., *Readings on English as a Second Language* (For Teachers and Teachers Trainees), 2nd Edition, Cambridge: Winthrop Publishers.
Swales, J., 1985, 'ESP-The Heart of the Matter or the End of the Affair?', in R. Quirk and H.G. Widdowson, eds, *English in the World: Teaching and Learning the Langua-ge and Literatures*, Cambridge: Cambridge University Press.

Appendix 1

The University of Ngaoundere—Faculty of Science
Pre-Test: Experimental and Control Study
Time allowed: 2 hrs

Part A : G.E. (General English)

Task 1.

Describe the person you admire most (mention name, age, physical characteristics, character, etc. (about 6 lines). (8 pts)

Task 2.

In about 10 lines, describe your last weekend. (6 pts)

Part B: EST (English for Science and Technology)

Task 3.

a) Give the names of the following elements and compounds in English
.i) Cu; (ii) Pb; (iii) Au; (iv) Ag; (v) NaCI; (vi) $CaCO_3$; (vii) $AgNO_3$; and (viii) H_2SO_4 (5pts)

b) Write out the following figure as you would read it to a friend on the telephone: 114,313,730 FCFA. (3pts)

Task 4.

a) Compare and contrast the following: Cu and Au
b) Complete the following equation and, in a short paragraph, describe the reaction which takes place:
$Zn + H_2SO_4$?   (10pts)
LNM

Appendix 2

Masters in Applied Biology
Second Semester Examinations

English Language Paper
Time Allowed: 3 Hours
Do tasks 3, 5, 6, and one other

Task 1. Micro-EST Skills

A) Write out these figures as you would read them out to an audience: (5 point)
   i) The project would cost 14, 313, 730 FCFA
   ii) 18.58 + 12.33 + 1.67= ?

B) Translate into English : Un baromètre est un instrument météorologique utilisé pour mesurer la pression atmosphérique. Les baromètres peuvent être classés en deux grands types en fonction de la manière dont l'enregistrement de la pression atmosphérique est effectué. (5 points)

Task 2. Giving Directions

You are at the University of Ngaoundere Round About with a visiting student from England /USA. This student would like to meet Dr. Nso whose office is located at the ENSAI Brewery Complex. Sketch out a rough map, and in a short paragraph, describe how this student can find Dr. Nso. (10 points)

Task 3. Comparing and Contrasting

Most people do not realize that a plant cell is fundamentally different from an animal cell. Explain, highlighting the major differences, if any (10 points).

Task 4. Community Related Development Issues

Imagine you are employed at the Ngaoundere General Hospital. Write a short essay of about 250 words explaining to the people of your community why it is not advisable for girls to begin to have children before the age of 18. (10 points)

Task 5. EST Rhetorical Skills

Do either
a) $Zn + H_2SO_4$? OR
b) $AgNO_3 + HCl$? (10 points)

In either case, complete the chemical equation and describe the reaction that takes place.

Task 6. Make a report of any scientific experiment you know

(10 points)

Section III

Sociolinguistics

17

The Pidgin Factor in the Development of the Niger Delta Region of Nigeria

Rose O. Aziza

Introduction

Pidgin is a language that is made up of elements of two or more languages and is used mainly for contact, especially trade contacts, between speakers who do not share a common language. It is not the mother tongue of any speech community. Its grammar and vocabulary are usually greatly reduced. Essentially, it is an unstable language, which quickly dies out when the circumstances that triggered its development disappear (see, for example, Todd 1974; Kamwangamalu 2000).

Pidgin emerged in Nigeria around the eighteenth century as a result of the need for communication between European traders and their multi-ethnic Nigerian hosts along the coast. The Niger Delta region (ND) covered by this study spans seven of the thirty-six states of Nigeria, namely, Abia, Akwa-Ibom, Bayelsa, Cross-River, Delta, Edo, Ondo and Rivers.

The indigenous languages spoken in the area include Edo, Efik, Igbo, Ijo, Itsekiri, Isoko, Oron, Urhobo and Yoruba. It should be noted that the Igbo and Yoruba speaking areas are a very small part of the ND. The main languages of the area are minority languages, which, as earlier indicated, attract very little central government attention. The urban centres of focus in this work are Benin City, Calabar, Port Harcourt and Warri. Oil companies are located in them and these have attracted many people of diverse tongues and cultures to settle there for work and for business.

Pidgin in the Niger Delta

Communicative Function of Pidgin

The Nigerian Pidgin (NP) is virtually indispensable in its communicative function in the home, school, church, market place, office—in fact, for most interpersonal communication needs, including inter and intra-ethnic communication. It eases the language barrier that the many languages in the area would have created.

In the mass media, NP is extensively used in the radio and television for both entertainment and educational purposes. Adverts are common in the language and even government announcements are regularly relayed in NP for a wider reach. There are also pidgin columns in a number of periodicals.

In spite of its widespread use, NP is not recognized formally as a language of instruction at any level in the school system, although it is common to find teachers resorting to it every now and then in order to explain difficult points. It is also not used for serious government or administrative deliberations.

Language Repertoire

Most people in the area have at their disposal the use of one or more Nigerian languages (NL), Pidgin (NP) and English language (EL).

The sample for this study was made up of 300 adults and 300 youths. A half of each group was literate (i.e., with O' levels and above) and the other half was illiterate (i.e., with below O' levels). Ages 18–40 belonged to the youth group while the adult group was made up of those over 40 years.

Data were collected through a questionnaire, oral interviews and secrettape recordings of conversations.[1]

The noticeable patterns that emerged from our study in the order of frequency of usage are as follows:

> All the 300 adults involved in the study can communicate reasonably in their NL but only 35 per cent can speak it well. All the 300 youths speak NP very well and for 18 per cent that is the only language they know. 67per cent can communicate only in NP and EL.

Varieties of Pidgin

In the literature, regional varieties as well as varieties according to age, educational status, socio-economic status, etc of living languages have been identified.

(i)	Adult Illiterate:	NL→	NP	
(ii)	Adult Literate:	EL→	NP→	NL
(iii)	Youth Illiterate:	NP→	NL	
(iv)	Youth Literate:	NP→	EL→	NL

In the four cities covered by this study, regional varieties that reflect the languages, cultures and habits of the people of each area were identified. The following are a few examples:

1a) Warri: *Omome, I dey koko di money* (My child, I am trying to put the money together

Omome and *koko* are Urhobo words for 'My child' and 'gather (something)'.

1b) Port Harcourt: *Chei, see dis Agbani* (Ah! This girl is very pretty)

(*Chei* is an Ikwerre exclamation while Agbani (Darego) is the name of the current Miss World who hails from Okrika in Rivers State. The name is now a slang for describing a slim, beautiful girl.)

1c) Benin City: *Comot! You be oyi* (Get out ! You are a thief; *oyi* is an Edo word for 'thief')

Noticeable varieties also exist according to age and educational background of speakers. The youth variety is markedly different from the adult variety. While the latter is like a typical pidgin with simplified grammar and vocabulary and, thus, easy to understand, the former has many slangs that vary from one social circle to another. The expressions in 2a and b below are presented in standard English; what follows in 2c and d are rendtions of the same expression by adults while 2e and f represent renditions by youths.

(2)   a) the foolish man drank native gin with all the money.
           b) when trouble came, the old man went mad.

           c) di *mumu* just take all di money drink *ogogoro*.
           d) when trouble kom burst, di papa kom dey crase.

           c) di *mugu* just take di pepper level *ogofi*.
           e) when *yawa* gas, pale kom *kolo*.

In addition, differences exist between the NP of the literate and that of the illiterate. The literate variety has more of English vocabulary and grammatical structures while that of the illiterate contains a lot of elements traceable to the indigenous languages of the area.

Effect of NP on the Languages of the Area

We shall be concerned here with only linguistic and social effects.

Linguistic Effects

Rather than the indigenous languages interfering with NP, it is the other way round, particularly among the youths. A number of sounds in the NLs are being dropped and replaced by those of NP. For example, Urhobo has the voiceless and voiced palatal plosives /c, ɟ/ spelt as *ch* and *dj* respectively, and the voiceless and voiced velar fricatives /x,ɣ/ spelt as *h* and *gh* respectively in its sound inventory. Our study shows that many youths cannot produce these sounds because they do not exist in NP. As a result, they commonly substitute [ʃ,ʒ] the voiceless and voiced palatal fricatives commonly spelt as *sh* and *j* respectively, for the palatal plosives and substitute [h] the glottal fricative commonly spelt as *h* for both the voiceless and voiced velar fricatives. Thus one commonly hears the following:

Ochuko [ɔcuko] pronounced as [ɔʃuko] 'personal name'
Odje [oɟɛ] pronounced as [oje] 'personal name'
Aghogho [aɣɔɣɔ] pronounced as [ahɔhɔ] 'personal name'

Prof Kay Williamson, in a personal communication, reports a similar situation, citing her experiences at the University of Port Harcourt. Abua, a dialect of Ijo, has ten vowels in its sound inventory and operates a vowel harmony system. However, most of her students of Abua origin can only produce the seven vowels of NP and have difficulty with the vowels [ɨ, ʉ, ə], thereby gradually reducing a 10-vowel system to a seven-vowel system. Besides, there is a lot of code mixing and code-switching between NP and NL in favour of NP.

Social Effects

As has been commonly reported in the literature, most Africans have a poor attitude to their languages and regard European languages as being more useful and prestigious (see, for example, Aziza 1993; Bamgbose 2000). The Niger Delta area is no exception. Even pidgin, which is supposed to be a non-standard or inferior form, has a higher social status in the eyes of the natives than the NLs. Thus, whereas the old illiterate woman is trying to improve on her NP because she feels that that gives her a better self-esteem, and, by so doing, swelling the number of NP speakers, the youths are showing a strong lack of interest in their NL, thereby reducing the number of potential speakers.

Besides, NP is the major language used to ease communication barriers among the different groups in the area. People speak it everywhere, irrespective of age, social status, sex ethnicity/nationality, from the home to government offices. With NP, everyone can participate in a communication process vertically and horizontally and it helps to remove the feeling of inferiority that should have existed between people of different socio-economic and educational backgrounds.

Implications for the Overall Development of the Niger Delta

Research has shown very clearly that there is a correlation between language and development such that the loss of a language means the loss of an important component of a people's rich natural heritage and an effective tool for national development (see, for example, Chia 2002; Tadadjeu 2002). The indigenous languages are the embodiment of the physical, spiritual and psychological well being of the people and such rich heritage can only be made available for tapping and development through the languages. The people's technological prowess, their medicare, etc., are embodied in their language. NP, although it performs a number of social functions, lacks a cultural base.

Since language promotes development, a lack of interest in the languages of the Niger Delta region by both the people and the government can be seen as a principal factor in the lack of development of the area. This is because it is only through the language that the people understand that they can properly articulate their needs as well as develop their potentials. Although the region is responsible for over 90 per cent of the nation's wealth, it is the least developed part of Nigeria. Most people live in abject poverty with no roads to link the mainly riverine communities, no water or electricity, and the speakers of the three major languages of Hausa, Igbo and Yoruba dominate even the oil companies. The central government is more interested in what it can get out of the region than in improving the lot of the people that live there. Their languages are in the minority group, which lack social prestige and are not given serious consideration. Besides, speakers of the dominant languages are at the helm of affairs in decision making in the country. The result is that the people lack the facilities to properly articulate their needs to attract the attention of government.

The Way Forward

A few suggestions are made below:

(i) The status of these languages has to be enhanced to reduce the dependence on NP and change the negative attitude towards them. One way of doing so is for government to properly implement the language provisions of the National Policy on Education (1981) and not merely pay lip service to them. What we find now in Nigeria is that the languages are approved as languages of formal and informal education on paper but in reality they are far from playing the role.

(ii) A committed pursuit of this goal by the organs of government will improve the prestige of these languages and the people will embrace them better.

(iii) The languages should be used more extensively in the mass media. Right now, most serious discussions on radio and television are conducted in English. More educational programmes and discussions of government and its policies need to feature regularly in these NLs so that the people would be better informed, which means airtime for English and NP programmes would be reduced.

(iv) We need to develop literacy programmes in these languages. This will lead to lexical expansion to cover new terms that need to be reflected in writing, production of literature, e.g., writing novels, drama pieces, etc. Government should encourage more vigorously the development of these languages. The time for rhetoric is over.

(v) Funds must be made available for the study and development of these languages. In this regard, every sector must be involved, including the three tiers of government, i.e., local, state and federal, as well as individuals, language committees, non-governmental agencies, experts and lay people, etc. All must be committed towards helping these languages take their proper place in the lives of the people and making them more relevant to modern technological needs.

(vi) The youths must be sensitized to see the benefits of using their NLs for more of their communicative needs than NP. After all, none of the 600 people involved in this study wanted NP to be used in education. Unless there is intergenerational transmission, these languages are on the path of death.

Conclusion

Although the Niger Delta region is heterogeneous there can be no meaningful development in the area without the development of the languages that make the people unique. Most of the people are not even aware of the intrinsic similarities between their languages and cultures because they are not exposed to them. This has given room to the exploitation of the people by some political manipulators who stand to gain more by emphasizing the differences between the ethnic groups. Our contention is that the ethnic unity that seems to elude the people will be better achieved if the languages of the people are made more relevant and functional and are given their desired pride of place in the scheme of things in the country.

Note

1. The data were taped without the knowledge of the informant so as to get a natural rendition of the necessary data. If the informant were to know that his conversation was being recorded, he would have been influenced and the data would have been distorted.

References

Aziza, R.O., 1993, 'Teaching and Learning in Nigerian Languages: Developed Versus Developing Languages', *Teaching Nigerian Languages: Experiences from the Delta*, Rose O. Aziza and Nolue E. Emenanjo, eds, Warri: COEWA Publishers, pp.112-21.

Bamgbose, A., 2000, 'Urban Multilingualism in Nigeria', paper presented at the 3rd World Congress on African Linguistics, Lome, 21-26 August.

Chia, E., 2002, 'The Endangered Languages of Cameroon', paper presented at the 23rd Congress of the West African Linguistics Society, Buea, 7-9 August.

Kamwangamalu, N.M., 2000, 'Languages in Contact', Vic Webb and Kembo-Sure, eds, *African Voices*, Oxford: Oxford University Press, pp.88-108.

Tadadjeu, M., 2002, 'Langues Africaines, Garant du Succès du NEPAD,' paper presented at the 23rd Congress of the West African Linguistics Society, Buea, 7-9 August.

Todd, L,. 1974, *Pidgins and Creoles*, London: Routledge.

18

Kamtok (Pidgin) Is Gaining Ground in Cameroon

Miriam Ayafor

Introduction

A Pidgin or a Creole?

A pidgin, in the real sense of the word, is a simple makeshift contact language that develops when people of different linguistic backgrounds meet and must interact with one another. Todd (1990) says a pidgin is a marginal language that arises to fulfil certain restricted communication needs among people who have no common language. It does not, and cannot, satisfy all the linguistic needs of the people using it. But what most people are still calling 'pidgin' in Cameroon today has long since passed the level of a pidgin. As far back as 1982, Ngome argued spiritedly for its status as an African language. It has grown into maturity as a language and can and does satisfy the linguistic needs of many people (Ayafor 2000:6). After examining the situation of pidgin in Cameroon with the aid of a questionnaire, Kouega (2001:21) draws the conclusion, and rightly so, that 'Pidgin is now being used in all functional domains in the country'.

A creole, on the other hand, is a pidgin that has become so developed that it is no longer only a makeshift language but has become the mother tongue of a people. In Cameroon today, there are families for which 'pidgin' is a mother tongue, especially families whose parents come from different linguistic backgrounds. To continue to call it a pidgin is to continue to do injustice to a language that deserves better.

Its Name Is 'Kamtok'

Languages have names. In 1963 the name 'Weskos' was used by Schneider to describe this West African coastal pidgin-derived language. In 1980 a Cameroonian journalist baptized the language 'Kamtok' over radio Buea. This name has been accepted and used ever since by prominent professors of language like Todd (1990: 2, 6-16), Mbangwana (1991:59), and McArthur (1998:177), and by language students like Ayafor (1996:53; 2000:4). Commenting on the use of this name by Todd & Jumbam, Mbangwana (1991) says:

> The authors' labelling of this speech form as Kamtok lends it descriptive and evaluative quality that invests it with a badge of identity as a Cameroonised Language since it is actively responsive to the linguistic environment of Cameroon.

As other African scholars accept and use this name, they give status and dignity to the language.

Kamtok in Literary Tradition

Codification/Standardization

Languages that are codified are more powerful and stand higher chances of survival than those that are not. Kamtok can be said to be codified in the sense that it has a certain form that is being used in writing. There have been liturgical texts in Kamtok since the 1920s, and in 1966, a more complete text by the Société biblique Cameroun-Gabon was produced: The Gospel according to St. Mark. Since then, other Christian church documents have been printed in Kamtok (Kouega 2001:18). Today, there is the complete New Testament of the Bible, entitled, GUD NYUS FO OL PIPUL in that language published by The Bible Society of Cameroon, Yaounde, in the year 2000. Following is a quotation from this Bible:

> Joseph yi na Mary haid Jesus Afta de pipul fo ist dem bin don go, Masa yi angel e kam fo Joseph fo insaid Drim, e tok fo yi sei, ' Herod e go di fain de pikin fo kil-am. So, weikop teik De pikin an yi mami, an wuna ron go fo Egypt bigin di stei fo dei sotee A kam Tok sei meik yu komot kam bak'. Joseph e weikop an e teik de pikin an de Mami, e komot daso fo nait, e go fo Egypt. E bigin de stei dei sotee herod kam Dai. Dis ting din happen so fo meik de ting weh Masa bin tok fo korekt hau weh De profet bin tok sei: 'A kol ma pikin e komot fo Egypt.

Matthew 1: 13-15.

The literature of some Cameroonian writers, too, contains portions of Kamtok. Such Cameroonian writers as Kenjo Jumbam, Bole Butake, Bate Besong, John Menget, and Anne Tanyi Tang have used Kamtok in their works. In his collection of short stories entitled *Lukong and the Leopard* (1975:46), Jumbam uses quite a lot of Kamtok, especially in the second story, 'The White Man of Cattle'. Wirnkar, the man whom Major Walters takes along to show him round the village of Jakiri, speaks to the major in Kamtok. Once during their village tour, when the Major takes a wrong turn on the road and misses his way, Wirnkar shouts:

> Massa! Massa! Na road dis. You done teik wrong road. Massa! Go for woman-hand. No go for man-handi.

In Bole Butake's *Lake God* (1986:18-9), the Fon speaks with Dewa, the cattle-rearer, in Kamtok:

Fon: You been talk all that foolish talk?

Dewa: Kai! Me no talkam no noting.

Fon: Na weti happen?

Dewa: Cow dong go drinki water for Ngangba sai wey na Kontri for Bororo.

Fon: For sika sey me tell you for go shiddon dere da wan mean sey na wuna Kontri?

Dewa: No bi gomna don talk sey na place for cow?

Fon: Which gomna, you bloody fool? You look the palaver wey you dong Bringam for my head?

Dewa: Allah! Me no bringam no trobou for Mbe.

Fon: You go pay all that chop wey you cow don choppam.

Dewa: No be ma nyun, Mbe! Na you nyun don choppam corn.

Fon: Shutup you mup, you bloody fool! [2]

The second drama in Bate Besong's *Beasts of No Nation* (1990:15) starts with the following song in Kamtok:

Solo: I fit tief one hundred million. I fit tief five hundred million sef.

Chorus: Because my umbrella dey for capital city

Because my umbrella dey for Ednuoay city.

Solo: I fit bury one thousand million for my ceiling

I fit bury meme ten thousand for my ceiling.

Chorus: Because Ednuoay city done spoil-oh

Because Ednuoay done spoil.[3]

Not only does John Menget include Kamtok portions in his writings, but he also writes complete poems and plays in this language. In his unpublished tragi-comedy, Mimbo Hos, only one of the sixteen members of the cast speaks English. All the rest speak Kamtok. Following are the opening lines of the play:

Mr. Bluemoon: Service! Service! Se- r- vi- ce!

Service: (from without) S- a- a- h!

Mr. Bluemoon: Why you no fit bring de glass quick? Dis massa done open yi beer Leav'am I de cold or sika glass. See de time you de clean bar...

For apass time. If you no want work more, tell me.

Munde: How you want sey make yi work? Yi work for bar den yi work for Bed; work for san-time, work for night. Two man work one man Do'am.[4]

Mr. Bluemoon: Munde shut up dey! Who call you here?

In Anne Tanyi Tang's collection of plays, entitled *Ewa and Other Plays* (2000:46-47), the play, 'My Bundle Of Joy' has a scene depicting the traditional healer's residence, where the Mallam, the traditional healer, his servant, and his client or patient interact in Kamtok:

Boy: Madam, mallam sey make you come inside. No forget for remove your shoes.

Kechem: I don hear. Thank you.

Mallam: Madam. I think sey you don forget we. Wuna dey fine?

Kechem: Yes, but.....

Mallam: I know. I be tell you say make you come back. But you nobi come. So I be Think sey all thing fine. Wait make I finam. (Throws cowries....) Madam, Your papa ye people dem dee vex with you for sika sey since you married, Your masa nodi give dem money. Dey wan one swine, one bag rice, Mukanjo, salt and tobacco. No forget strong mimbo. Tell your masa. After you give them all these things, come back for me and I go give you Medicine. After three months, you go carry bele.

Kechem: So na so ngambe talk?[5]

Actually, it is very difficult for any Anglophone Cameroonian of today to write a complete play without making use of Kamtok from time to time. Such a play would not really satisfy the entertainment needs of the Cameroonian audience, and would not reflect the sociolinguistic situation of the country. It is true that Kamtok is not yet standardized. But the fact that writing in that language is going on shows that there is a tendency towards standardization. It is a question of time and efforts will be consolidated to bring about its standardization.

Kamtok as Medium of Instruction

As mentioned earlier, for many families in Cameroon, and in homes where father and mother do not come from the same ethnic or linguistic background, especially in the Anglophone region of the country, Kamtok is the language of the home. It is true that a handful of elitist families of such mixed marriages would ban Kamtok from their homes, but the end result is still victory for the language. Children from such homes still get to know and speak Kamtok with their peers in school and in the neighbourhood, and when they grow older and are no longer under parental pressure they interact freely in that language even in their homes.

Most Cameroonians grow up acquiring their mother tongues first before going to learn English or French in schools. Since in plantations and towns of English speaking Cameroon, children grow up speaking Kamtok, the operational language education project (PROPELCA) should include Kamtok as one of the mother tongues for the children in these areas though unofficially. Kouega (2001:21), talking about Pidgin (Kamtok), says:

> Teachers make use of it in the classroom. If teachers who are the specialists in the field make use of Kamtok in class, it is because they have found that it works. They must have realized that our young children can only understand certain concepts when these are explained to them in a language they master well; and Kamtok is such a language.

In a study of the language profile of Cameroon, Koenig (1983:47) reveals that:

> in the Northwestern and Southwestern Provinces, the percentage of children who do not speak a Cameroonian language is considerably higher in two of the towns. Percentages are as follows: Kumba, 4 percent; Bamenda, 5 percent; Mamfe, 5 percent; Buea, 10 percent and Victoria, 16 percent.

In the same study, it is shown that 'not even one out of two children attending primary school the first year in the Anglophone towns can speak Standard English' (ibid.:100). But all these children can speak Kamtok. It is normal, therefore, for some teachers to use Kamtok in their classes.

It is worth noting that children whose first language (L1) is Kamtok are found in Anglophone and Francophone towns. Koenig's study (p. 48) reveals percentages of Pidgin as L1 in the towns listed in table below. It is needless to say that the first five on the list being Francophone towns. With the increase in the use of Kamtok today in the press, the media and public places, something that was very rare twenty years ago, it is likely that these figures would be higher if the study were repeated now.

Town	(%)
Douala	2
Yaounde	1
Nkongsamba	1
Bafoussam	1
Edea	2
Mamfe	25
Bamenda	22
Kumba	19
Buea	26
Victoria	31

Kamtok in Meeting Houses

An extra-linguistic or sociological factor that further empowers Kamtok is ethnic loyalty in Cameroon. People in this country are very proud of their origins; and every group, no matter how small it is, wants to promote the culture and language of its people. That is what accounts for the various 'family meetings' existing in

urban areas all over the country. Consider, for example, the city of Yaounde as an urban centre, and the people of the North West Province of Cameroon as immigrants into that city. The North West Province is made up of seven administrative divisions. Mezam is made up of five sub-divisions, Santa being one of them. From Santa alone, there are nine 'Manjong' groups registered in Yaounde as separate cultural associations. They come from the following villages: Akum, Alateneng, Awing, Baba, Baforchu, Baligham, Mbei, Njong and Pinyin. The principal difference between these groups is language. During their meetings, which are held at least once every month, the culture and language of these 'families' are strongly encouraged and promoted. Members of a 'Manjong' group come from the same village and speak the same language. Thousands of such groups from all over the national territory are registered in big cities like Yaounde and Douala, and they function very successfully. This common practice in all urban areas of the nation is the very promoter of Kamtok in the sense that when people from the different linguistic backgrounds must interact with one another, in their daily activities, they need a common language. That language is Kamtok.

Kamtok in the Media and the Press

Domains that were hitherto reserved only for the official languages of the country are now readily lending themselves to Kamtok. An example of this is the *Cameroon Tribune*, the nation's official newspaper, which features a Kamtok column entitled 'Tory Man'. In this column, anecdotes are written in Kamtok. The argument, therefore, is that if the language can be tolerated in such a publication, then it is really being empowered. In addition, the electronic media are contributing well to the empowerment of the language through the advertisements and educative programmes they target at the rural communities as well as the complete newscasts they relay in Kamtok. 'Tory Time' in the FM radio station of Buea and 'Afrique Nouvelle' in Radio Bamenda are ready examples.

Attitudes Towards the Language

Despite the foregoing evidence of the popularity of Kamtok in Cameroon, there are many (including those who use it most) who legislate against the language and seek to kill it. These people have advanced a number of flimsy excuses to ban the use of Kamtok.

They argue that the language is the cause of the falling standards of English in Cameroon. They argue that speaking Kamtok would mar their knowledge and mastery of the English language and that of their children. These people close their eyes to the real factors (unrelated to the use of Kamtok) that contribute immensely to the problem of low standards of English in Cameroon today. Some of these problems are related to large classes, unqualified teaching staff, poverty, lack of extensive general reading, negative influence from the media, language interference, etc. This writer is strongly of the opinion that once these problems are addressed, a solution would have been found for the problems of poor standards in English in Cameroon, perhaps the critics will then spare Kamtok.

But for now the language has to contend with verbal and written assaults, and unofficial ban of its use in academic milieus, such as the following found on bill boards in the University of Buea campus:

> English is the password, not Pidgin
>
> English is the language of the Commonwealth, not Pidgin.
>
> If you speak Pidgin you'll write pidgin
>
> Pidgin is taking a negative toll on your English; shun it.

However, the fact that Kamtok is being banned by such written orders only goes a long way to show how popular it has become; so much so that extra measures have to be taken to dissuade university students from speaking it on campus. The most the university can do is to indicate where the use of Kamtok is appropriate, not ban it since it has no way of implementing its ban anyway.

Conclusion

The discussion above reveals one fact: that Cameroonian Pidgin English (Kamtok) is part and parcel of the Cameroonian society. That it is the language of all and sundry, the rich and the poor, the young and the old, the uneducated and educated. It cuts across the fabric of the society and it is growing and spreading like wild fire; hence the need to officially recognize and adopt it as an official language so that it can be standardized and promoted, and with its functions defined.

As I have made clear, the solution to falling standards of English does not lie in banning Pidgin English but in promoting and controlling its use. This promotion can be done by codifying and standardizing it. In this regard, we recommend that linguists interested in creolistics should come together and agree on a common script for Kamtok.

Just as other Cameroonian national languages are being used in literacy, Kamtok, too, could be used for the same purpose. Instructional material could be developed in the language so that it can begin to serve as a language of wider communication in Cameroon and, of course, the society will then begin to enjoy the numerous benefits of empowering the language.

Notes

1. Translated into English this would be: Sir! Sir! This is the way. You've missed the way. Sir! Go to the left. Don't go to the right.
2. The Fon is asking Dewa what happened that his cows had to destroy some villagers' crops. Dewa explains and defends himself.
3. The singer is saying that he could steal any amount of money and go free because he has a God-father (umbrella) in the capital city. The capital is corrupt.
4. The waitress (service) is called to bring a glass for a customer. She is slow in coming because she was busy cleaning up the bar. The customer accuses her of cleaning the bar late. Munde comes to her defence by saying that she woke up late because she had been working in the night.
5. Kechem goes back to a traditional healer she had earlier consulted. The healer says he had been expecting her, but since she did not come back, he had thought all was well. He then inquires through divination and finds out the Kechem's paternal relatives are not happy with her. They need a pig, a bag of rice, some stockfish, some salt, some tobacco and strong drinks from her husband and then she will be able to conceive.

References

Ayafor, M., 1996, 'An Orthography for Kamtok' in *English Today*, Vol. 12, No 4. Cambridge: Cambridge University Press.

Ayafor, M., 2000, 'Kamtok: The Ultimate Unifying Language for Cameroon', in *The Carrier Pidgin*, Vol. 28, Nos 1-3, January-December, Florida International University.

Barber, C., 1993, *The English Language: A Historical Introduction*, Cambridge: Cambridge University Press.

Bate, Besong, 1990, *Beasts of No Nation*, Yaounde: Edition CLE.

Bole, Butake, 1986, *Lake God*, Yaounde: Edition CLE.

Chumbow, B. S., 2000, 'Transborder Languages of Africa', in *The Journal of Social Issues*, South Africa.

Jumbam, K., 1975, *Lukong and the Leopard*, Yaounde: Edition CLE.

Koenig, E. L., Chia, E., Povey, J., eds, 1983, *A Sociolinguistic Profile of Urban Centers in Cameroon*, Los Angeles: Crossroads Press.

Kouega, J. P., 2001, 'Pidgin Facing Death in Cameroon', Discussion Paper No 17 (online), York, Mouton de Gruyter. Available online at www.terralingua.org.

Mbangwana, P.,1991, 'Kamtok is Achieving its Lettres de Noblesse', in *Lore & Language*, 10/2.

McArthur, T., 1998, *The English Languages*, Cambridge: Cambridge University Press.

Ngome, M.,1982, 'Cameroon Pidgin English Vocabulary: A Lexico-SemanticStudy', Dissertation, University of Yaounde.

Tanyi Tang, A., 2000, *Ewa and Other Plays*, Yaounde: Edition CLE.

The Bible Society of Cameroon, 2000,*Gud NyusFo ol PipuL*, Yaounde: The Bible Society of Cameroon

The Daily Mail, 23 September 1991.

The Guardian, 6 October 1991.

The Observer, 24 December 1989.

Todd, L., 1990, *Pidgins and Creoles*, New edition, London: Routledge & Kegan Paul.

Todd & Jumbam, M., 1992, 'Kamtok: Anatomy of a Pidgin, in *English Today*, 8, 3.

Schneider, G., 1963, 'First Steps in Wes-kos', in *Harford Studies in Linguistics* , 6, V11-81 p. 004. Pidgin

Simo Bobda, A., 1992, 'Common Deviations in Cameroon English Usage' Yaounde.

Sure, K., 1992, 'Falling Standards of English in Kenya', in *English Today*, Vol. 8, No. 4.

19

Towards the Universals of Loan Adaptation:[1] The Case of Cameroonian Languages

Ayu'nwi N. Neba, Beban S. Chumbow and Pius N. Tamanji

Introduction

With the great technological advancement the world is currently experiencing and the pace with which the world is shrinking into a global village, the lexical expansion of languages has become all the more crucial. This is because languages need to accommodate new concepts (especially in modern technology, which is introduced to Africa mainly in English and French) if this knowledge is to be available to all in the global village.

This chapter is centred on one of the mechanisms for lexical expansion[2] in almost all the world languages—loan adaptation. Since African languages share a number of structural characteristics, the strategies employed for loan adaptation (for example cluster simplification, sound interpretation, etc.,) are largely the same as one moves from one language to another. The chapter demonstrates this thesis with data drawn from some Cameroonian/African languages. It is hoped that once these common characteristics are identified, loan adaptation and lexical expansion of African languages will be facilitated, as computers could then be programmed to do the work easily and faster. However, what is presented here is essentially a hypothesis that can be verified empirically as more research results become available from other language families.

In the first part of the chapter, some structural characteristics common to Cameroonian/African languages are discussed. This is followed by an overview of some of the mechanisms commonly employed by these languages for loan adaptation. The chapter ends with a discussion of how different languages make use of these processes, highlighting the point that the same processes are employed by different languages to tackle the same structural problems.

Structural Characteristics Common to African Languages

The Sound System

Nasal-Consonant Sequences

One characteristic common to African languages is the use of nasals followed immediately by other consonants. In most cases, the prenasals are syllabic (constituting the nucleus of a syllable); in other cases the consonant and the nasal constitute a single sound. This is illustrated in (1) below.

(1)
a. Bafut (Mfonyam 1989)

(i) ǹdâ 'house'
(ii) m̀fɔ 'chief'
(iii) m̀bo 'hands'
(iv) ŋ̀gàŋ 'root'
(v) bɔ́ɔ́ntə̂ 'build a little'

b. Kom (Keh (2002)

(i) ǹdɔ̀ŋ 'potato'
(ii) m̀bɨ̀jntɨ́ 'pants'
(iii) ŋ̀kám 'thousand'
(iv) ǹdó 'school'
(v) ŋ̀gvɨ̄ 'fowl'

c. Mokpe (Nkwenti (2002)

(i) ńdáwò 'house'
(ii) m̀bólì 'goat'
(iii) ǹdə̀ndə̀kì 'needle'
(iv) ǹdă 'cocoyams'
(v) ŋ̀gàŋgò 'umbrella'

d. Kenyang (Enouchuo (2002))

(i) m̀fɔ 'chief'
(ii) ǹnɔ̀ 'mother'
(iii) ŋ̀kɔ̀k 'fowls'
(iv) ǹsók 'cow'

In these data, the syllabic nasals are nominal class prefixes and, as noticed, they are always homorganic (i.e., fprmed in the same place of articulation) and following consonant. A majority of African languages have at least some morphemes that have initial syllabic prenasals.

Monophthongs

While diphthongs and triphthongs are common in English, which is one of the languages from which African languages borrow, most African languages make use of monophthongs. This means that there is a tendency for African languages to employ vowel reduction processes to adapt words borrowed from English to suit the indigenous language structure. This is the case in the examples below.

(2)

Word in Receptor Language	Receptor Language	Donor Language	Word in Donor Language	Gloss
(i) tòrísà	Bafut	English	traʊsəz	'trousers'
(ii) sìtúfɨ	Kom	English	stəʊv	'stove'
(iii) àdɨlɔ́lìkɨ	Kenyang	English	haɪdrɔlik	'hydraulic'
(iv) wíndò	Mbu	English	wɪndəʊ	'window'

As it is the case with diphthongs and triphthongs, many African languages do not make use of consonant clusters. Since these clusters are commonly used in English and French, which are donors to African languages, they are often simplified. The data in (3) below illustrate this.

(3)

Word in Receptor Language	Word in Donor Language	Receptor Language	Donor Language	Gloss
sɨkúlɨ	skul	Bafut	English	'school'
kɨlísəmẽ	krɪsməs	Kom	English	'Christmas'
màtìmàtííkì	mæəmætɪks	Yoruba	English	'mathematics'
sɨtɨríkɨ	strɪkt	Kenyang	English	'strict'
kɔ̀ré	krE	Ewondo	French	(craie) 'chalk'

Syllable Structure

Most African languages prefer an open syllable type (one that is not arrested by a consonant). Thus, the V, and CV types are dominant given that consonant clusters are disfavoured by these languages (cf 1.1.3). Although some of these languages allow consonants in coda/word final position, they are relatively fewer in number and the consonants are highly restricted. For example Bafut does not allow consonants in coda position and if they must occur, then they must be nasals (Neba 1998). As a result, Ito (1986) postulates a universal constraint on consonants in coda/word final position. The nasal consonants in word final position in Bafut are as a result of the deletion of a postnasal word final vowel in non-imperatives. The data in (4) below are illustrative of this.

(4) *Bafut*

	UR	Non-final	Final	Gloss
a.	/sɨŋi/	b. [sɨŋ]	c. [sɨŋə́]	'bird'
	/lə́ŋə/	[lə́ŋ]	[lə́ŋə́]	'horse'
	/bɨ́nɨ/	[bɨ̂n]	[bɨ́nəɪ̯]	'dance'

Noun Classes

Many African languages are characterised by nouns that pattern into classes. This feature makes them different from the Indo-European languages - English and French. Borrowed words from these languages and others will need to be assigned to appropriate noun classes. In some cases, they are subjected to prothesis and the inserted vowel is usually the noun class prefix. This is shown in the data below.

(5)

Borrowed Word	Loan Word	Receptor Language	Donor Language	Gloss
à-bɔ́sà	pɜːs	Bafut	English	'purse'
à-kànúʔú	kənuː	Bafut	English	'canoe'
è-rísí	raɪs	Kenyang	English	'rice'
è-rúlá	ruːlə	Kanyang	English	'ruler'

Prosody

While Indo-European languages are stress-timed, most African languages are tonal. That is, African languages make use of contrastive pitch. The data in 6 below illustrate this.

(6)

	a. Bafut		b. Mankon		c. Kom	
	lə́ŋə́	'hang' (imp)	ŋ̀kɪə̀	'basket'	bó	'weave'
	lə́ŋə́	'horse'	ŋ̀kɪə́	'water'	bō	'hill'
	lə̀ŋə̂	'tap' (imp)	ŋ̀kɪə̂	'charcoal'	bò	'bag'

In the data above, the words in each language differ in meaning as a result of a change in pitch (tone). In some of these languages verbs are grouped into tone classes. In Bafut, for example, there are two verb groups depending on the tone that a verb bears. These two classes are the low tone and the high tone verb classes. These are illustrated in (7) below.

(7)

a. Low Tone Verbs

(i) lɔ̀gɔ̂ 'take'
(ii) lɔ̀gɨ̀nɔ̂ 'begin'
(iii) lɨ̀gɨ̀tɔ̂ 'doubt'
(iv) ŋwà?ànɔ̂ 'write'

b. High Tone Verbs

(i) lɔ́ŋɔ̂ 'hang'
(ii) bɔ́gɔ̂ 'break of stick'
(iii) bɔ́gɨ́tɔ̂ 'break one by one'
(iv) sɨ́gɨ́tɔ̂ 'bend a little'

The above discussion implies that once an African language borrows a word from English or French, there must be a harmonization of prosodic features.

Summary of Expectations

In sum, one expects that once a word is borrowed into an African language, the following processes should take place: sound replacement, cluster simplification, noun class assignment, prosodic harmonization (tone and intonation assignment) and syllable structure adjustment.

In the next section, we discuss how different Cameroonian languages implement these processes, showing that this implementation is fairly uniform as one moves from one language to another. That is, for example cluster simplification is done through the insertion of the same or almost identical vowel and that borrowed nouns are assigned to the same noun classes in the various languages.

Loan Adaptation Strategies

Cluster Simplification

As mentioned above, many Cameroonian languages have the tendency to simplify consonant clusters when they are attested in borrowed words. In this section of the work, we will examine how a number of languages simplify clusters. Consider the data below chosen from different languages.

(8)a. Bafut (Numfor 1999)

Loan word	Donor	Bafut Equivalent	Gloss
ʊ́kul	English	sɨ̀kúlɨ̀	'school'
mætʃiz	English	mátsɨ́sɨ̀	'matches'
krisməs	English	kɨ̀rɨ́sɨ̀	Christmas'
trosa	Pidgin English	tòrɨ́sà	'trousers'
laımz	English	lámɨ̀ʃɨ̀	'limes'

Bafut is a language whose syllable structure is dominantly open. Codas are, therefore, stigmatized and, as mentioned earlier, the language does not welcome consonant clusters. One of the strategies employed to avoid consonant clusters and codas is the insertion of vowels. We notice consistently in (8) that it is the high central unrounded vowel [ɨ] that is inserted for this purpose. Notice that in the case of [laImz] 'limes' an [i] is inserted at word final position.

Numfor (1999) postulates the following rule to describe cluster breaking in Bafut.

8) b. ø → [ɨ] / C — C (#)
                      [-nas]

9)   Kom (Kay 2000)

Borrowed Word	Donor Language	Kom Word	Gloss
krismǝs	English	kɨ́lísǝmē̄	'Christmas'
skul	English	sɨkúlɨ	'school'
skɜ:t	English	sɨkɨ́tɨ	'skirt'
trosa	Pidgin English	tɨlɔ̀sí	'trousers'
stǝuv	English	sɨtúfɨ	'stove'
fla:sk	English	fɨ́lásɨ	'flask'
plæŋk	English	bzɨ̌lâŋ	'plank'

It can be observed in these data that the dominant vowel inserted either to break consonant clusters or open syllables is the central vowel [ɨ].

(10)

Borrowed Word	Donor	Kenyang language word	Gloss
haɪdrɔlɪk	English	àdɨrɔ́lɨ́kɨ̀	'hydraulic'
hɒspɪtǝl	English	wàsɨ̀pítà	'hospital'
sɪlvǝ	English	sɨ̀ríβá	'silver'
dɪvelǝpmǝnt	English	déβéróp̄ɨmén	'development'
testǝment	English	tèsɨ́támén	'testament'
test	English	tîsɨ	'test'
strɪkt	English	sɨ̀tɨ́rɨ́kɨ̀	'strict'
fɜst	English	fɛ́sɨ	'first'

Again, as it was the case with the two languages, Bafut and Kom, already discussed above, the dominant vowel that is inserted between consonant clusters is still the central high-unrounded vowel [ɨ]. To account for consonant cluster simplification, Enoachuo (2002) postulates the rule in (10b) below.

10) b. ø → [ɨ] / C — C (#)

We will recall that a similar rule (8b) was postulated to account for vowel insertion in Bafut.

As a general observation, most languages will use the central high vowel to break consonant clusters as has been illustrated in the three languages above—Bafut, Kom and Kenyang. In all these three languages, the [ɨ] sound is attested in the sound inventories. The question that arises is what will happen in a situation where this vowel is not attested in a language. The data in (11) are from Mokpe, an example of such a language. It will be realized that cluster breaking in this language is done with the dominant insertion of the high front vowel [i]. This is natural because [i] is the most acoustically and articulatorily similar vowel to [ɨ]. That is, they share quite a number of phonetic features in common. Thus, as a general remark, we will expect that [ɨ] should be used for breaking consonant clusters in most words borrowed into Cameroonian languages and in situations where the [ɨ] is not attested in the sound inventory of the language in question, the high front vowel [i] should be used. This is probably why in the Yoruba data in (12); it is the [i] that is used in most cases to break consonant clusters.

(11)   Mokpe (Nkwenti 2000)³

Borrowed Word	Donor language	Mokpe word	Gloss
brʌʃ	English	bìlɔ́ʒì	'brush'
kəut	English	kótì	'coat'
trausəs	English	tɔ̀ʒríʒrì	'trousers'
pæstəu	English	páʒrítò	'pastor'
skul	English	zrùkúlù	'school'

(12)   Yoruba (Awobuluyi ms)

Borrowed word	Gloss	Source
kɔ́nsɔ́nántì	'consonant'	English
ásɛ́ntì	'accent'	English
físíìsì	'physics'	English
fónímù	'phoneme'	English
fáwèlì	'vowel'	English
síntáàsì	'syntax'	English
músíìkì	'music'	English
màtìmátíìkì	'mathematics'	English

Sound Reinterpretation

This is a situation whereby some segments attested in a donor language but absent in a receptor language are replaced. It has been discovered that in such situations the strange sounds are approximated to the indigenous sound segment with which they have the highest degree of phonetic similarity [Chumbow and Tamanji (1994), Mutaka and Tamanji (1995)]. This section of the chapter examines the ways in which different languages reinterpret their sounds, in a bid to establish the sounds commonly used for this purpose. Essentially, our attention will be on diphthong and triphthong simplification given that most African languages have only monophthongs whereas the English language, which lends many lexical items to African languages, makes use of diphthongs and triphthongs.

Triphthong and Diphthong Simplication

Many African languages replace diphthongs either by separating the two sounds that make up the diphthong or by reducing it to a monophthong. The discussion that follows shows how some of the languages treat different diphthongs.

[aɪ] is generally reduced to [a]. The data below illustrate this.

(13)

a. Bafut

Borrowed word	Donor word	Gloss	Source
lâmʃì	[laɪms]	'limes'	English
básíkò	[baɪsɪkl]	'bicycle'	English
fân	[faɪn]	'fine'	English

b. Kom

Borrowed word	Donor word	Gloss	Source
filabãn	[fraɪpæn]	'frypan'	English
lâmsɨ	[laɪms]	'limes'	English

c. Kenyang

Borrowed word	Donor word	Gloss	Source
san	[saɪn]	'sign'	English
fajin	[faɪn]	'fine'	English

d. Ngamambo

Borrowed word	Donor word	Gloss	Source
básíkò	[baɪsɪkl]	'bicycle'	English
lâmʃì	[laɪms]	'limes'	English

[aʊ] is generally replaced with [o] or [u] as illustrated by the data in 14 below.

(14)

a. Ngamambo (Nangang 2002)

Borrowed word	Loan word	Donor Language	Gloss
wíndo	wɪndəʊ	English	'window'
mútù	məʊtə	English	'motor'
fótò	fəʊtə	English	'photo'

b. Kom

Borrowed word	Loan word	Donor Language	Gloss
sfìgè?è	səʊldʒə	English	'soldier'
sìtûfì	stəʊv	English	'stove'
bzɨl:	pɪləʊ	English	'pillow'
kúntâ	kəltɑ¹	English	'coal tar'
kûsɨ	kəʊst	English	'coast'
kût	kəʊt	English	'coat'

c. Bafut

Borrowed Word	Loan word	Donor Language	Gloss
mángòlɨ	mæŋɡ əʊ	English	'mango'
kótɨ	kəʊt	English	'coat'
bílò	pɪl əʊ	English	'pillow'
sìtófɨ	stəʊv	English	'stove'
pólìjò	pəʊlio	English	'polio'

d. Mokpe

Borrowed word	Loan word	Donor Language	Gloss
kótɨ	kəʊt	English	'coat'
mòtó	məʊtə	English	'motor'

e. Kenyang

Borrowed word	Loan word	Donor Language	Gloss
Mòtó	məʊtə	English	'motor'
tòmátò	təmaːtəʊ	English	'tomato'

As observed in the data above, even though both [o] and [u] are used to replace the diphthong [əʊ], [o] is more recurrent. It is only Kom that make use of [u] all other languages use [o]. The former is apparently an exceptional case and the norm is, therefore, the case where [aʊ] is reduced to [ɔ]. The data in (15) illustrate this.

(15)

Borrowed word	Receptor language	Gloss	
bɔ́dà	Kom	pɑʊdə	'powder'
tɔ̂ŋ	Mbu	tɑʊn	'town'
tɔ̂ŋ	Bafut	tɑʊn	'town'

The diphthongs [ɔɪ] and [ɪə]; and the triphthongs [aʊə], [ɔɪə] and [aɪə] are adapted into these languages by transforming the [ɪ] and [ʊ] into the glides [j] and [w] respectively as illustrated in (16) below.

(16)

a. [ɪə]

Borrowed word	Receptor language	Gloss	
jèlíŋ	Bafut	ɪərɪŋ	'earring'
bíjà	Bafut	bɪə	'beer'
jèli	Akum	ɪərɪŋ	'earring'

b. [aɪə]

Borrowed word	Receptor language	Gloss	
ájòn	Bafut	ɑɪən	'iron'
ájɔ̀n	Kom	ɑɪən	'iron'

c. ɔɪ(ə)

Borrowed word	Receptor language	Gloss	
ɔ́jà	Kenyang	ɔɪl	'oil'
lójà	Bafut	lɔɪə	'lawyer'

d. [aʊə]

Borrowed word	Receptor language	Gloss	
páwà	Bafut	pɑʊə	'power'
áwa	Bafut	ɑʊə	'hour'
táwòrɨ	Bafut	tɑʊəl	'towel'
tówà	Bafut	tɑʊə	'tower'
fɨ́láwà	Bafut	flɑʊə	'flower'
táwùla	Kom	tɑʊəl	'towel'

In sum, diphthongs and triphthongs are reduced to monophthongs as summarized in (17) below.

(17)

Diphthong/Triphthong	/Replacing Monophthong
aɪ	a
əʊ	o/u
aʊ	ɔ
ɔɪ	ɔj
ɪə	jɛ/ja
aʊə	awa
ɔɪə	ɔjə, ɔja

Note: High vowel quality in initial position of diphthongs or medial position of triphthongs becomes corresponding glides {I, ɪ}→ j , {ʏ, u} → w

Noun Class Prefixes

As mentioned earlier, most African languages of the Bantu and related language family have noun classes. That is, the nouns of these languages pattern into classes. What this means is that once a word is borrowed, it has to be given a noun class prefix. This section of the chapter examines how borrowed words from English and French are assigned to the noun classes of some African languages. The data presented in (18) illustrate this.

(18)

Bafut

a.
Word (sg)	Plural	Gloss
tòrɨ̀sà	bɨ̀ tòrɨ̀sà	'trouser'
mɨ́tù	bɨ̀ mɨ́tù	'motor'
bɨ́tà	bɨ̀ bɨ́tà	'Peter'
bɛ́bǎ	bɨ̀ bɛ́bà	'paper'
nómbà	bɨ̀ nómbà	'number'

b.
Singular	Plural	Gloss
à kàlɛ́ndà	ɨ̀ kàlɛ̃̀ndà	'calendar'
à kɔ̀mfɛsɔ́n	ɨ̀ kɔ̀mfɛ́sɔ́n	'confession'
à bɔ̀sà	ɨ̀ bɔ̀sà	'purse'
à tàbúrə̀	ɨ̀ tàbúrə̀	'tarpaulin'
à kànú?ú	ɨ̀ kànú?ú	'canoe'

In this language, borrowed nouns fall into two genders. Either they are in gender ½ which has a ø prefix as singular nominal class prefix (18a) or in gender 7/8 with a vowel nominal prefix (18b). There is no borrowed noun with a *cv* prefix.

On the assignment of borrowed nouns into grammatical classes, Numfor (1999) says:

> ... loan adapted words are put in genders a 1/2 and 7/8. Out of 56 loan adapted words collected from Bĭfĭ̀ (Bafut) speakers, 54 of them are found in gender ½ and 2 are found in gender 7/8. That is, 96% of the words fall in classes ½ and 4% in gender 7/8.

This excerpt reveals that most loan-adapted nouns into Bafut are assigned to class 1. A few of them are assigned to class 7. In a nutshell, any loan-adapted noun into Bafut will either carry ø or [a] as a singular nominal prefix and bɨ/ɨ respectively as a plural prefix.

This situation is not very much different in Kenyang where borrowed nouns are put into three gender classes with singular nouns either carrying a ø nominal prefix or ʊ/ŋ. Enoachuo (2002) summarizes this in the following words:

We realize that most loan adapted nouns fall in classes 1/2. In a word list of 20 loan nouns, 35 per cent fall under gender 1/2 and the rest of the 65 per cent unevenly distributed among classes 7/8 and 9/10.

The Kenyang data in (19) below illustrate the noun classes of borrowed words in this language.

(19) Kenyang

	Singular	Plural	Gloss	
a.	è - rísí	-	'rice'	cl_7
	è̩ rulà	bèrúlà	'ruler'	$cl_{7/6}$
b.	tɨ̀rɔ̀sá	bɔ̀ tɨ̀rɔ̀sá	'trouser'	$cl_{1/2}$
	mòtó	bɔ̀ mótó	'motor'	$cl_{1/2}$
	pèn	bɔ̀ pèn	'pen'	$cl_{1/2}$
c.	ŋ̀gwáβa	ŋ̀gwáa	'guava'	$cl_{9/10}$
	ŋ̀kɔ̀k	ŋ̀kɔ̀k	'cock'	$cl_{9/10}$

In Kom, typical loan adapted words fall in the same singular class and the plural is formed by suffixing [sɨ] to the singular. This is not very different from the other examples treated above, as these nouns still fall in the singular prefix class. The data in (20) below illustrate this.

(20) Kom

	Singular	Plural	Gloss	
a.	bɨléd	bɨlédsɨ	'bread'	$cl_{9/10}$
	bɨlàŋgî	bɨlàŋgísɨ	'blanket'	$cl_{9/10}$
	kàká	kàkásɨ	'cocoa'	$cl_{9/10}$
	lâm	bɨlmsɨ	'lamp'	$cl_{1/2}$

b. a báŋ   ɨ bʷaŋ   'bench' cl$_{7/8}$

In most of the languages, almost all the loan-adapted nouns have a (nominal prefix. The data below illustrate this point as far as Mokpe, Feʔfeʔ, Yoruba and Ewondo are concerned.

(21) *Mokpe (Nkweti 2000)*

Noun	Gloss
kótì	'coat'
mótò	'motor'
wíndà	'window'
tɔ̀ʒríʒrí	'trouser'
páʒrítò	'pastor'
pɔ́ʃrè	'purse'
zrùkúlù	'school'

(22) *Feʔfeʔ (Mutaka and Tamanji 1995)*

Noun (sg)	Gloss
kàjê	'exercise book'
sìmî	'cement'
vɔ̂t	'vote'
tápèlè	'table'
pítʃà	'picture'
mòtòsákù	'motor cycle.'

(23) *Yoruba (Mutaka and Tamanji 1995)*   (24) *Ewondo*

Noun (sg)	gloss	Noun	Gloss
kɔ́nsónántì	'consonant'	lám	'blade'
kóódú	'code'	bǝlǝ́d	'bread'
jéndà	'gender'	fàdà	'father'
áséntì	'accent'	kə̀rɛ́	'chalk'
físìisì	'physics'	tórs	'torchlight'
fɔ́tò	'photo'		
fóníìmù	'phoneme'		
sílébù	'syllable'		

As a conclusion, we can say that loan adapted nouns will either mostly be put in a noun class with a zero singular nominal prefix or to a class that has a vowel or a syllabic nasal prefix.

Prosody

Unlike English and French, which are stress-timed languages, African languages are tonal. As a result, one of the loan adaptation strategies employed is to assign tone to words that are borrowed from either the English or French languages. We examine how this is done in the following lines.

As noted in Chumbow and Tamanji (1994) and Mutaka and Tamanji (1995), the general tendency is that receptor African languages tend to match stressed syllables bearing primary stress in the donor language with high tones and unstressed syllables with low tones. The data in (25) illustrate this.

(25)

	Borrowed word	Donor word	Donor language	Gloss
Fe'fe'				
a.	kàje	'cahier'	French	'book'
	sìmî	'ciment'	French	'cement'
	vɔ̂t	'vote'	French	'vote'
	tápɨlɛ	'table'	French	'table'
Kom				
b.	ájɔ̀jìn	aıən	English	'iron'
	bzɨ́lù	pıləʊ	English	'pillow'
	tábɨ̀lə̀	teıbəl	English	'table'
	bzɨ́bà	peıpə	English	'paper'
	táwùlà	taʊəl	English	'towel'
	tɛ́là	teılə	English	'tailor'
	tósin	θaʊznd	English	'thousand'
	fálà	faðə	English	'father'
Bafut				
c.	mátà	mæt	English	'mat'
	matsɨ́sɨ̀	mætʃıs	English	'matches'
	bábà	ba:bə	English	'barber'
	nómbà	nʌmbə	English	'number'
	tòrɨ́sà	traʊzə	English	'trouser'
	bɛ́bǎ	peıpə̣	English	'paper'
Mokpe				
d.	windǎ	wındəʊ	English	'window'
	máŋgò	mæŋgəʊ	English	'mango'
	bɔ́là	bɔ:l	English	'ball'

Notice that in the case of words that are borrowed from the English language with stress on the first syllable, high tones are also assigned to those syllables when the words come to African languages. In the case of the Feʔfeʔ data, most of the words are borrowed from French whose words are generally stressed on the final syllable except when the final syllable contains a [ə]. We notice here that high tones assigned to the final syllables except in tapèlè 'table' from French [table]. The initial syllable contains a stress because the original word also contained a stress on that syllable.

Inserted vowels are generally assigned low tones whereas high tones are generally assigned to vowels that are stressed in the source language. This explains why the inserted initial vowels in the Bafut data below are assigned low tones whereas the root vowels carry high tones.

(26)

Bafut

à - bɔ̀sà	'purse'
à - tàbúrə̀	'tarpaulin'
à - kànú/ú	'canoe'
à-wàsɨbɨtà	'hospital'
à -bɔ́kɛ́	'bucket'
à -kàtàbílà	'caterpillar'

Phrasal falling intonation in the donor language is marked by a low tone. This explains why the Kom loan adapted words in (27) below have falling tones on the final syllables.

(27)

Kom

bîlêd	'bread'	fîlâs	'flask'
tôs	'torch lamp'	lâm	'lamp'
tʃôs	'church'	wâs	'watch'
kût	'coat'	dʒɔ̂k	'jug'
kâ	'car'	bzê	'pear'
lûm	'room'		

Summary of Findings

Since loan adaptation seems to be constrained and conditioned by morpheme structure constraints (Chumbow and Tamanji 1994), characteristic features of loan adaptation arrived at in this study are best presented along the lines of the two main components of morpheme structure constraints: segmental structure and sequence structure constraints (Schane 1973). We, therefore, close this work with a summary of our findings along these lines.

Characteristics Due to Segment Structure Constraints

Phonetically Similar Sounds

The first point to make here is that segments of a foreign lending language not attested in the receptor language are systematically replaced by other attested segments, sharing with the foreign segments a high degree of phonetic similarity (as evident in the number of shared distinctive features between the two). This is summarized in (28) below:

(28)

English	Mankon/ Pidgin	English	Donor A	Receptor B
'cup'	kʌp	kɔ́b(ə)	ʌ	ɔ
'purse'	pɜːs	pɔ́sà	ɜ	ɔ
'pan'	pæn	mân	æ	a
'foot'	fʊt	fût	ʊ	u
'sit (down)'	sɪt(daʊn)	sǐdɔ́ŋ	ɪ	i
'thick'	θɪk	tîk	θ	t
'thunder'	θʌndə	tóndà	θ	t
'brother'	brʌθə	bùrɔ́dà	ð	d
'vowel'	vaʊəl	fáwèli(Yoruba)	v	f

An inspection of the sounds of an IPA chart and the distinctive feature/matrix will indicate that the sounds of the donor language in A have a high degree of phonetic similarity with those of the receptor language in B.

Diphthong and Triphthongs Simplification

Diphthongs and triphthongs, generally unattested in African languages, tend to be monophthongs or simplified in one of two possibilities. This is summarized in (29) below.

29a. Simple monophthongs

	English	African Language	Gloss
aɪ → a	kaɪn	kan	'kind'
əʊ → o	kəʊt	kóti	'coat'
aʊ → ɔ	paʊdə	póda	'powder'
eɪ → e	təmeɪtəʊ	tɔ̀métò	'tomato'

29b. Glide formation and disyllabification

	English	African Language	Gloss
ɔɪ → ɔj	bɔɪ	bɔ̂j	'boy'
ɪə → jɛ/ja	ɪərɪŋ	jɛrɪŋ/jarɪŋ	'earring'

	fɪə	fjə/ fja	'fear'
auə → awa	flauə	filawa	'flower'
	auə	awa	'hour'
ɔɪə → ɔɪə/ɔja	lɔɪə	lɔja	'lawyer'

High vowels of diphthongs (in the case of (b)) become corresponding glides and, ipso facto, modifying the syllable structure of loan words. The structures in (30) below are illustrative of this fact.

	English	Bafut	
ɪə → jɛ/ja	ɪə rɪ ŋ V – CV C	jɛ ri ŋ CV– CV C	'earring'
auə → awa	f l auə C C V	fɨ la wa CV–CV CV	'flower'
	auə V	a wa V CV	'hour'

Prosody Harmonization

Since most African languages are tone languages while English and French (the main sources of borrowing) are stress-timed, the conversion of stress to tone in loanwords is generally characterized by the following rules:

(31) (i)
  a. stressed syllables bear high tone
  b. unstressed syllables bear low tone
  c. inserted vowels bear low tone
     (ii) other tone rules in the language are applicable

Adaptation Characteristics Due to Sequence Structure Constraints

Cluster Simplification

By far the most important sequence structure adjustment that loan words have to undergo is consonant cluster simplification arising from the fact that most African languages either do not allow a contiguous sequence of consonants at all, or do allow only a restricted combination of much consonant sequences.

Theoretically, to conform to these sequence structure constraints, loan words that violate it can be made to achieve consonant cluster simplification either by (i) consonant deletion by which a CCV(C) syllable (or word) structure becomes CVC[4] or by (ii) vowel insertion whereby a CCV(C) structure becomes CVCV(C).

The cross-linguistic data examined in this chapter indicates a general preference for vowel insertion with two variations as follows:

a. Languages with Coda Syllable Structure (CVC or VC):

Two processes are required to satisfy segment structure constraints.

(32)

(i) A rule of epenthesis that inserts a vowel between consonants to break up consonant clusters (within or across syllable and word boundaries): $\emptyset \rightarrow V/C\text{-}C$

(ii) A rule of prothesis that adds a vowel to a syllable or word final consonant to avoid closed syllables:

$$\emptyset \rightarrow V/(C)\ V\ C - \begin{Bmatrix} C \\ \# \end{Bmatrix}$$

b. Languages with Codaless Syllables, i.e., Open Syllables of the Canonical Shape (C) V:

In such languages, only the first rule (epenthesis) applies and the second rule does not apply because its structural description is not met (since there are no closed syllables in the language). The type of vowel to be inserted in the two rules above is an empirical issue to be determined by cross-language data. The evidence presented so far indicates that /ɨ/ a high central unrounded vowel or /i/ high front unrounded vowel where the former is unattested, are epenthetic or prothetic, as appropriate, in many languages. However, there is evidence that in languages where vowel harmony operates, the vowel to be inserted may be determined by the harmonic categories involved in the vowel harmony process or by consonant properties of the consonant sequences to be broken up. This explains (in part, at least) why Bafut (language with no harmony) differs from Yoruba (a language with a partial vowel harmony) system, as illustrated below:

(33)

English	Bafut	Yoruba	Gloss
brɛd	bɨrédɨ	bùrédi	'bread'
krɪsməs	kɨrísɨmɨsɨ	kèrísíméṣɨ	'Christmas'
skul	sɨkúlɨ	sìkúlu	'school'
mæθmatɪk	màtɨmátɨkɨ	màtɨmátíki	'mathematics'
brʌðə	bɨlɔ́dà	bùrɔ́dà	'brother'

Other Forms of Adjustments

Loan words tend to conform to other morphological characteristics of the borrowing language. These include, for instance, noun class and related concord morphemes in Bantu noun and verb morphology:

i. With respect to noun morphology, borrowed nouns are generally assigned to a noun class that has no nominal prefixes in the singular, especially gender ½ otherwise they are assigned to other classes with a vowel or syllabic nasal as nominal prefix.

ii. In general, in loan adaptation, morphological alternation tends to be reduced or simplified to a minimum. Thus a language with ten to fifteen productive noun classes may retain only one or two for all loan words. The implication of this for terminological creation or lexical expansion in language planning to express new knowledge in science and technology is clear. Loan words in the borrowing mechanisms of lexical expansion can be legitimately and systematically standardized into one (or two) noun classes.

While the discussions in this chapter cannot claim to be exhaustive, it is hoped that avenues for further cross language exploration of highly diversified language families have been identified to generate interest and further research, leading to universal constraints that can clarify the issues in loan adaptation as well as serve the interest of output- oriented and computer-based theories like the Optimality Theory (OT).

Conclusion

This chapter set out to examine cross-language characteristics of the mechanisms of loan adaptation in African languages with particular reference to Bantu languages of Cameroon and occasionally input from Yoruba (a Kwa language) and other languages in an attempt to build what could be ultimately termed the universals of loan adaptation in African languages.

Notes

1. We have used the term 'universal' here with a limitation to African languages only, which share a number of structural characteristics, which non-African languages do not. It should, therefore, not be perceived as referring to all the world languages.
2. For a detailed description of the other mechanisms of lexical expansion commonly employed by African languages, see Chumbow and Tamanji (1994), Mutaka and Tamanji (1995).
3. [zr] and [ʒr] are some kind of retroflex sounds.
4. Witness for instance k- deletion in Yoruba: æk-sɛnt (CVC-CV from English VC-CVCC) kən-sɔ-nænt→ kən-sɔ-nænti.

References

Chumbow, B.S. and Tamanji, P. N., 1994, 'Development of Terminology in African Language: Mechanisms of Lexical Expansion', Paper presented at the First Mozambican Workshop on Educational Use of African Languages and the Role of LWCS. Maputo, Mozambique, 21-23 November.

Enoachuo, E., 2002, 'The Development of a Thematic Glossary for Kenyang', an MA Thesis, University of Buea.

Ito, Junko, 1988, *Syllable Theory in Prosodic Phonology*, New York: Garland Press.

Keh, Victorine, 2000, 'The Phonology and Morphology of Borrowed Words in Kom', a B.A. Long Essay, University of Buea.

Mfonyam, J.N., 1989, 'Tone in Orthography. The Case of Bafut and Related Languages', a doctorat d'Etat Dissertation, University of Yaounde.

Mutaka, P.N. and Tamanji, P.N., 1995, 'Introduction to African Linguistics', Unpublished Manuscript, Université Catholique Centrale, ICY & University of Yaounde I.

Nangang, N.S., 2002, 'Morpho-Phonology of Borrowed Words in Ngamambo', a B. A. Long Essay, University of Buea.

Neba, Ayu'nwi N., 1998, 'Tone in the Bafut Noun Phrase', an MA Thesis, University of Buea.

Numfor, C. N., 1999, 'A Thematic Glossary of **Bîfĩ** an MA Thesis, University of Buea.

Schane, Sanford, 1973, *Generative Phonology*, New York: Prentice Hall Eaglewood Cliff,.

Section IV

Syntax

20

Feature Checking in Optional Wh-Phrasal Movement in Denya

Samson Negbo Abangma

Introduction

In this chapter, we claim that Denya exhibits optional wh-phrasal movements. The analysis and the explanations are given in terms of the Minimalist assumptions (Chomsky 1993, 1995). Following Pesetsky (2000:2), we shall use the term movement or displacement to describe a situation where a syntactic unit, for example, a word or phrase 'appears to occupy more than one position in syntactic structure and is pronounced in a position where we do not expect it to be pronounced'. In this respect, it is not additionally pronounced in its expected 'trace' position.

The wh-phrasal movement is probably one of the best-studied instances of displacement/movement in English and other languages (Chomsky 1970; May 1977, 1985; Huang 1981, 1982; etc.). Rizzi (1990), Cinque (1990), Lasnik & Saito (1992), and Mazini (1992) consider the example of overt wh-phrasal movement in English.

(1) Which car did John give t (a) to his wife?

In this example, the wh-phrase is pronounced in its position in front of the clause/question, although we know that it originates as object of the verb 'give'. This position is marked t (a), its trace, and where it is assumed to be interpreted.

The Issue

It is well documented within the generative tradition, especially the Principles and Parametres model, that cross-linguistically, wh-phrasal movement is probably parametric variation. There are languages like English where wh-movement is obligatory in overt syntax and others like Chinese (Huang 1982) where it is not possible, probably only covertly. The Minimalist assumptions (Chomsky 1993, 1995) favour covert movement. If we consider an economy principle like Procrastinate (Chomsky 1993) which favours covert movement over overt, all things being equal, we expect no movement to be overt. If movement is overt rather than covert, then it must have been forced to operate 'early' by some special requirement or need. Chomsky solves this riddle by postulating the mechanism of feature checking and by an appeal to the 'strong' feature analysis. In this connection, wh-phrases do not move for their own sake, but in order to check the strong wh-feature (-Q- in feature) in C, which they are attracted to. Where the features are not strong (i.e. weak), the wh-element would not have to move in order to do the checking. If the movement is not necessary, economy makes it impossible. The problem one faces in the case of languages like Denya, with respect to wh-phrasal movement is that the movement appears to be optional. In other words, the constituent which undergoes wh-movement in the interrogative clauses, subject, object or adjunct, may stay in situ as in (2a) or appear at the beginning of the sentence/clause as in (2b).

(2)
a. | Eva | a-na | <u>ndé</u> |
| Eva | AGR-buy | what. |
| What | did | Eva buy? |

b. | Ndé | Eva | á- na- mé |
| What | Eva | AGR buy. |
| What | did | Eva buy? |

Considering that (2a,b) mean exactly the same in equivalent discourse contexts, Abangma (1987, 1992) concluded that wh-movement in Denya must be an optional process. This conclusion is purely intuitive. Accepting that wh-phrasal movement is an optional operation in the language, one still has a number of issues/questions to answer. Some of these include:

- What evidence is there to confirm this claim?
- Can the same language have 'strong' and 'weak' features in a given checking domain?
- Although optionality of wh-movement can explain cross-linguistic variations, is it permissible within a given language?

In this chapter, an attempt will be made to answer these questions. As regards the optionality of wh-constituents, empirical evidence will be given to support our claim. Seizing on Denham's (1997) suggestion, I will explain that the source of optionality in wh-movement in the language is due to the presence or absence of the functional head, C, in the numeration. If the numeration includes C, the derivation will involve obligatory raising of the wh-element to spec-CP. However, where the numeration does not involve C, then the wh-phrase will remain in situ.

Basic Data and Analysis

In this section, we present data as supporting evidence to the claim that wh fronting in Denya is wh-phrasal movement, a process different from topicalization, focalization and clefting.

The first diagnostic of wh-movement is meaning diagnostic.

(3)
a. Eva   a-nye   ndé
    Eva   AGR-eat   what.
    What   did Eva   eat?
b. Ndé   Eva   á-nyɛɛ e?   t (a) ?
    What   Eva   AGR-eat
    What   did   Eva eat?

(4)
a. Eva   a-do   waá
    Eva   AGR-beat   who
    Who   did   Eva beat?

Consider the following sentences:
b. Waá   Eva   á-   doó   t(a)i ?
    Who   Eva   AGR   beat
    Who   did   Eva   beat?

(5)
a. Eva a-belé   ŋka   yá   nde   mbaá
     Eva AGR-keep   money my   what   place
     Where did   Eva   keep my   money?
b. nde mbaá Eva á-belé   ŋka   yá
     Where Eva   AGR-keep   money my
     Where did   Eva   keep my   money?

In the above, the (a) examples have the wh-phrase in its base-generated position. While in the (b) examples the wh-elements are fronted. In other words, they have been displaced or moved. From the translations given, the pair of sentences has exactly the same meaning. If we accept the suggestion (Denham 2000) that if two sentences with the same lexical items have identical meanings and are discourse equivalents, then an optional process must relate them, we can conclude that wh-phrasal movement is an optional process in the language. On the contrary, if two sentences with the same lexical items differ in meaning in the same way, then they are not likely to be related by an optional process.

Compare the following sentences in (b).

(6)
a. Eva   a-do   ɛnó
    Eva   AGR-beat   Eno
    Eva   beat   Eno

b. Eno,   Eva   a-do
    Eno,   Eva   AGR-beat
    Eva,   Eno   beat

c. ɛnó   ne   Eva   á-doó
    Eno   that   Eva   AGR-beat
    It is Eno that Eva beat.

d. le   ɛnó   ne   Eva   á-doó
    It   Eno   that   Eva   beat
    It is Eno that Eva beat.

If we compare (6a) and (6b), we notice that the two sentences have the same lexical items but they do not have the same meaning. The fronting of the object NP, makes (a) prominent and emphatic. The (b) example does not mean the same as the (a) example. The same is true of (6c) where the fronted object NP is followed by a focus marker *ne*. This means that the two sentences do not mean the same. The process of focalization relates the two sentences.

In (6d), the fronted object is not only focused but also clefted. *le*, as the clefted marker, precedes the fronted object NP.

We have shown that wh-phrases can occur in situ and in spec-CP. The position of wh-phrases is variable. In other words, wh-phrases have the freedom of movement. This is not true of non-wh-phrases, as (7) below demonstrates.

(7)
a. Eva   a-nyɛ   ∈risi
    Eva   AGR-eat   rice
    Eva   ate   rice.

b. *Erisi   Eva   á-nyɛ
    Rice   Eva   AGR-eat
    *Rice   Eva   eat.

c. ∈ risi   ∈-nyε Eva

In (7b), the fronting of the object NP results in ungrammaticality except it is given an emphatic or focused meaning. In (7c), it will be grammatical if it is given the improbable meaning of the rice eating Eva.

The point we wish to emphasize here is that since non-wh-nominals do not have the same variable positions as wh-phrases, there is wh-movement.

Feature Checking and Wh-Phrasal Movement

In the Minimalist Programme (Chomsky 1993, 1995), the property of displacement is thought of as movement or attraction which is driven by the need to eliminate uninterpretable morphological features in lexical items through the mechanism of feature checking. As Pesetsky (2000:9) remarks, 'Chomsky's (1995) proposal starts with the idea that movement is a 'repair strategy' by which an interpretable F on a head K is deleted in response to movement to K of another instance of F (typically an interpretable instance of F). Failure to repair a structure that contains an uninterpretable feature renders the derivation non-convergent. Movement for any other reason is 'banned'.

It is claimed (Chomsky 1995, Uriagereka 2000, Pesetsky 2000, etc.) that the feature that triggers wh-phrasal movement in English is not only uninterpretable but also strong and, therefore, has to be erased after it is selected. As Uriagereka (2000:367) notes, wh- elements do not move for their own sake, but in order to check the strong Q-feature in Comp, which they are attracted to.

Consider (10a) below with its structure in (10b).

(10)
 a. **What did John buy?**
 b. [CP [CØ [IP John I [VP [V buy [DP what]

Attracts wh-features

In the above example, we have to assume a Q (question) feature in Comp is attracting a wh-feature in the wh-element, forcing the wh-element into a checking domain of Comp. The reason why the wh-element can move at all is that its wh-features are interpretable and, as such, always accessible to CHL. Of course, this justifies the movement/attraction in terms of the Last Resort Condition (LRC) since the moved wh-phrase does emerge in checking relation with one of the sub-labels of the hosting Comp, which attracts the wh-element to check its strong features. So English wh-elements move because the Q in Comp is strong. In some languages like Chinese (Chomsky 1993, 1995, Uriagereka 2000, Ura 2000, Huang; 1982, etc., a wh-element does not have to be moved to C since in this type of language a wh-feature cannot be moved/attracted to C. As we very well know, if movement is not necessary, economy makes it impossible.

From the illustrations in English and Chinese, we can conclude that categories which move by PF in one language do not move at all in another, not even at LF.

The explanation given about obligatory wh-movement in English root clauses and wh- in situ in Chinese ones appears satisfactory and suggests parametric variation cross linguistically. The point of view expressed so far is Chomsky's (1995) who argues that +interpretable features, such as wh-, will only ever require checking when strong on a functional head. This brings us back to the question of optional wh-movement in Denya. If, as Chomsky claims for English that wh-phrases move in overt syntax because they carry +interpretable, +strong features requiring checking, it remains unexplained why Denya should at one moment allow wh-movement and at another allow wh-in situ. Simpson (2000) attempts to explain this phenomenon in Iraqi Arabic, when he argues that wh-phrases cross linguistically carry wh-features in need of checking. He stresses that 'the relevant features which are checked by movement of a wh-phrase are wh-features on the wh-phrase itself and not among operator features in Comp'. He argues that if this were not the case, then wh-raising to Comp would have to take place in all wh-questions. Iraqi Arabic is similar to Denya in this respect. His other main argument is that although it is accepted that wh-features carried by wh-phrases must be checked prior to spell-out, raising to Comp is not forced where a wh-phrase occurs base-generated in the tense domain of +Qcomp and a wh-phrase remains in situ. Since Simpson assumes that all wh-features on wh-phrases must be checked somehow, how are the features on wh- in situ checked since the wh-phrase will not be in a Spec-head relation in order to obey the Strict Locality Condition (SLC) required for such checking to take place. Simpson argued, using Iraqi Arabic data, that it must be conceded that not being in the specifier of the checking head (C°) at the point in which wh-checking takes place, it be accepted that 'feature checking is in fact not subject to Strict Locality Condition'. Simpson's explanation attempts to account for the licensing of wh-phrases, but fails to account for arbitrariness in the choice of either raised wh-phrase to Comp or remaining in the base-generated position.

In the rest of this chapter, following the suggestion by Denhams (1997, 2000), I shall argue that the possibility of a language like Denya having optional wh-phrasal movement should be imputed to the presence or absence of C in the numeration upon which the derivational outcome is based. In other words, the selection of C from the lexicon is optional in wh-questions in Denya. What is the motivation for such a point of view? The Minimalist assumptions encourage the free selection of lexical and functional items from the lexicon to form a given numeration. Also, an economy principle like (11) (Chomsky 1995:294) gives a leeway to explaining this rather baffling situation of optionality in a theory that discourages it.

(11) a enters into a numeration only if it has an effect on output.

We do claim here that two derivations succeed in Denya wh-questions because the arrays of items selected from the lexicon and constituting the numeration for each question are distinct. One numeration contains C while the other does not. The one that contains C will result in wh-movement to check off the wh-features in C.

Summary and Conclusion

In this chapter, we have attempted to demonstrate that Denya exhibits the properties of optional wh-movement/attraction. In doing this, we have shown that the fronting of wh-phrases in the language is a different process from topicalization, focusing and clefting. It was explained that the phenomenon of optional wh-movement was due to the fact that in the language C may or may not be selected from the lexicon in a resultant numeration. Whatever the case, both options lead to convergent derivations.

It was earlier argued that Chomsky (1995) feature 'strength analysis' might account for cross-linguistic variation between English type languages where wh-movement is obligatory and Chinese-type languages where wh-movement is barred. But it poses problems where such variation is within a single language. We further observed that Simpson's (2000) attempt to account for the same phenomenon in Iraqi Arabic and some other languages by relaxing the Strict Locality Condition on feature checking, does not appear to solve the problem. There is some degree of arbitrariness in deciding when C must be selected for the SLC to apply, and when wh-elements must remain in situ and have the SLC relaxed.

References

Abangma, S.N., 1987, 'Modes in Denya Discourse', Dallas: SIL & University of Texas at Arlington.

Abangma, S.N., 1992, 'Empty Categories in Denya', PhD Thesis, University of London.

Chomsky, N., 1970, 'Remarks on Nominalisation', in R. Jacobs and E. Rosenbaum, eds, *Readings in English Transformational Grammar*, Waltham, Mass: Ginn and co.

Chomsky, N., 1977, 'On Wh-Movement', in T. Cullicover et al., eds, *Formal Syntax*, New York: Academic Press.

Chomsky, N., 1993, 'Minimalist Program for Linguistic Theory', in K. Hale, & S. J. Keyser, eds, *The View from Building 20*, Cambridge, Mass.: MIT Press.

Chomsky, N., 1995, *The Minimalist Program*, Cambridge, Mass.: MIT Press.

Cinque, G., 1990, *Types of Dependencies*, Cambridge, Mass.: MIT Press.

Denham, K., 1997, *A Minimalist Account of Optional Wh-Movement*, PhD Dissertation, University of Washington.

Denham, K., 2000, 'Optional Wh-Movement in Babine WITSU WITEN', in *Natural Language and Linguistic Theory* 18.1, 198-251.

Huang, J., 1981, 'Move Wh- in a Language without Wh-Movement', in *The Linguistic Review* 1, 396-416.

Huang, J., 1982, *Logical Theory in Chinese and the Theory of Grammar*, Cambridge, Mass.: MIT Press.

Lasnik, H. & Saito, M., 1992, *Move a: Conditions on Its Application and Output*, Cambridge, Mass.: MIT Press.

Manzini, M.R., 1992, *Locality*, Cambridge, Mass.: MIT Press.

May, R., 1977, 'The Grammar of Quantification', PhD Dissertation, Cambridge, Mass.: MIT Press.

May, R., 1985, *Logical Form*, Cambridge, Mass.: MIT Press.

Pesetsky, D., 2000, *Phrasal Movement and Its Kin*, Cambridge, Mass.: MIT Press.

Rizzi, L., 1990, *Relativized Minimality*, Cambridge, Mass.: MIT Press.

Simpson, A., 2000, 'Wh-Movement, licensing and Locality of Feature Checking', in D. Adger et al., eds, *Specifiers: Minimalist Approaches*, Oxford: OUP.

Ura, H., 2000, *Checking Theory and Grammatical Functions in Universal Grammar*, Oxford: Oxford University Press.

Uriageraka, J., 2000, *Rhyme and Reason*, Cambridge, Mass.: MIT Press.

21

Constituent Structure of the Associative Construction in Grassfields Bantu

Pius N. Tamanji and Gratiana L. Ndamsah

Introduction

The associative construction (N of N structure) is a characteristic feature of Grassfields Bantu languages, which offers interesting research possibilities. Its treatment in the literature has, however, been limited since researchers do not explore, in depth, the various semantic interpretations and structural relations attested in this rather peculiar construction. Many research endeavours focus only on the possessive relation to which they invariably attribute the structure of a genitive construction. Many other semantic and pragmatic relations, such as theme, agent, source, material make-up, etc., are neglected and, consequently, the related interesting phrase structure representations are not often highlighted.

This chapter attempts an in-depth examination of the constituent structure and related pragmatic/semantic interpretations of the associative construction in Grassfields Bantu, using Bafut and Limbum for illustration. We analyse the different semantic interpretations attested and propose that in a framework that seeks to preserve some form of isomorphic relation between form and meaning, the various semantic relations should be captured differently in the phrase structure (PS) representations. The PS representations posited explain the intriguing patterns of agreement observed in the associative construction. Especially, we are able to account for why despite the intrinsic relations between the head noun and the associative noun; there is no agreement between the two.

In the first section of the chapter, we present a broad outline of the structure of the associative construction. The first section focuses on the status and function of the associative morpheme (AM). In the second, we present the different semantic and pragmatic interpretations attested in the associative construction and posit a PS representation for each interpretation. Next, we discuss agreement proposing that the absence of agreement between the head noun and the associative noun follows from the *Feature Uniqueness Condition* (Tamanji 2001) and requirements of Merge (Carstens 2000). Finally, we conclude the chapter with the observation that this analysis that focuses on Grassfields Bantu can easily extend to other Bantu languages spoken in Cameroon.

Structure of the Associative Construction

The associative construction in Grassfields Bantu, on the surface, subdivides into two classes. In one, the genitive relation between the head noun and the dependent (associative) noun is marked by a segmentally realized associative morpheme (AM), while in the other, the AM is not segmentally realized.

(1) Bafut

a. nǐ-bɔ́ʔɔ́ n.í tsítsa   b. ǹ-dá tsítsà
    pumpkin AM teacher   house teacher
    'A teacher's pumpkin'.   'A teacher's house'.

(2) Limbum

a. r-bɔ́ʔɔ́ y.í tícà   b. ǹ-dáp tíca
    pumpkin AM teacher   house teacher
    'A teacher's pumpkin.'   'A teacher's house.'

The structural difference between (1a) and (1b/2) leaves one with the false impression that we are dealing here with two different constructions similar to Free State and Construct State Nominals in Semitic (Ritter 1987). This structural difference is only illusory. In both examples, the head noun is linked to the second by an AM but, whereas the AM in (1a) is made up of a consonant plus vowel plus tone, in (1b and 2), it is marked by a floating tone only.

It has been established for most Bantu languages that the AM that links nouns of various classes to the associative noun is simply tonal (see Hyman 1977; Mfonyam 1989; Nkemnji 1995; Boum 1980). The following is a representative sample of genitive morphemes from four Bantu languages, including Bafut and Limbum. The letters *L* and *H* represent low and high tonal AMs. The Nweh examples are adapted from Nkemnji (1995); the Befang from Boum (1980).

Table 1. Genitive Morphemes in four Bantu Languages

LAN / Noun Class	Bafut	Limbum	Nweh	Befang
1	L		L	L
2	bɨ			bə́
3	N			ú
4				kə́
5	nɨ́		H	é
6	mɨ		H	á
7	á		á	á
8	ɨ́			ó
9	N		L	L
10	H			e
19	fɨ			fó

Notice that in all four languages the AM for classes 1 and 9 is an L tone. In Bafut, classes 7, 8 and 10 are marked by a vowel/nasal plus H tone and classes 3 and 9 are marked by a vowel/nasal plus L tone. On the surface, the vowel/nasal segment is deleted leaving the tone that then associates to the final syllable of the first noun in the associative construction if it is H. The L tonal genitive morpheme, on the other hand, remains floating, provoking downstep on following H tones.[1] In the following examples, we illustrate the association of an H associative tone in Bafut. Example (3) contains nouns in their citation forms with each syllable bearing its underlying tone. Examples (4-6) show the nouns in association.

(3)

à-bàa 'bag',   ɨ̀-bàŋ   'retaining walls',
ɨ̀-bɔ̀ʔɔ 'mushroom',   ø-tsítsa   'teacher.'

(4)
à-báá tsítsa
bag   teacher
'A teacher's bag'

(5)
ɨ̀-báŋ   tsítsà
retaining walls   teacher
'A teacher's retaining walls.'

(6)
ɨ̀-bɔ̀ʔɔ́   tsítsa
mushroom   teacher
'A teacher's mushroom'

Whereas, in (3), the final syllables of the nouns bear an L tone, in (4-6) they bear an H tone. The change from an L to an H tone is accounted for if we assume that in the underlying form there was an H tonal morpheme which resulted from the deletion of a segment. In the surface realization, this H tone associates to the final syllable of N1 delinking the underlying L tone.

This leads to the conclusion that the two types of associative construction in (1 and 2) are structurally identical. In both types the head noun is linked to the associative noun by an AM that in some cases is marked by a floating tonal morpheme that results from the loss of an associative vowel/nasal. Since tones cannot be realized independently of a segment, the tonal AM associates to the first noun and, as such, the construction appears to be missing an AM.[2] At this stage in the discussion, one could temporarily propose the following underlying structure for the associative construction.

(7) [N1 [AM N2]] (N1 = head noun, AM = associative morpheme, N2 = genitive noun)

We will provide a detailed representation of this structure below after analysing the syntactic status and role of what we have referred to as the associative morpheme (AM). In the rest of the discussion, the expression 'head noun' will be used to refer to N1, and N2 will be referred to as the 'genitive noun'.

Role and Syntactic Status of the Associative Morpheme

The associative morpheme (AM) has been referred to variously in the literature as a relational element (Carstens 1991), an associative morpheme (following Bantuist tradition) (Mfonyam 1989; Ambe 1989; Nkemnji 1995), a genitival connective (Vitale 1981), etc. Most often, it is referred to simply as an agreement/concord element (see Hyman 1979, 1981). The fact that the segmental content of the AM in, for example, some Bafut associative constructions are identical to the prefix of the head noun makes it tempting to analyse it simply as an agreement marker. We argue that the AM is not simply an agreement marker but the surface realization of a complex unit comprising an AM and a concord consonant.

An empirical fact which argues against treating the AM simply as an agreement marker comes from comparing its form to that of the adjective prefix. Compare the form of the adjective prefix in (8) to that of the AM in (9).

BAFUT

(8) a. bɨ̀-lūʔū bɨ́.sɨ́gɨ̀nɨ̀   b. nɨ̀-bɔ̀ʔɔ̀ nɨ́.sɨ́gɨ̀nɨ̀
    2-spoons 2-nice   5-pumpkin 5-nice
    'Nice spoons.'   'A nice pumpkin.'

(9)
a. bɨ-lūʔū bɨ́
    2-spoons 2-AM 1-teacher
    'A teacher's spoons.'

b. ø-tsítsà
    5-pumpkin 5-AM 1-teacher
    'A teacher's pumpkin.'

The claim that the AM is an agreement morpheme stems from the observation that its segmental form is identical to that of the nominal prefix of the head noun. This suggests that the agreement marker is simply a copy of the nominal prefix of the head noun. If agreement is a copy of the nominal prefix of the head noun, the minimal expectation is that, in the examples in (8), the morpheme preceding the adjective should be identical to the prefix of the head noun. We, however, notice that in addition to a tonal difference (the adjective prefix has a high tone while the nominal prefix has a low tone) the adjective prefix takes the vowel i while the nominal prefix takes the vowel [ɨ]. Also, observe that a change in the class of the head noun entails a change in the consonant of the adjective prefix. We propose that the adjective prefix is the surface realization of two morphemes: a class plus number agreement element [cɨ] and a morpheme [i] that links the adjective to the head noun. Let us call the latter an adjective vowel. The number plus class agreement morpheme combines with the adjective vowel as sketched below to yield the surface adjective prefix.

(10)

    cɨ̀   í   → cí-
    Num + Class   Adj. Vowel   Adj. Prefix

In the process, the vowel of the number/class agreement morpheme is deleted, and the adjective prefix which surfaces is a combination of the number/class agreement consonant [c] and the adjective vowel [í].

To return to the AM, and pursuing the line of argument developed above for the adjective prefix, it makes sense to claim that the AM in the examples in (9) is the surface realization of a number plus class agreement morpheme [cɨ] and an associative vowel [ɨ], which establishes the associative relation between the head noun and the associative noun. The combination of the morphemes is sketched out below.

(11)

    cɨ̀   ɨ́   → Cɨ
    Num + Ass. Vowel   AM

The vowel and tone of the number/class agreement element is deleted and the AM surfaces as a combination of the number/class agreement consonant plus the associative vowel.[3] The form of the agreement consonant depends on the class of the head noun.

Having determined the parts of the associative morpheme, we can now examine its syntactic status and function. At first sight, at least from the translation of an associative construction such as (12), it seems reasonable to claim that the AM is a preposition similar to 'of' in English or 'de/di' in Romance.

BAFUT

(12)

a. nɨ̀-bɔ̀/ɔ n.ɨ́ m-fɔ̀ ny.a   b. bɨ̀-lū/ū b.ɨ́ m-fɔ̀ by.a
   pumpkin AM chief the   spoons AM chief the
   'The pumpkins of a chief.'   'The spoons of a chief.'

A closer look, however, reveals that the associative morpheme is not a preposition. First of all, prepositions in Bafut do not bear agreement morphology. Thus, in a construction like (13), for instance, the preposition nɨ́ 'with' relates a head noun to a following noun just like the associative morphemes nɨ́ and bɨ in (12), but it does not agree with the head noun.

BAFUT

(13)

a. m-àŋgyè nɨ́ mɨ̀-tʃe   b. bɨ̀-fɔ̀ nɨ́ mɨ̀-tʃè
    women with wisdom   chiefs with wisdom
    'Wise women.'   'Wise chiefs (village sages).

Agreement on prepositions is, however, not altogether unprecedented since something like it is attested in Celtic and Berber languages. There is, however, a significant difference in that, in these languages, the agreement-like property holds with respect to the object of the preposition. In the Bafut examples in (12), agreement is with the head noun and not with the object of the associative morpheme. Treating the associative morpheme in Bafut as a preposition, therefore, seems untenable first because ordinary prepositions in Bafut do not bear agreement and second because where Bafut appears to pattern with Celtic and Berber languages, the associative morpheme agrees with the head noun and not with its object.

We will treat the associative morpheme simply as relational element that links the associative noun to the head noun and also establishes the associative relation between the two. The fact that this element links the two nouns can at least explain why it bears agreement determined by the head noun. In the syntax, the relational element projects a functional projection which we refer to as a genitive phrase (GenP). Based on the foregoing, we propose the following tentative structure for the associative construction in Grassfields Bantu. It does not matter for present purposes whether the genitive phrase is a complement

(14)

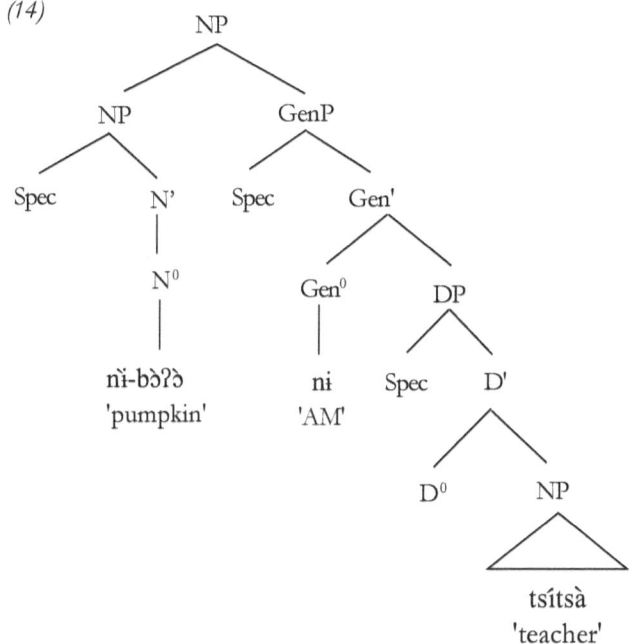

of the head noun or adjunct of NP. What is important is that the associative morpheme (AM) which is often treated in Bantu morphology as a simple agreement marker is actually a functional head category which projects an XP.

As the structure shows, the head of the associative construction (the noun) takes GenP as complement. GenP agrees with the head noun and the agreement is marked on the associative morpheme.

The Head of GenP Takes Another DP as Complement

To recapitulate, we have argued in this section that the AM is not an agreement marker, as is traditionally assumed in the literature on Bantu morphology. Rather, it is a functional element, akin to determiners, demonstratives and quantifiers, which is underlyingly comprised of a vowel segment only. In the surface form, this vowel segment takes on a number/class concord consonant determined by the morphological class of the head noun. Analysing the AM as a functional category at par with determiners led us to project a GenP headed by the AM. In the sections that follow, we focus on the relation of GenP to the head noun with a view to determining the structural positions of genitive phrases.

Genitive Relations

Genitive phrases stand in different relations to the head noun. Some simply modify the head nouns as possessors, some are frozen with the head noun into some sort of compound, others are arguments of the head noun and yet others are related to the head noun in ways that are difficult to describe. We discuss these different relations below proposing that, in a framework that seeks to preserve some kind of isomorphism between form and meaning, the different genitive phrases should occupy distinct positions in the phrase structure (PS) representation. This allows the PS system to capture the intuitive contrast between associative phrases and also provide a stepping-stone on which to build an analysis of nominalizations.

Genitives of Possession

The most common type of relation that holds between two members of an associative construction is a possessive type, where possessor must be understood in a very broad sense. This is the kind of relation that holds between the two members of the following:

(15) BAFUT

a. mɨ̀-lùʔù m.ɨ́ máŋgye
    wine   AM woman
    'A woman's wine.'

b. bɨ̀-lūʔū b.ɨ́ m-fɔ̀
    spoons AM chief
    'A chief's spoons.'

(16) LIMBUM

a.   nta'   muu
        chair   child
        'child's chair'

b. mta'   boo
    chairs children
    'children's chairs'

In these examples, the genitive phrase can be interpreted in one of two ways:

    (a) as a pure possessor, i.e., the entity to which the first noun belongs; and

    (b) as indicating a quality or distinguishing mark by which a person or a thing is characterized. It is adjectival (being a genitive of description or quality). Thus, for instance (15a) means 'wine belonging to a woman or a brand of wine that women like drinking (sweet wine) while (16a) means a chair belonging to a child or a chair meant for children to sit on'. What is, however, common between the two interpretations is that the genitive phrase answers the question 'which' and its meaning determines the reference of the entire associative construction.

Included in this group of genitives of possession is what we call *Genitives of Source/Origin* (following the Oxford English Dictionary) and *Classifying Genitives*. The genitive of source/origin indicates the person, thing or place from which N_1 comes, is acquired or sought. It also expresses racial, local or native origin, descent etc. or the notion of belonging to place as deriving a title from it as its ruler. The classifying genitive on the other hand is adjectival as it expresses a kind of quality. These relations are exemplified below:

Genitive of Source/Origin

(17) BAFUT

a. ŋ-ù (à)mēlíka
    person America
    'An American.'

b. fi-bwè f.i sōriwàtá
   fish AM ocean
   'Fish from the ocean.'

c. m-fɔ̄ bi-fii
   1-chief Bafut
   'The chief of Bafut'

(18) LIMBUM

a. muu   taŋ
    child   tang
    'child from Tabenken'

b. nyaa   riŋ
   animal   forest
   'animal from the forest'

Classifying Genitives

(19) LIMBUM   *(20) Bafut*

a. shaa   byeŋge
    cornbeer women
    'cornbeer of women'

b. laba' mboroŋ
   shoe Bororo
   'shoe of Bororo people'

ø-lú?ú m-fɔ̄
spoon chief
'A spoon typical of chiefs.'

The question we want to answer at this point is what the structural position of genitives of possession and genitives of source/origin is. The syntactic characteristics of these genitives give us a clue. One common characteristic of genitives of source/origin and the genitives of possession in (15-20) is that the relation between the genitive phrase and the head noun is not intrinsic in the sense that the choice of one noun does not depend on that of the other. The head noun and the genitive noun in both cases are like two distinct terms in a relation: two separate entities that are loosely related to each other. Another interesting property of the class is that, syntactically, genitives of possession and source are treated as denoting separate entities from the head noun. For instance, the possessor/source genitive noun can be pluralized independently of the head noun, can be post- or pre-modified, and can be pronominalized. We illustrate this in (21-23). The examples in (21-22) illustrate pluralization while those in (23) illustrate post-modification.

(21) LIMBUM

a. mbaŋ ŋku
    staff   chief
    'chief's 'staff'

b. mmbaŋ ŋku
   staffs   chief
   "chief's staffs"

c. mbaŋ   bku   d.   mmbaŋ   bku
    staff   chiefs   staffs   chiefs
    'chiefs' staff'   'chiefs' staffs'

(22) BAFUT

a. ø-lú?ú   m-fɔ   c. ø-lú?ú   bɨ-fɔ
    sing–spoon sing–chief   sing-spoon   pl-chief
    'A chief's spoon.'   'A spoon for chiefs.'

b. bɨ-lū?ū   bɨ m-fɔ   d. bɨ-lū?ū   bɨ bɨ-fɔ
    pl–spoon   AM sing–chief   pl-spoon   AM sing-chief
    'A chief's spoons.'   'Chiefs' spoons.'

The (a) examples show the head noun and the genitive noun in the singular form. In (b) and (c) one of the two is pluralized and in (d) both are pluralized.

The Limbum examples in (23) illustrate post-modification. Each of the nouns can be post-modified independently of the other.

(23). LIMBUM

a. muu   tang   c. muu   tang   mbo
    child Tabenken   child Tabenken plain
    'child from Tabenken'   'child from Tabenken plain'

b. muu ber   taŋ   d. muu ber   taŋ   mbo
    child tender Tabenken   child tender Tabenken plain
    'Baby from Tabenken'   'Baby from Tabenken plain'

In (23a), both nouns are not modified. In (b) and (c), one of them is post-modified and in (d) both are post-modified. These illustrations show us that, although the head noun and the genitive noun are in a relation, they are, in a way, independent of each other. The genitive phrase is not intrinsically linked to the head noun in the same way that [of John], for instance, is related to [father] in [father of John]. The genitive phrase is simply an adjunct modifier, which serves to describe/specify the type of the head noun in the same way that adjectives would attribute a quality to the head noun. Notice also that when used with another genitive phrase in the same construction, the genitive of possession/source is always further away from the head noun than the other genitive phrase. The examples in (24-25a) show a genitive of source in the same construction with another type of genitive. In (24-24b) the two genitives have switched positions and the construction is ungrammatical. The genitive of source is italicized.

(24) BAFUT

a. bɨ̀-tà b.ɨ́ Johnb.ɨ́ yàmndè   b. *bɨ̀-à b.ɨ́ yàmndè b.ɨ́ John
    fathers AM John AM Yaounde   fathers AM Yaounde AM John
    'John's fathers from Yaounde.'

(25) LIMBUM

a.   muu   Nfo   ta?   b.*   muu   taŋ   Nfo
    child   Nfor   Tabenken   child   Tabenken   Nfor
    "Nfor's child from tabenken"

Considering this linear order and the fact that possessor/source genitives are modificational adjuncts, we propose that, in the PS representation, a possessor/source genitive phrase is adjoined to NP as sketched out below. In the structure, we indicate the position of the other genitive phrase [of John] just for clarity. We return to a more detailed discussion of it later.

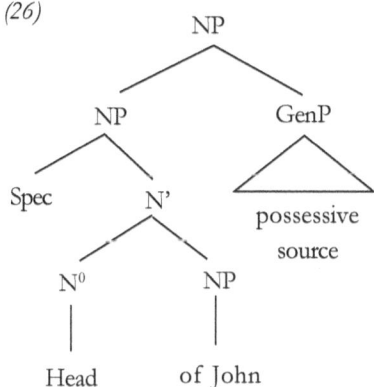

(26)

Compound Genitives

This class of genitives includes genitive phrases which are intrinsically linked to the head noun, where intrinsically linked means that they are treated along with the head noun as a unit, a sort of compound. The genitive phrases that constitute this class of compound genitives are presented below.

A. Genitives of Purpose/Place/Time

As the name indicates, these genitives indicate the purpose for which the referent of the head noun is used as well as the time and/or place generally associated with its use. Some examples are:

(27) LIMBUM

a. mcɛp tu [purpose]
   medicine head
   'Headache medicine'

b. cɛ' mbɛp [time]
   dress cold
   'dress used when it is cold'

(28) BAFUT

a.   fɨ-kùù f.ɨ n-dānwɨ̀ [place of use]
    bench AM church
    'A church bench.'

B. Genitives of Substance

These indicate the material of which something is made or consists of or holds/contains as a kind of extension of sense.

(29) BAFUT

a. ɨ̀-kùú (ɨ)-khɨ [material make-up]
   bed   cane
   'A cane bed.'

b. ǹ-tsɨ́ŋ ŋ-ki [content]
   bottle water
   'A water bottle.'

In the interpretation of the foregoing examples of compound genitives, the genitive phrase serves to restrict the reference of the head noun. In contrast to the identificatory relation in genitives of possession/source, the genitive noun, in this case, specifies the kind of the reference of the head noun. The semantic relation between the two nouns is such that the denotation of the construction as a whole is a subset of the denotation of the head noun alone.

    Other forms included in this class are kinship terms and some body parts such as:

(30) BAFUT

a. ǹ-tɨ́ɨ (à)-bo [body parts]
   heart hand
   'Palm of hand.'

b. m-ú n-tɔ̃ʔ ɔ
   child palace
   'Prince/princess.'

c. ǹ-dzààntɨ́ ø-tāà [kinship terms]
   sister   father
      'Aunt.'

A syntactic property that characterizes compound genitive constructions and which helps in determining their structural position, is that the genitive phrase is bound to the head noun. 'Bound' is used here in a morphological sense to mean that the genitive phrase is inseparable from the head noun. In the case of the genitives of possession and source/origin treated earlier, we observed a number of properties, which indicated that the head noun and the genitive phrase are two separate entities loosely linked together. Thus, for instance, each of the nouns could be freely pluralized, pre- or post-modified or pronominalized. Compound genitives do not exhibit this freedom. In the compound genitive construction, the genitive noun cannot be treated as a separate entity from the head noun. The two nouns are treated compositionally such that the overall meaning of the construction is the combined meanings of the head noun and the genitive noun. Inflections such as the plural morpheme as well as any modifiers in the construction are associated with the head noun only. As the examples below show, only the head noun can be pluralized in the compound genitive construction.

(31) BAFUT

a. ɨ̀-kùú (ɨ)-khɨ   b. mɨ̀-kùù m.ɨ́ (ɨ)-khɨ   c. *ɨ̀-kùú mɨ̀-khɨ
sing-bed sing-cane   pl-bed AM sing-cane sing-bed   pl-cane
   'A cane bed.'   'Cane beds.'

Also, only the head noun, but not the genitive noun, can be pre- or post-modified. In (32), 'small' can modify the head noun 'bed' but not the genitive noun 'cane'. In (33), the demonstrative can only modify the head noun (witness the agreement on the demonstrative), but not the genitive noun.

(32) BAFUT

a. múnchíri ɨ̀-kùú   (ɨ)-khɨ   b. *ɨ̀-kùú múnchíri (ɨ)-khɨ̀
   small sing-bed   sing-cane   bed   small
   'A small cane bed.'

(33) LIMBUM

a. cǎ' mbåp ana   b. bcɛ' mbɛp bwana   c. * bcɛ' mbɛp mwana
   dress cold that   dresses cold those   dresses cold those
   "That pullover"   "Those pullovers"

It is obvious that the genitive phrase in the compound genitive construction cannot be treated like the one in possessive genitive constructions. Specifically, the compound genitive phrase cannot be analysed as an adjunct/modifier like a possessive genitive. The compound genitive phrase, rather, appears to form a constituent with the head noun such that the plural morpheme in (31b) and the pre- and post-modifiers in (32-33) are actually associated with the entire construction and not just the head. If they appear to be associated with the head noun, it is simply because it is the head of the construction (see Hudson (1987) for a discussion along these lines in which inflections are generally located on the head of a constituent). Based on these observations, we propose that the genitive phrase is frozen with the head noun into a single constituent; a sort of compound. This proposal receives independent confirmation from pronominalization facts. In (34) below, it is possible to replace the entire genitive construction in (a) with an interrogative pronoun but not the head noun alone (c) or the genitive noun alone (d).

(34) LIMBUM

a. mɛ fyɛni cɛ' mbɛp
   I sell dress cold
   'I have sold the pullover'

b. mɛ fyɛni kɛɛ?
   I sell what
   'what have I sold?'

c. *mɛ fyɛni cɛ' kɛɛ?
   I sell dress what

d. *mɛ fyɛni kɛ cɛ?
   I sell what dress

If we have to ask a question relating to the kind of material, then we will have to add another morpheme, as in (25) below:

(35)
   mɛ fyɛni njɛr cɛ' kɛɛ?
   I sell kind dress what
   "What kind of dress have I sold?"

The sentences in (34c-d) are ungrammatical perhaps because the head noun and the genitive noun form an inseparable constituent, a compound. This constituent, as a whole, is the head of the NP as represented in the structure below.

(36)

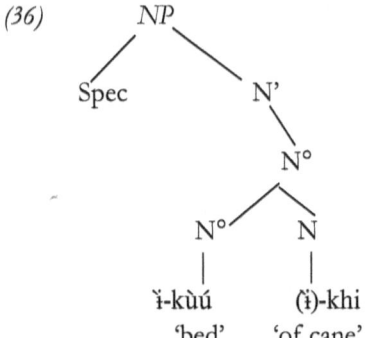

Dependent Genitives

Dependent genitives comprise genitive phrases that stand in a close relation to the head noun akin to the one between the verb and its object. Dependent genitives are interpreted as denoting separate entities from what the head noun denotes. However, the relation between the two entities is not as loose as that between the head noun and the possessor genitives in the sense that, in their distribution, the dependent genitive is always in a position adjacent to the head noun. At the same time, the relation between the two is not as close as that between the head noun and a compound genitive. Unlike the compound genitive, the dependent genitive is not frozen with the head noun. These properties will be exemplified and clarified as the discussion progresses. Let us first review relevant examples.

The most common type of dependent genitives are genitive phrases which mark inalienable possession. Some examples are given below.

(37) BAFUT

a. nɨ̀-lɨ́ʔɨ́ n.ɨ́ Suh   b. mɨ̀bɛ̀ m.ɨ́ Suh
    eye AM Suh   chest AM Suh
    'Suh's eye.'   'Suh's chest.'

(38) LIMBUM

a. rkoo Nfo   b. mer   Nju'
    arm Nfor   eyes   Njuh
    "Nfor's arm"   "Njuh's eyes"

Also included in this group are genitives which are interpreted as themes. In the example below, 'chiefs' is interpreted as a theme, in the sense that the statue represents chiefs.

(39)
    fɨ-ŋkōbɨ f.ɨ́ bɨ́-fɔ́
    statue   AM chiefs
    'A statue of chiefs.'

An outstanding characteristic of the dependent genitive is that, when it occurs in the same genitive construction with a possessive genitive phrase, it (i.e., the dependent genitive phrase) is always in a position immediately adjacent to the head noun. Consider the examples below that contain a dependent genitive and a possessor genitive. The dependent genitive is italicised.

(40) BAFUT   (41) Limbum

a. nɨ̀-lɨ́ʔɨ́ n.ɨ́ Suh n.ɨ́ nɨ́-kwābɨ́   ŋkuŋ   na'   Nju'
    eye *AM Suh* AM fortune-telling   tail   *cow* Njuh
    'Suh's eye of fortune-telling'   "Njuh's cow tail"
    (Suh's eye which he uses for fortune-telling).'

b. fɨ-ŋkōbɨ f.ɨ́ bɨ́-fɔ́ f.ɨ́   Bih
    statue *AM chiefs* AM   Bih
    'Bih's statue of chiefs.'

In each of these examples, the two genitive phrases modify the head noun (witness the form of the AM in (40). The dependent genitive is immediately adjacent to the head noun. Were we to reverse the positions of the two genitive phrases, either the meaning of the construction will change completely or the utterance will be ungrammatical.

(42) BAFUT

a. nì-lî?i n.í ní-kwābí   n.í Suh
    eye AM fortune-telling AM Suh
    'Suh's fortune-telling eye
    (an eye (not Suh's) which Suh uses for fortune-telling).'

b. fí-ŋkōbí f.í Bih f.í bí-fɔ̃
    statue AM Bih *AM chiefs*
    'Chiefs's statue of Bih.'

(43) *Limbum*

* ŋkuŋ   Nju   na'
   tail   Njuh Cow

The example in (40a), with [of Suh] adjacent to the head noun, refers to Suh's own eye (as part of his body). In its counterpart in (42a) where [of Suh] is no longer adjacent to the head noun, we are no longer referring to Suh's eye. Rather, we are referring to an object which has the shape of an eye and which Suh uses for fortune-telling. Both DPs, in this case, act as adjunct modifiers. Similarly, in (40b), where [of chiefs] is adjacent to the head noun, the statue represents chiefs but in (42b), where [of chiefs] is further away, the statue represents Bih. We observe, therefore, that the dependent genitive is always adjacent to the head noun while the possessor genitive could be further away. One may wonder at this point how the PS system would represent this contrast.

Earlier on, based on linear order and the interpretation of possessor genitives as adjuncts/modifiers, we proposed that possessor genitives are adjoined to NP. In a phrase structure compatible with the examples in (40-43), the possessor genitive would be in NP adjoined position. We are now left with the position of

(44)

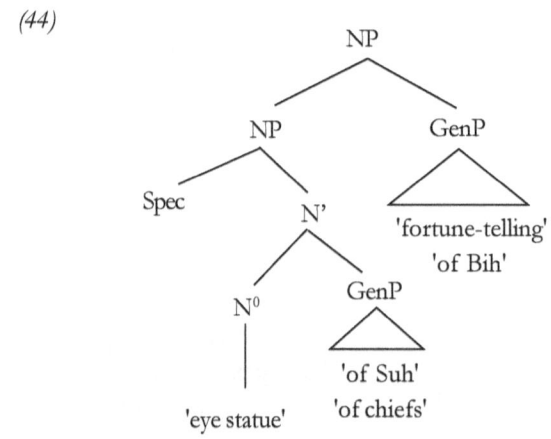

(45)

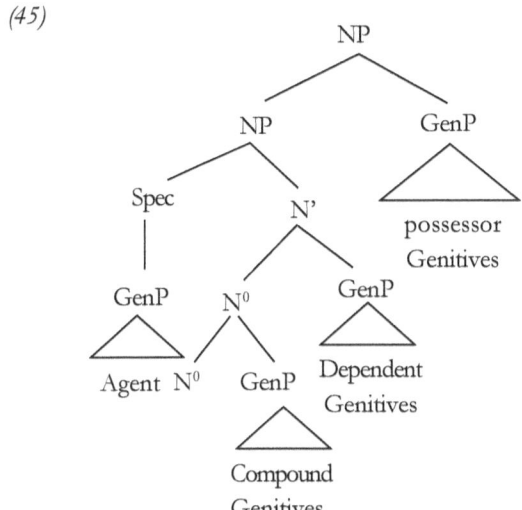

the dependent genitive. Considering the similarities in the distribution of the 'chiefs' and 'Suh' in (40 and 42) we propose that the dependent genitive [of Suh] is an internal argument of the head noun; that is, we propose that all dependent genitives (which include themes) are in complement of N° position. The examples in (40) would, therefore, have the structure in (44).

If we now incorporate the proposal in Giorgi and Longobardi (1991) that agents are generated in Spec-NP position, we end up with the following generalized base structure for the NP in Grassfields Bantu.

In the derivation of an associative construction containing an agent in Spec-NP, movement of the head noun to Num° produces the correct word order in which the head noun precedes the genitive phrase (see section 4 for details on this movement). Movement of the head noun to Num° in constructions containing the possessor genitives, themes or dependent genitives is not visible since these phrases are base generated in a position to the right of the head noun. In compound genitives, the entire construction comprising the two members of the compound, that is the head noun and genitive phrase, raises to Num°.

Agreement Relations in the Associative Construction

In the course of the discussion, we noticed manifestations of interesting patterns of agreement that need to be accounted for. In the genitives of possession, for instance, we observed that that the head noun or the genitive noun can take a determiner, which agrees with it in number and class. The examples below illustrate agreement between the definite determiner and the two nouns in the associative construction.

(46) BAFUT

a.   nì-bɔ́ʔɔ́   n.í   bí-fɔ́   ny.â
     5-pumpkin 5-AM 2-chiefs 5-the
     "The pumpkin of the chiefs (the one already mentioned)"

b.   nì-bɔ́ʔɔ́   n.í   bí-fɔ́   by.â
     5-pumpkin 5-AM 2-chiefs 2-the
     "The pumpkin of the chiefs (the chiefs already mentioned)"

In the example in (a), the definite determiner agrees with the head noun while in the (b) example, agreement is between the definite determiner and the genitive noun. This pattern of agreement extends to adjectives and other such modifiers, which can agree either with the head noun or the genitive noun.

(47) BAFUT

a.   nì-bɔ́ʔɔ́   n.í   bí-fɔ́   ni.sígìnì   ny.â
     5-pumpkin 5-AM 2-chiefs 5-nice   5-the
     "The nice pumpkin of the chiefs (the one already mentioned)"

b.   ì-bɔ́ʔɔ́ n.í bí-fɔ́ bi.sígìnì by.â
     5-pumpkin 5-AM 2-chiefs 2-nice 2-the
     "The pumpkin of the nice chiefs (the nice chiefs already mentioned)"

Interestingly, in spite of this manifestation of rich agreement and despite the intrinsic relation between the head noun and the genitive noun, there is no direct agreement between the two. In all the examples we have examined, the genitive noun does not agree with the head noun. Rather, agreement is between the head noun and the associative morpheme. We account for these facts in the subsections that follow.

Agreement Between Noun and Determiner/Adjective

As pointed out immediately above, the head noun or the genitive noun can take a determiner which agrees with it in number and class. The Bafut examples are repeated below for convenience.

(48) BAFUT

a.   nì-bɔ́ʔɔ́   n.í   bí-fɔ́   ny.a
     5-pumpkin 5-AM 2-chiefs 5-the
     "The pumpkin of the chiefs (the one already mentioned)"

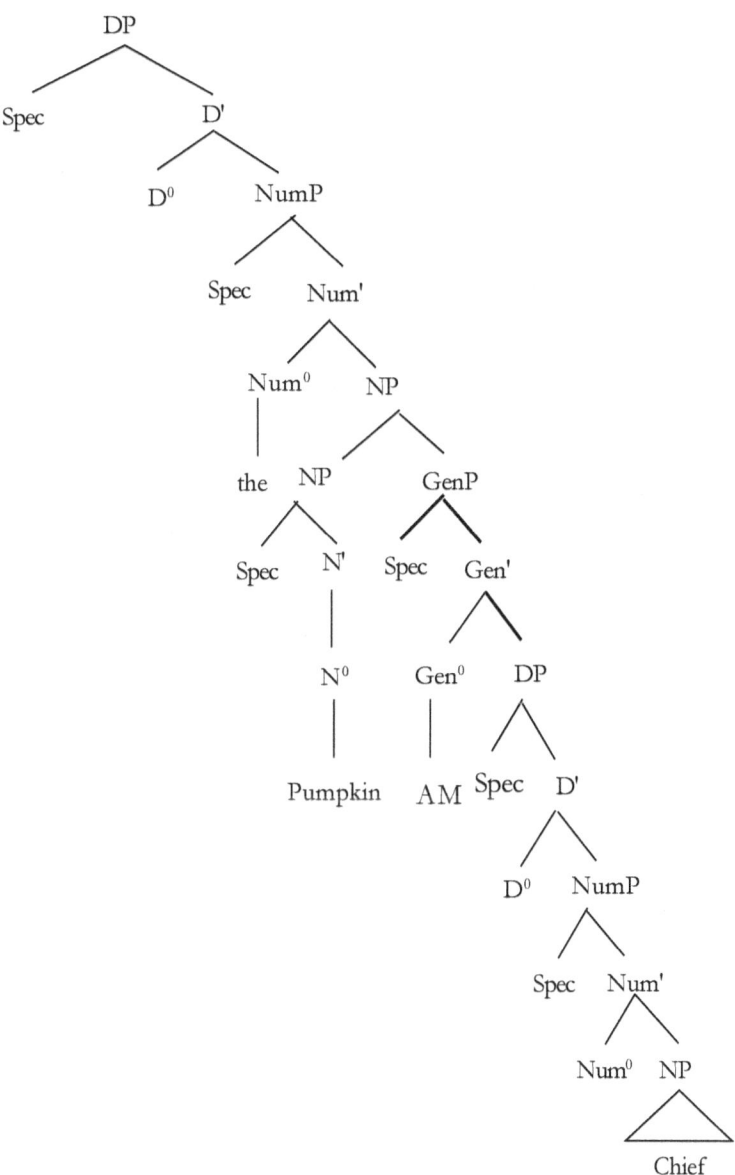

In these examples, the determiner agrees either with the head noun or the genitive noun. Two questions arise:

1. How does the determiner and head noun, for instance, which are linearly far from apart, come to agree?
2. How does feature checking operate to reflect the fact that the determiner/ adjective agrees either with the head noun or the genitive noun?

To answer the first question, we propose that the constituent structure ensures that the head noun agrees with the determiner that is linearly far away. Concretely, in (46a), for instance, where the determiner agrees with the head noun, both constitute a constituent and, in (46b) where agreement is between the genitive noun and the determiner, both determiner and genitive are also in the same constituent. Let us illustrate this. Following Abney's (1987) DP hypothesis and modifications contained in Carstens (1991, 2000), we assume that each noun projects a DP headed by a determiner. Thus, in the associative construction, the head noun projects the core DP while the genitive noun projects a modifying DP. In (46a), where agreement is between head noun and determiner, the determiner is in the head position of the core DP and in (46b), where the determiner agrees with the genitive noun, the determiner is in the head position of the modifying DP. The PS representation is sketched below. The PS representation includes a Number Phrase (NumP) proposed in Carstens (1991).

In this structure, the higher DP is what we have called the core DP while the lower is the modifying DP. In (46a), the determiner is in the head position of the core DP which also contains the head noun. Therefore, although the two are linearly far apart, they are structurally in the same constituent; the same core DP. In the example in (46b), the determiner is in the head position of the lower DP and so both are in the same constituent structure.

Now, to answer the second question regarding the manner in which the checking process operates in order to ensure that each noun checks features on the relevant determiner, we propose the following: In (46b), where the determiner agrees with the genitive noun 'chief', the genitive noun will have to check the number plus class features on the determiner. In order to do this, the genitive noun will first raise to the lower Num° position. Subsequently, all of the modifying NumP will move to the Spec position of the lower DP and so the noun can check the features of the determiner in the regular Spec-Head configuration of Chomsky (1995). This process is sketched below using only the relevant section of the tree diagram.

As the arrows indicate, the genitive noun first raises to Num°. Then all of NumP moves to Spec-DP giving rise to the surface word order in which the noun precedes the determiner. In Spec-DP position, the noun then checks the agreement features on the determiner.

(49)

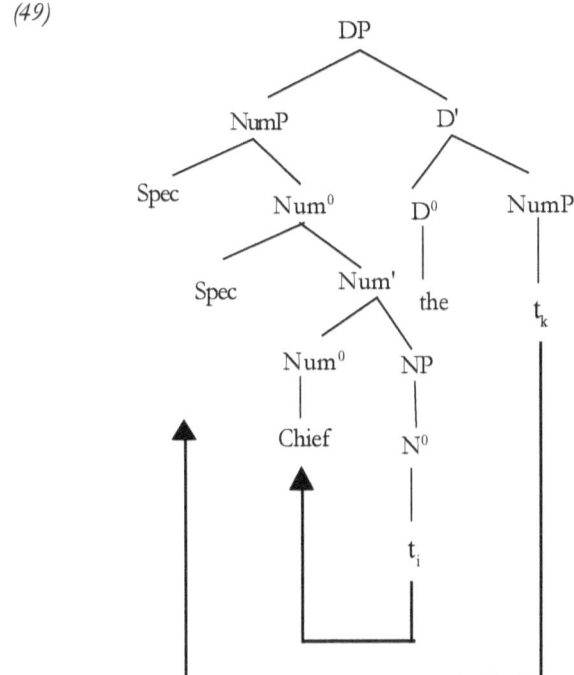

In the case in (46a), the same process occurs in the core DP, that is the head noun 'pumpkin' raises to Num° and, subsequently, all of core NumP moves to Spec of core DP. Here again, the number plus class features on the determiner are checked by the head noun in the usual Spec-Head configuration. We notice then that the system ensures that an agreement relation holds between two items by placing them in the same constituent structure. Thus, the head noun agrees with a determiner as in (46a) if they are both in the core DP and it agrees with the genitive noun as in (46b) if they are both in the modifying DP. In the same manner, an adjective will agree with the head noun if it is adjoined to core NP and will agree with the genitive noun if it is adjoined to the modifying NP.

Absence of Agreement on Genitive Noun

We observed in the introduction to this section that in spite of the manifestation of rich agreement in the associative construction and despite the intrinsic relation between the head noun and the genitive noun, there is no direct agreement between the two. Rather, agreement is between the head noun and the associative morpheme. There are actually two problems here; first, why does the genitive noun does not exhibit overt agreement with the head noun, and, second, why does the AM agree with the head noun and not with its object. The facts of Grassfields Bantu are very similar to those of Swahili. Thus, in both language groups, we can have (50a) but not (50b) and (50c).

(50) BAFUT   SWAHILI

a. nìkà'à ní fínjɔ́ɔ   a.   Kiti cha mtoto
   5leg 5AM 19 toad   7chair 7of 1child
   "A toad's leg"   "The child's chair" [AM/of agree with head N]
b. *nìkà'à fí fínjɔ́ɔ   b.   *kiti wa mtoto
   5leg   19AM 19toad   7chair 1of 1child [*AM/of and object agree]
c. *nìkà'à í nífínjɔ́ɔ   c.   *Kiti   a wmtoto
   5leg AM 5/19 toad   7 chair of 7/1 child
                                        [*Head N and object agree]

Considering the second problem first, the fact that the genitive noun does not exhibit overt agreement with the head noun supports an analysis whereby the genitive noun should not be in a relevant (head-head or Spec-head) relation with the head noun. In Carstens' (2000) proposal for Swahili, and the one we have outlined in this paper for Grassfields Bantu, the genitive noun is quite low down in the structure. Raising it into a head-head or Spec-head relation with the head noun (so that it can check the relevant features) will violate a number of locality conditions on movement. Observe also that each noun has intrinsic number and class features and the agreement morphology is also specified for the number and class features of the head noun. Were the genitive noun to exhibit overt agreement with the head, it would end up with two class features and two number features. One can imagine what this will entail for the checking theory assumed in this paper. The number + class features borne by the associative morpheme require the genitive noun to raise to matrix Num° (through Num° embedded inside GenP) in violation of locality conditions on movement, as pointed out immediately above.

Since the genitive noun does not exhibit overt agreement with the head noun, one could imagine a condition like the one in (51) which militates against a single noun bearing two distinct class or number features.

(51) *Feature Uniqueness Condition*

$*X^{f_1,f_2}$ where f_1, f_2 are two instantiations of the same feature, F. (Tamanji 2001).

Under (51), the genitive noun cannot bear concord morphology and so the concord morphology controlled by the head noun is obliged to associate to the AM/of.[4]

Turning now to the other problem why the AM does not agree with the genitive noun, Carstens (2000) exploits Chomsky's (1995, 1998) ideas about

Merge to account for the failure of agreement between 'of' and its object in Swahili. According to her proposal, checking between 'of' and its object fails because the two items are co-terms of merge, i.e., the two items are adjacent to each other as a result of merging and not movement. We adopt her proposal and add to it the fact that in addition to being co-terms of merge, the syntactic relation between 'of' and its object is not like the one between other heads (e.g., verbs) and their objects. According to Chomsky (1998), Case is a manifestation of agreement. Assuming this to be true, we expect the AM to agree with the genitive noun which it case-marks. An explanation as to why the AM does not agree with the genitive noun concerns the status of AM as a Case assignor. Recall that the issue of genitive Case had been debated for long and one of the conclusions arrived at was that genitive Case is inherent. If we return to this assumption, we can provide an explanation for why the AM does not agree with the genitive noun. Genitive Case is inherent, implying that it is not assigned by any particular category. Assuming this to be correct, and holding on to the idea that Case is a manifestation of agreement, we do not, therefore, expect the AM to agree with the genitive noun (since the AM does not case mark the genitive noun).

Conclusion

This article set out to describe the internal constituent structure of the associative construction in Grassfields Bantu languages. First we examined the role and syntactic status of the associative morpheme, pointing out that it is a relational element that bears agreement morphology and not simply a concord element as has generally been assumed in the literature. The next part of the discussion focused on the different semantic/pragmatic interpretations of the associative construction and the relevant PS representations. We proposed that while some genitives simply modify the head nouns as possessors, some are frozen with it (the head noun) into some sort of compound, and others are arguments (theme, agent) of the head noun. In order to preserve some form of isomorphism between form and meaning, we proposed different PS representations for these different relations.

Finally, we examined prominent agreement relations inside the associative construction such as determiner-noun, adjective-noun and AM-noun. Modifiers of the head noun such as adjectives and determiners are either in the core DP, in which case they agree with the head noun, or they are in the modifying DP, in which case they agree with the genitive noun. On the other hand, the genitive noun does not agree with the head noun because of the Feature Uniqueness Condition. Similarly, the genitive noun fails to agree with the AM because they are co-terms of merge and because the AM does not case-mark the genitive noun.

Notes

1. See Tamanji (1998b) for a detailed description of the patterns of floating tone association in Bafut.
2. This conclusion regarding the syntax of the associative construction incidentally bears on the question of whether the examples in (1b and 2) are similar to a construct state NP in Semitic. In the Construct state NP; an associative noun with no relational element to indicate the assocaitive relation between the two nouns immediately follows the head noun. Compare the Hebrew example in (I) to Bafut in (II).

    I. beyt ha-'is   [Hebrew]   II. ǹ-dá tsítsà [Bafut]
    house the-man   house teacher
    'The man's house.' (Siloni 1997:21)   'A teacher's house.'

    On the surface, the Bafut example is very similar to the Semitic Construct State NP in that there is no visible relational element indicating the genitival relation between the two nouns. However, as the discussion above has shown, there is no such similarity between the two languages. In Bafut, the head noun is always linked to the associative noun by an AM which happens to be tonal in (II).
3. This process of deriving the associative morpheme by combining a concord consonant and an associative vowel is quite transparent in a genetically related language—Kiswahili. In Kiswahili, the AM is marked by the vowel -a which takes a concord consonant determined by the class of the head noun as in the following:

    a. mtoto w-a Hamisi   b. vitu vy-a watu   c. kitapu ch-a Ali   d. nyuso z-a watoto
    child AM Hamisi   things AM people   basket AM Ali   faces AM children
    'Hamisi's child'   'People's things.'   'Ali's basket.'   'The children's faces.'
4. The *Feature Uniqueness Condition* is reminiscent of other modules of grammar (e.g. *Theta Criterion, Case theory*, etc.) which require that an item be specified for a unique syntactic role.

References

Abney, S.P., 1987, 'The English Noun Phrase in its Sentential Aspect', Ph.D. dissertation, MIT.

Ambe, S.A., 1989, 'The Structure of Bafut', Ph.D. dissertation, Georgetown University.

Boum, M. A., 1980, 'Le groupe Menchoum: Morphologie Nominale' in L.M. Hyman, ed. *Noun Classes in the Grassfields Bantu Borderland*. SCOPIL 8: 73-82

Carstens, V.M., 1991, 'The Morphology and Syntax of Determiner Phrases in Kiswahili', Ph.D. dissertation, UCLA.

Carstens, V.M., 2000, 'Concord in Minimalist Theory', Linguistic Inquiry, 31:319-55.

Chomsky, N., 1995, The Minimalist Program, Cambridge, Mass.: MIT Press.

Chomsky, N., 1998, *Minimalist Inquiries: The Framework*, (MIT Occasional Papers in Linguistics 15.) MITWL, Department of Linguistics and Philosophy, MIT, Cambridge Mass.

Giorgi, A. and G. Longobardi, 1991, *The Syntax of Noun Phrases: Configuration, Parameters and Empty Categories*, Cambridge: Cambridge University Press.

Hudson, R., 1987, 'Zwiky on Heads', *Journal of Linguistics*, 23: 109-136.

Hyman, L. M., 1977, 'Noni (Misaje Group)', in Larry M. Hyman and Jan Voorhoeve, eds., *Noun Classes in Grassfields Bantu*, Paris: Centre National de la Researche Scientifique.

Hyman, L. M., 1981, *Noni Grammatical Structure*, SCOPIL 9: University of Southern California, Los Angeles.

Mfonyam, J.N., 1989, 'Tone in Orthography: The Case of Bafut and Related Languages', Ph.D. dissertation, Universite de Yaounde, Cameroun.

Nkemnji, M., 1995, 'Heavy Pied-Piping in Nweh', Ph.D. dissertation, UCLA.

Ritter, E., 1987, 'Genitive NPs in Hebrew: A Functor Analysis', *Generals Paper*, MIT, Cambridge MA..

Rizzi, L., 1997, 'The Fine Structure of the Left Periphery', in Liliane Haegeman, ed., *Elements of Grammar*, Kluwer, Dordecht, pp. 281-337.

Siloni, T., 1997, *Noun Phrases and Nominalizations: The Syntax of DPs*, Dordrecht, Boston, London: Kluwer Academic Publishers.

Tamanji, P., 2001, 'Concord and DP Structure in Bafut', Ms University of Yaounde I.

Vitale, A., 1981, *Swahili Syntax*, Foris: Dordrecht.